PERGAMON GENERAL PSYCHOLOGY SERIES

Editors: Arnold P. Goldstein, *Syracuse University*
           Leonard A. Krasner, *SUNY, Stony Brook*

THE PRACTICE OF
BEHAVIOR THERAPY

D0724851

". . . . It is the business of epistemology to arrange the propositions which constitute our knowledge in a certain logical order, in which the later propositions are accepted because of their logical relation to those that come before them. It is not necessary that the later propositions should be logically deducible from the earlier ones; what is necessary is that the earlier ones should supply whatever grounds exist for thinking it likely that the later ones are true."

Bertrand Russell

An Inquiry into Meaning and Truth

THE PRACTICE OF BEHAVIOR THERAPY

by

Joseph Wolpe, M.D.

*Professor of Psychiatry, Temple University School of Medicine
and Eastern Pennsylvania Psychiatric Institute,
Philadelphia, Pennsylvania*

PERGAMON PRESS

New York • Toronto • Oxford • London • Mexico City
Edinburgh • Sydney • Paris • Braunschweig • Tokyo
Buenos Aires

PERGAMON PRESS INC.
Maxwell House, Fairview Park, Elmsford, N.Y. 10523
PERGAMON OF CANADA LTD.
207 Queen's Quay West, Toronto 117, Ontario
PERGAMON PRESS LTD.
Headington Hill Hall, Oxford;
4 & 5 Fitzroy Square, London W. 1
PERGAMON PRESS S.A.
Villalongin 32, Mexico 5, D.F.
PERGAMON PRESS (SCOTLAND) LTD.
2 & 3 Teviot Place, Edinburgh 1
PERGAMON PRESS (AUST.) PTY. LTD.
Rushcutters Bay, Sydney, N.S.W.
PERGAMON PRESS S.A.R.L.
24 rue des Ecoles, Paris 5e
VIEWEG & SOHN GmbH
Burgplatz 1, Braunschweig
PERGAMON PRESS DIVISION
BARTON TRADING K.K.
French Bank Building
1-1-2 Akasaka, Minato-ku, Tokyo

Copyright © 1969, Pergamon Press Inc.
First edition, First printing 1969
Second printing 1970
Library of Congress Catalog Card No. 71-84737

All rights reserved. No part of this publication may be reproduced,
stored in a retrieval system or transmitted, in any form, or by any
means, electronic, mechanical, photocopying, recording or otherwise, without prior permission of the copyright holder.

08 006563 5 (hard)
08 006390 X (soft)

Contents

To

Allan and David

Preface

BEHAVIOR THERAPY, or conditioning therapy, is the use of experimentally established principles of learning for the purpose of changing unadaptive behavior. Unadaptive habits are weakened and eliminated; adaptive habits are initiated and strengthened. The now popular term, *behavior therapy*, introduced by Skinner and Lindsley (1954), owes its wide promulgation and acceptance to Eysenck (1959, 1960, 1965).

Before the advent of behavior therapy, psychological medicine was a medley of speculative systems and intuitive methods. Behavior therapy is an applied science, in every way parallel to other modern technologies, and in particular those that constitute modern medical therapeutics. Therapeutic possibilities radiate from the uncovering of the lawful relations of organismal processes. Since learning is the organismal process most relevant to psychological medicine, the establishment of lawful relations relevant to the learning process is the main road to therapeutic power in this field.

However, the scientifically-minded behavior therapist need not confine himself to methods derived from principles. For the welfare of his patients he employs, whenever necessary, methods that have been *empirically* shown to be effective. Colchicum was a well-authenticated and widely-used remedy for attacks of gout long before colchicine was isolated or the metabolism of gout understood (Stetten, 1968). In the same way, in present-day behavior therapy, we use mixtures of carbon dioxide and oxygen to alleviate pervasive anxiety without knowing the mechanism of their action. The criterion is the existence of compelling evidence of a relationship between the administration of the agent and clinical change. Unless it meets this criterion no technique is clinically acceptable. But whereas in other fields of medicine empirical effectiveness is often quite easy to establish — as, for example, when a medicament consistently clears up a chronic skin infection in a few days — in psychotherapy it is a more complicated matter. Unusual care is needed to ensure the unequivocal specification of the technique. For example, if interpretation is claimed to be an effective technique, the character and conditions of the interpretations need to be exactly specified. A very special difficulty in evaluating how much a psychotherapeutic technique *per se* contributes to change resides in the fact that almost any form of psychotherapy produces substantial benefit in about fifty per cent of cases, apparently because of anxiety-inhibiting emotional reactions that therapists evoke in patients (Wolpe, 1958). Therefore, a particular technique must be, *prima facie* at least, effective beyond that level if it is to be even provisionally recommended on empirical grounds. Failure to observe this rule can lead to the gullible acceptance of almost anything that is touted, and back to the pre-scientific chaos of recipes from which modern technological principles have extricated us.

PREFACE

Two themes have recently been prominent among the criticisms voiced by opponents of behavior therapy. One is that it is "mechanistic and non-humanistic." The two adjectives are usually combined as though they belong together like face and beard. Insofar as behavior therapy leans on mechanisms it is indeed mechanistic. But nobody can fairly call it non-humanistic. No basis exists for the idea that others have more compassion than the behavioristic psychotherapist. Internal medicine is not dehumanized when penicillin replaces bloodletting as a treatment for infections; and no more is psychotherapy when conditioning replaces free association. The therapist's concern for his patients and his sympathy with their sufferings is not diminished by his having at his command methods that are based on knowledge of mechanisms.

The other criticism is that there is a narrowness of vision involved in the attempt to apply a "simple" model to the complexities of the human personality (see, for example, Breger and McGaugh, 1965). There are several answers. First the stimulus-response model is not simple. Second, the methods that this model has generated are evidently more effective in changing the neurotic personality than the more involved frameworks that these critics favor. How can these other frameworks be "better" without the validation of experimental testing which none of them have? One is reminded of the interchange between Pavlov and Paul Schilder (Pavlov, 1941). Schilder had asserted, "We cannot interpret the neurosis by means of the conditioned reflex, but by means of the psychic mechanism we have studied in the neurosis we can well explain what occurs in the conditioned reflex." Pavlov replied, "What is the meaning of the term 'interpretation' or 'understanding' of the phenomenon? The reduction of the more complex to the more elemental is a simple thing. Consequently the human neuroses should be explained, understood, i.e., analysed, by the help of the animal neuroses, as naturally the more simple, and not by the reverse procedure."

This volume, *The Practice of Behavior Therapy,* has grown out of my personal contribution to an earlier book, *Behavior Therapy Techniques,* by J. Wolpe and A. A. Lazarus, Pergamon Press (1966). In this new volume, I have included additional material not formerly available, in particular the results of work conducted since the preparation of the first book.

This volume gives major prominence to the principles expounded in *Psychotherapy by Reciprocal Inhibition.* The emphasis is very much on the treatment of *neuroses.* Much of the research on techniques that has appeared in the past two or three years is incorporated. There are augmented accounts of the variants of systematic desensitization, the treatment of frigidity, aversion therapy, "flooding" techniques, the use of drugs, and a chapter on operant conditioning. The many illustrative cases include four complex ones given at length. I should like to draw particular attention to the table of "consequences of neurotic anxiety" in Chapter III.

I am grateful to those who have helped in the literary side of the book's production — Mrs. Barbara Srinivasan, Mrs. Aviva Wanderer, and my wife; and to my old friend and colleague, Dr. L.J. Reyna, who, as so often in the past, has been a fount of information and ideas.

CHAPTER I

Introduction

A HABIT is a consistent way of responding to defined stimulus conditions. Ordinarily a habit declines — undergoes extinction — when its consequences become unadaptive, i.e. when it fails either to subserve the needs of the organism or to avoid injury, pain or fatigue. Neurotic habits are distinguished by their resistance to extinction in the face of their unadaptiveness.[1] Behavior therapy, as far as neurotic habits are concerned, is mainly the application of experimentally established principles of learning to overcoming these habits, but sometimes the conditioning of positive new habits is a major goal. In order to change a habit it is always necessary to involve the individual responses that constitute it. Change depends on eliciting behavior that can compete with these individual responses.

HISTORICAL PERSPECTIVE

While the modern behavior therapist deliberately applies principles of learning to his therapeutic operations, therapeutic prescriptions involving behavior are probably

[1] For a detailed discussion see Wolpe (1958)

as old as civilization — if we consider civilization as having begun when man first did things to further the well-being of other men. From the time that this became a feature of human life there must have been occasions when a man complained of his ills to another who advised or persuaded him on a course of action. This could be regarded as a behavioral therapy whenever the behavior itself was conceived as the therapeutic agent.

Ancient writings contain innumerable accounts of the therapeutic advice which constituted behavioral therapy in this sense. It is irrelevant whether the methods worked or not; but a good many of them undoubtably did at times. Often, surely, there were "suggestion" effects or "placebo" effects, by virtue of the responses to which words or things had previously been conditioned; and sometimes the instigated changes in behavior would have led to re-conditioning, with beneficial consequences for emotionally disturbed states.

Despite the derogation he usually receives, Mesmer (1779) deserves our salutation as perhaps the first therapist to base his efforts at behavior change on a general behavioral principle. Though that principle did not stand up to scientific testing it generated procedures that *were* often successful. Their essential elements were subsequently elucidated by the researches of de Puysegur, Bernheim and later investigators, and were the fountainhead of later techniques of suggestion and hypnosis (and other forms of verbal control of behavior) which have continued to play a part in behavior therapy — and probably always will.

The classical forms of suggestion are designed to substitute desirable for undesirable behavior by direct verbal prescription. As it now seems, when this works it is because the new response competes with the old, and, if it dominates, inhibits the latter. Whenever, either immediately or after repetition, this is followed by lasting diminution (or elimination) of the old response we have an instance of conditioned inhibition based on reciprocal inhibition (see below). Unfortunately, it does not work very often.

An early example of a less direct use of competing responses that is remarkably close to some modern practices was recently unearthed by Stewart (1961) from a book by Leuret (1846). The patient was a thirty-year-old wine merchant with a ten year history of obsessional thoughts which had become so insistent that he had ceased to be able to carry on his business. Having admitted the patient to hospital, Leuret ordered him to read and learn songs which he could recite the next day. The patient's food ration depended upon how much he had learnt. This regime continued for about six weeks during which the patient's recitals steadily improved. Meanwhile his obsessional thoughts were interfering less and less, and at the end of the six weeks he told Leuret that he had not had the thoughts for several days and that he felt much better. Leuret found him work as a nurse, and a year later noted that he was still well and a very successful nurse.

The 19th century therapist had some empirical guidelines for his techniques, but each therapeutic foray was an experiment whose outcome could not be predicted. The arrival of Sigmund Freud led to the appearance of a new group of techniques that were based on coherent theoretical principles, and that must be regarded as constituting a more systematic attempt at behavioral therapy; for again it was through behavior that his techniques were intended to accomplish his therapeutic goals. They did not, in fact, afford the hoped-for increase in favorable and predictable outcomes, but they fascinated the mind because they were set in a remarkably ingenious and colorful theoretical framework, and stimulated tremendous interest in problems of human behavior.

Nevertheless, during the first half of the twentieth century, in terms of scientific advancement, no other field of knowledge lay more stagnant than behavioral therapeutics. No hypotheses were being put to the test; no lawful relations were being established; and no reliable rules existed for procuring therapeutic change. The explanation for this is that modern therapy is applied science; and behavior therapy could not enter the world of science before there was a sufficient foundation for it in the basic studies of the experimental laboratory.

THE DEVELOPMENT OF SCIENTIFIC BEHAVIOR THERAPY

Eventually, as studies of normal behavior, largely in the laboratory, revealed more and more about the factors determining the acquisition, elicitation, maintenance, and decline of habits, some of this knowledge lent itself to the construction of hypotheses to account for the special characteristics of certain types of abnormal behavior. Certain of these hypotheses subsequently withstood testing by observation, and thereby acquired scientific standing.

Behavior therapy had its conceptual origin in 1920 in Watson and Rayner's famous experiment on Little Albert. When the child had been conditioned to fear a white rat, and, by generalization, other furry objects, they suggested that the conditioning might be overcome in four possible ways — by experimental extinction, by "constructive" activities around the feared object, by "reconditioning" through feeding the child candy in the presence of the feared object, or by procuring competition with fear by stimulating erogenous zones in the presence of the feared object. The last three of these suggestions are all on the counterconditioning model, but none of them were attempted because Albert left the hospital.

A few years later, one of Watson and Rayner's suggestions was adopted by Mary Cover Jones (1924) in connection with children's phobias. She described the method she employed as follows:

> During a period of craving for food, the child is placed in a high chair and given something to eat. The feared object is brought in, starting a negative response. It is then moved away gradually until it is at a sufficient distance not to interfere with the child's eating. The relative strength of the fear impulse and the hunger impulse may be gauged by the distance to which it is necessary to remove the feared object. While the child is eating, the object is slowly brought nearer to the table, then placed upon the table and finally, as the tolerance increases, it is brought close enough to be touched. Since we could not interfere with the regular schedule of meals, we chose the time of the mid-morning lunch for the experiment. This usually assured some degree of interest in the food and corresponding success in our treatment.

The details of the use of this method are illustrated (Jones, 1924b) by the case of a boy, Peter — "one of our most serious problem cases" who recovered after daily treatment over a period of two months. Jones was clearly aware of the role of hunger in the overcoming of the fear habit, noting that the effectiveness of the method increased as hunger was greater, and that "the repeated presentation of a feared object, with no auxiliary attempt to eliminate the fear, is more likely to produce a summation effect than an adaptation."

It is this insight that gives her work an honored place in the history of the development of techniques of this kind. It was an insight that was not shared even years later by Herzberg (1941) and Terhune (1948) who also made use of graduated tasks in the therapy of neurotic patients.

In the meantime, the most studied habit-eliminating process was — and has continued to be — experimental extinction — the gradual decrement in strength and frequency of responses that follow their unreinforced evocation. Dunlap (1932) probed the therapeutic possibilities of this process, and evolved the technique called "negative practice," whereby undesirable motor habits are overcome through securing their repeated evocation. About the same time, Guthrie (1935) observed the general therapeutic applicability of the counterconditioning method that Jones had demonstrated, stating that the simplest rule for breaking a habit is "to find the cues that initiate the action and to practice another response to these cues." (Guthrie, 1935, p. 138). He stressed the need to control the situation so that the cue to the original response is present while "other behavior prevails."

The next step forward occurred when Guthrie's principle was applied to the experimental neuroses, which had first been produced in Pavlov's laboratories early in the 20th century, and many times subsequently.[2]

Because the behavior of neurotic animals is strikingly different from normal, and is moreover exceedingly persistent, all the earlier experimenters shared the opinion that some kind of lesion or physiopathology was

[2]Some of the following material has been slightly modified from Psychotherapy: the nonscientific heritage and the new science. Wolpe, J., Behav. Res. Ther. 1:23-28. 1963.

the basis of these neuroses. The Russian workers believed this opinion to be supported by the finding that in certain instances the neuroses were overcome by giving the animals depressant or excitant drugs. However, in 1943, grounds for dissent from this view emerged. Masserman, in the course of a fascinating series of experiments on cats that had been made neurotic by being shocked in a small cage, observed that the neuroses could be overcome if the animals could be induced to feed in that cage. The fact that the mere evocation of the eating patterns of behavior could 'cure' the neuroses spoke against a lesion theory, and the fact that in order to procure the change the behavior had to be evoked in the experimental cage (in contrast to the living cage) strongly suggested that learning was at play. It must be said that these were not the conclusions reached by Masserman who, deeply steeped in "psychodynamic" thinking, interpreted the facts in terms of "breaking through the motivational conflict" — a view whose inadequacy was pointed out several years later (Wolpe, 1956).

The next requirement was to devise tests for the learning hypothesis. To begin with it was necessary to define 'learning' rather clearly. The following definition was adopted:

> Learning may be said to have occurred if a response has been evoked in temporal contiguity with a given sensory stimulus and it is subsequently found that the stimulus can evoke the response although it could not have done so before. If the stimulus could have evoked the response before but subsequently evokes it more strongly, then, too, learning may be said to have occurred (Wolpe, 1952a).

Several predictions were then made that would necessarily be fulfilled if the neurotic behavior were indeed learned. If they were not fulfilled the learning hypothesis would have to be abandoned. They were:

(1) The behavior manifested in an experimental neurosis must be essentially the same as that elicited by the stimulus situation that precipitates the neurosis.

(2) The neurotic behavior must be at greatest intensity when the animal is exposed to stimuli most like those in whose presence the neurosis was precipitated, and the intensity must decrease as a direct function of diminishing resemblance (according to the principle of primary stimulus generalization).

(3) Unlearning of neurotic behavior should occur in circumstances like those that produce unlearning in other contexts, i.e., extinction and/or counterconditioning.

Each of these predictions was submitted to experimental test[3] in 1947 (Wolpe, 1952, 1958) in cat neuroses produced by high-voltage low-amperage shocks in an experimental cage similar to that used by Masserman, and each prediction was sustained. In every animal the features of the reactions to shock were duplicated in the reactions of the neurosis; the intensity of neurotic response decreased as the environment to which the neurotic animal was exposed was less similar to that of the experimental cage, and while the reactions could not be overcome by the extinction process (partly, it seems, because of the small amount of reactive inhibition evoked by autonomic responses — Wolpe, 1958), it was possible to eliminate them through the reciprocal inhibition of weak anxiety responses by feeding. The animals would first be fed in a place where only slight anxiety was aroused — by stimuli remote

[3] I was extremely fortunate at that time to have the collaboration of Dr. L.J. Reyna in working out the conceptual and practical problems this involved.

on a generalization continuum — and when the anxiety had disappeared would advance along the continuum.

The foregoing having provided some assurance that experimental neuroses were learned, the next proposition that called for testing was that *human* neuroses are parallel to experimental neuroses in respect of the three features at issue: acquisition by learning, primary stimulus generalization, and elimination by unlearning.

With regard to the first, a study was made of the historical antecedents of the 'symptoms' in clinical cases of neurosis. In a large proportion of them a clear history of the time of onset of particular reactions was obtained. In these instances the patient recalled either a particular occasion of great distress or else the repeated arousal of anxiety in a recurrent situation involving, for example, a threatening parent or a hostile schoolteacher. It was invariably found that neurotic reactions whose origin could be dated to such experiences, had come to be evocable by stimuli similar to those that were to the forefront in the precipitating situations (although other stimuli later became effective in many cases, through second-order conditioning (see Wolpe, 1958).

It was also evident that human neurotic reactions obey the principle of primary stimulus generalization (Wolpe, 1958, 1961a). As in the animal neuroses, their intensity is determined by the degree of similarity of the evoking stimulus to a zenithal stimulus that is often identical with the original conditioned stimulus. In a particular case, there may be several physically unrelated classes of anxiety-arousing stimuli, each of which is found on examination to have a zenith and a generalization gradient. The ranked members of a gradient constitute a hierarchy. In man there are often hierarchies based upon similarities of internal effects (secondary generalization) — Osgood's "mediated generalization". For example, physically dissimilar situations may have the theme of rejection in common, and insofar as the patient is disturbed by rejection the situations can be placed in a hierarchial order determined by the relative strength of the reactions they evoke. To take a particular instance in another area (Wolpe, 1961), a patient with claustrophobia also had claustrophobic reactions in situations that had the mere 'feel' of enclosement, e.g. a tight zipper, or wanting to remove nailpolish while having no access to polish remover (see Chapter VII).

One basic question concerns the role of learning in bringing about recovery. Like animal neuroses, human neuroses are not usually extinguishable by repeated evocation of the neurotic responses. The first evidence that they may be overcome by graduated counter-conditioning was Mary Cover Jones' treatment of children's phobias cited above (p. 5), whose technique was almost identical with that used to overcome animal neuroses. In recent years, adult human neuroses have been treated by methods that employ responses other than feeding for the reciprocal inhibition and counterconditioning of anxiety (Wolpe, 1958; Eysenck, 1960); and these are the main subject-matter of this book.

The facts invoked to answer the question regarding human neuroses have been essentially 'clinical' but insofar as the observations have been consistent and have been confirmed by independent observers, it may be said that the learning hypothesis of neurosis has cleared its first hurdles and qualified as a scientific hypothesis.

But properly controlled experimental observations are necessary. While a great deal has to be done, some data is already available, and all of it accords with the clinical findings. Experiments on the *production* of human neuroses are naturally considered with hesitation, if not trepidation, so that it is not surprising that only three can be cited. One is the previously mentioned Watson and Rayner experiment (1920). The second is Krasnogorski's (1925) induction of experimental neuroses in children by exposing them to ambivalent stimuli in relation to the conditioning of alimentary responses — a procedure very similar to a common technique for producing experimental neuroses in Pavlov's laboratories (Pavlov, 1927). Finally, Campbell, Sanderson and Laverty (1964) have demonstrated (though not in a context of *neurosis-production*) that marked anxiety reactions can be conditioned by a single severe stress due to respiratory paralysis, and furthermore, that repeated evocation of the conditioned response is accompanied by increased strength of response, instead of extinction — in keeping with a common clinical experience (see Chapter X).

It is much more congenial to perform *therapeutic* experiments, and a growing output of process studies is now in evidence. For example, Lang and Lazovik (1963), Lang (1964), and Lang, Lazovik and Reynolds (1965) in controlled studies of the desensitization of snake phobias, have found that therapeutic change is apparently due to the conditioning procedure, and cannot be attributed to suggestion, rapport ('transference'), or muscle relaxation; and Rachman (1965) and Davison (1965) have both shown that the whole desensitization procedure is significantly more effective than either scene presentation or relaxation alone. In the field of therapy employing operant conditioning, process studies are already numerous. A considerable number of them have been collected by Krasner and Ullman (1965), Franks (1965) and Eysenck (1965).

THE EFFECTS OF BEHAVIOR THERAPY

The most distinctive feature of behavior therapy is in the command it gives to the therapist both in planning the general strategy of therapy and controlling its details as he goes along. When one type of maneuver fails to accomplish change, another is tried according to appropriate indications, each variation being an application of an experimentally established principle. When a procedure shows signs of inhibiting the patient's anxiety responses it is systematically applied to diminish the anxiety-evoking potential of the antecedent stimuli. The specificity of effect is often extremely clear, as shown, for example, in an experimental case study (Wolpe, 1962) involving a multi-faceted motor car phobia (reproduced in Chapter XIII). It has also been shown (Wolpe, 1963) that in the case of classical phobias treated by desensitization therapy, there is a mathematical relationship between the number of scene presentations and the degree of procured recovery (see Chapter VII).

The foregoing is in strong contrast to the conventional therapist's rather helpless position. In the conditions set for his interactions with the patient, he can only passively hope that some constructive result will emerge from his procedures.

Therefore in the conventional literature on psychotherapy much has been attributed to the patient-therapist relationship. A widely prevalent belief is that the quality of the therapeutic relationship is more basic to therapeutic outcome than the therapist's specific methods and techniques, and this is probably true of the conventional therapies. As Frank (1961) has shown, a relationship in which the therapist is able to mobilize the patient's expectation of help and hope of relief is in and of itself a powerful therapeutic instrument. The conditioning procedures add to its effects. The practice of behavior therapy may thus be viewed as a 'double-barrelled' means of alleviating neurotic distress.

Statistical studies of the effects of behavior therapy by competent therapists have shown that almost 90 per cent recovery or marked improvement may be expected among patients who have had a reasonable amount of exposure to behavioral methods. These studies are summarized in Chapter XIV, where they are also compared with statistics from other therapies. The comparisons are clearly favorable to behavior therapy; but vulnerable to the criticism of lack of control. The results of some well-controlled outcome studies, however, also emerge decisively on the side of behavior therapy. A point that must be given emphasis is that *behavior therapy is effective in all neuroses* and not only in unitary phobias.

All in all, there is reason for confidence in the future of behavior therapy. It is founded in biology and its principles and practices are determined by the rules of science. Its clinical results are encouraging. And it is still in its infancy. The methods in use today will look very rough-hewn a decade or two from now. We may anticipate the fulfillment of Reyna's (1964) expectation that "more rigorous applications of the laws of learning will render conditioning therapies even more effective; and will extend their use to a broader range of behavior problems."

CHAPTER II

Technical And
Moral Principles

TECHNICAL PRINCIPLES

THE AIM of behavior therapy is always to change habits judged undesirable. The achievement of this aim depends on the application of one or more of three categories of conditioning operations.

1. Counterconditioning

A basic premise about neuroses is that they are persistent unadaptive learned habits of reaction (see Chapter I). Almost universally, anxiety is a prominent constituent of neurotic reactions; and since anxiety involves a primitive (subcortical) level of neural organization, its unlearning can be procured only through processes that involve this primitive level. Neurotic anxiety cannot be overcome purely by intellectual action — logical argument, rational insight — except in the special case where it stems entirely from misconceptions (see p. 59).

The elimination of anxiety response habits is usually accomplished by the inhibition of anxiety by a competing response. The formal process is the development of conditioned inhibition through reciprocal inhibition (Wolpe, 1954). *If a response inhibitory of anxiety can be made to occur in the presence of anxiety-evoking stimuli it will weaken the bond between these stimuli and the anxiety.* In human neuroses, a considerable number of responses which empirically inhibit anxiety have been successfully used to overcome neurotic anxiety-response habits as well as other neurotic habits. For example, assertive responses (Chapter V) are used to overcome neurotic anxieties that inhibit effective action towards those persons with whom the patient has to interact. The essence of the therapist's role is to encourage the outward expression, under all reasonable circumstances, of the feelings and action tendencies previously inhibited by anxiety. Each act of assertion to some extent reciprocally inhibits the concurrent anxiety and slightly weakens the anxiety response habit. The reduction of anxiety drive is the main reinforcing agent of this habit change. Similarly, relaxation responses can be employed to bring about systematic decrements of anxiety response patterns to many classes of stimuli (Chapter VII).

The reciprocal inhibition principle also comes into play in overcoming responses other than anxiety. It is the basis of the conditioned inhibition of obsessional and compulsive habits by aversion therapy (Chapter XI). In this a painful faradic shock or similar stimulus inhibits the undesired behavior, with the result that conditioned inhibition of the latter is established, and accumulates with repetition. There are also many instances of positive conditioning which *ipso facto* include the conditioned inhibition of previous habits of response to the antecedent stimuli concerned. For example, when assertive behavior is instigated, while the expression of 'positive' feelings produces conditioned inhibition of anxiety, the motor actions involved in such expression inhibit and consequently displace the previous motor habit. It should be noted that here the reinforcement comprises the various 'rewarding' consequences of the new response.

2. Positive Reconditioning

The conditioning of new motor habits or ways of thinking may accompany the overcoming of unadaptive autonomic responses, as in the example just given. But frequently new habits of action or of thought are needed in contexts that do not involve anxiety. An instance of this is the conditioning treatment of enuresis nocturna. By arranging for the patient to be awakened by an alarm as soon as the first drop of urine is excreted during sleep, the waking reaction is conditioned to the imminence of urination, and this subsequently leads to the development of an inhibition of the tendency to urinate in response to bladder stimulation during sleep (Gwynne Jones, 1960, Lovibond, 1963). A further example is the conditioning of effective study habits in individuals who have unproductive habits and fritter away their time when they should be working (Sulzer, 1965).

Successful conditioning of new habits always involves the use of 'rewards' of one kind or another. It sometimes suffices to supply these on an *ad hoc* basis, but in recent years there has been increasing formal use of Skinner's (1953) operant conditioning principles to remove and replace undesirable habits. In order to establish a new behavior pattern in a particular situation, the desired response has to be elicited and each time rewarded, while the undesired behavior is consistently not rewarded and even punished. For example, anorexia nervosa has been successfully treated by making social rewards such as the use of a radio or the granting of companionship contingent on eating, withdrawing these rewards when the patient fails to eat (Bachrach, Erwin and Mohr, 1965). Various types of behavior in schizophrenics have been treated on the same principle (Lindsley, 1956, Williams, 1959, Ayllon, 1963, Davison, 1964) and major and lasting changes of behavior have been produced, even in patients who had been hospitalized for years. (see Chapter XII).

3. Experimental Extinction

This is the progressive weakening of a habit through the repeated nonreinforcement of the responses that manifest it. Thus, behavior that depends on food reinforcement becomes progressively weaker if its occurrences are not followed by food. The same is usually true of avoidance behavior if it is not reinforced by an occasional shock. The very evocation of the response has effects that are self-weakening (whether or not it should ultimately be proved that this depends on the fatigue-associated reactive inhibition mechanism proposed by Hull (1943).

Therapeutic techniques based on the extinction mechanism, introduced a quarter of a century ago by Dunlap (1932) under the name "negative practice," have in recent years again been employed in the treatment of such motor habits as tics (e.g. Yates, 1958). In correlation with a very large number of unreinforced trials spontaneous evocations of the undesired movement are progressively lessened.

MORAL PRINCIPLES

The *raison d'etre* of psychotherapy is the presumption that it can overcome certain kinds of human suffering. Neurotic symptoms and related disabilities are the commonest source of suffering for which patients seek psychiatric help. The neurotic patient calls upon the therapist to remove his distress no less than if it were due to an organic illness, and it becomes the central task of the therapist to remove this distress. It is small comfort to tell a patient whose neurotic anxieties remain undiminished after treatment that he is cured because his personality has matured.

One result of realizing that neurotic behavior is learned is to place the responsibility for the patient's recovery unequivocally on the therapist, just as in other branches of therapeutic practice; and the patient should know this. If he does not improve despite earnestly co-operating in the programs that have been set for him, it must be for reasons that attach to the therapeutic methods. Perhaps there has been a faulty analysis of the case, or the techniques have been inappropriately applied, or none of the available techniques can offer a solution to his particular case.

In this last instance the therapist should frankly admit defeat, though he may offer continued 'support' and also the hope that in time the advance in our knowledge of controlling mechanisms may bring a solution to hand. To several cases with whom I have maintained contact after acknowledging that I had no effective solution to offer, I have later proposed new methods as they have emerged. More often than not, success has ultimately been achieved.

It must be evident from the foregoing that the behavior therapist does not blame the patient when treatment fails. He cannot attribute failure to 'resistance', secondary gain, or other members of that family of popular alibis. He does not insistently 'plug away' at one technique because he 'knows' it is right and 'must' cure, if only the patient will allow it to succeed. Only evidence of change can justify a therapist in continuing with 'more of the same.'

Certain moral issues are brought up by patients. A good many of them question the morality of assertive behavior when it is required. They may be reassured in various ways. One useful approach has been to point out that there are three possible broad approaches to the conduct of interpersonal relations. The first is to consider one's self only and ride roughshod over others, if necessary, to get what one wants. The psychopathic personality is the extreme expression of this basic attitude, and often, of course, falls foul of society. He has not been conditioned to feel guilty or otherwise anxious in situations in which most people are so conditioned. The second possible approach to interpersonal relations is always to put others before one's self. Such unselfishness is the extreme opposite of the psychopathic personality. The patient fluctuates between guilt at falling short of his standards of selflessness and the frustrations that result from self-abnegation. No less than that of the psychopath, though in a different way, his behavior has unhappy results. The Talmudic saying, "If I am not for myself, who will be for me?" recognizes the biological truth that welfare of the organism begins with its own integrity. The third approach is the golden mean, dramatically conveyed in this fuller quotation from the Talmud: "If I am not for myself, who will be for me? But if I am for myself alone, what am I?" The individual places himself first, but takes others into account. He conforms to the requirements of social living while acceding to the biological principle that the adaptions of the individual organism *primarily* serve the needs and the individual and not those of others. He fulfills his obligations to the group, but claims and is prepared to defend what he believes are his reasonable rights.

In the setting of this practical philosophy, to decide what behavior is suitable to particular circumstances is usually a simple matter. While most of the resultant behavior would be acceptable to people of many backgrounds and many religious beliefs, there are instances that would arouse dissent. For example, if chronic unhappiness results from an unsatisfactory marriage and all efforts to rectify the situation have failed, it is reasonable and human to advise and aid the patient towards divorce, since the worth of a marriage should be weighed solely in terms of human happiness. Marriage is not a sacred entity to be preserved for its own sake. Similarly, it is justifiable to attack on rational grounds a patient's religious beliefs if they are a source of suffering. For example, finding that a patient (Case 12, Chapter XIII) was greatly distressed by the stern view taken by his church of some of his behavior, the foundations of the church's judgment were questioned and the patient was given a copy of Winwood Reade's splendid old book *The Martyrdom of Man* (1872). Though at first upset by its criticisms of religion, he later had a sense of relief. His more rational outlook was not only a good thing in itself but facilitated psychotherapeutic procedures that eventually met with complete success.

In adopting this line of positive action, it is vital that the therapist does not confuse different aspects. He must be able to distinguish technical decisions from moral ones, and separate the tenets of his own moral code from the moral requirements of the patient's situation. London (1964) summarizes the issues as follows in the course of an excellent and wide-ranging discussion:

> At the same level of abstraction, it is probably correct to declare that every aspect of psychotherapy presupposes some implicit moral doctrine, but it is not necessary to seek this level in order to say why it is important for therapists to recognize the moral concomitants of patients' problems and the implied moral position of some of their solutions. Some problems are inevitably moral ones from the perspective of either client or therapist, and some can be viewed as strategic or technical ones and treated without reference to particular value systems. In the one case, the therapist must fulfill a moral agency in order to function at all, whereas in the other he may restrict himself to the impartial helping or contractual function with which he is usually identified. But if he does not know the difference, then his own moral commitments may influence his technical functioning so that he willy-nilly strives to mold men to his own image, or his technical acts may imply moral positions which he might himself abhor.

Our discussion of the moral aspects of psychotherapy cannot be concluded without reference to an objection to behavior therapy that is frequently brought up at lectures and seminars. The complaint is that the behavior therapist assumes a kind of omnipotence by demanding the patient's complete acquiescense in his methods, which, it is felt, denudes the patient of human dignity. The truth is that the grade of acquiescense required is the same as in any other branch of medicine. Patients with pneumonia are ready to do what the medical man prescribes, because he is the expert. The same is the case when psychotherapy is the treatment required.

CHAPTER III

Investigating The Case: Stimulus-Response Relations

THE FIRST step in investigating a case for behavior therapy is necessarily the taking of a careful clinical history. This is broadly similar to the history that might be taken by almost any conscientious clinician; but the behavioristic orientation leads to differences in the direction and manner of questioning. The special features can be more effectively communicated to the reader by the transcripts given later in this chapter of the initial interviews of Cases 1 and 2, than by any description that might be attempted.

Having obtained from the patient such basic personal details as name, address, telephone number, age and occupation, the therapist at once proceeds to explore the patient's neurotic reactions. The circumstances surrounding the onset of each one of these reactions are meticulously explored in the hope of obtaining a coherent picture of its original determinants. In the case of an anxiety response habit, such as a fear of heights or of being the focus of attention, we try to establish both the circumstances in which it was conditioned and what later contingencies may have modified its form or led to its 'spread' to other stimuli by second-order conditioning. The conditioning history of each anxiety habit is traced in the same essential way.

The historical information provides a background for subsequent steps. At the very least, it gives the therapist a perspective on the case; but it may also provide important clues to the stimulus-response relationships that are currently relevant. These *current relationships* will naturally be the focus of therapy. Therefore, the most intensive scrutiny is given to them. If the patient is anxious in social situations, it is necessary to find out exactly what aspects of these situations upset him. He may have a conditioned anxiety reaction to being looked at, that increases with the number of people looking at him; or the reaction may depend on the degree of speaking-performance-demand that the situation seems to hold; or the social group may impose on him a fearful feeling of not being able to get away. The correct identification of the stimulus antecedents of reactions, indispensable to effective behavior therapy, depends, in the main, on stringent questioning (see Cases 1 & 2).

The relevant information is always more difficult to obtain when the presenting problem is not anxiety — when, for example, the patient has come for the treatment of a stutter, a compulsion, or a psychosomatic condition like asthma. These conditions are usually in one way or another consequents of neurotic anxiety habits — but not always. Therefore, the first question is whether or not the patient also has neurotic anxiety. If he has, we want to know whether there is any correlation between the anxiety and the stutter, com·

pulsion, or asthmatic attack. Usually, the correlation is quite clear and straightforward. For example, a stutter may be found to increase as a function of intensity of felt anxiety, which, in turn, depends upon the identity, number, and attitudes of the people in the patient's presence. But, especially in some psychosomatic cases, the correlation may be difficult to detect. An outstanding example of this was a case of asthma I saw several years ago, in whom the fact that the attack regularly took place four hours after a stressful event only became apparent after the patient had kept an hour-by-hour diary for several weeks.

Table 1 sets forth some of the consequences of neurotic anxiety. The deconditioning of the underlying anxiety generally brings these consequences to an end. Except for the rather rare cases of classical hysteria with *la belle indifference*, there are very few neuroses which can be overcome without eliminating anxiety. (see Chapter XII).

TABLE 1.
CONSEQUENCES OF NEUROTIC ANXIETY

Mechanism of Consequence	Manifestation
a. Autonomic	
1. Hyperventilation	Transient Somatic Effects, e.g. (a) Dizziness (b) Fainting attacks (d) Paresthesia (c) Headaches (e) Tachycardia
2. Protective Inhibition (hypothesized) when anxiety is very prolonged and intense	Depression

(Table 1. Continued)

Mechanism of Secondary Effect	Manifestation
3. Autonomic discharges especially channeled into one organ system	Psychosomatic Symptoms, e.g. (a) Neurodermatitis (b) Asthma (c) Vasomotor rhinitis (d) Peptic ulceration and peptic ulcer syndrome (e) Spastic colon (f) Frequency of micturition (g) Dysmenorrhea (h) Hypertension (i) Migraine

b. Motor

1. Prominent muscle tension, general or localized	Motor Disturbances, e.g. (a) Tremor (b) Stuttering (c) 'Fibrositic' pain, e.g. backache (d) Ocular dyskinesia
2. Motor avoidance conditioning (may be conditioned either simultaneous with anxiety or secondary to it)	Avoidance of anxiety evoking stimuli

3. Complex motor behavior conditioned by its anxiety-reducing consequences	1. Compulsions
	 2. "Character Neuroses", e.g.
	  (a) Sexual deviations (e.g. homosexuality, pedophilia)
	  (b) Exhibitionism
	  (c) Voyeurism
	  (d) Promiscuity

4. Anxiety interfering with complex functioning	1. Inability to work or impaired work capacity 2. Impaired capacity for social interaction (anxiety in social contexts) 3. Impaired sexual function (impotence or frigidity)

(Table 1. Continued)

Mechanism of Secondary Effect	Manifestation
c. Cognitive	
1. Cognitive distraction by anxiety-response-produced stimuli	Amnesia due to 'non-registration' of extrinsic stimuli
2. Cognitive distortion	Paranoid and related behavior

When the patient's presenting reactions have been sufficiently explored, the therapist elicits the basic facts of his past and present life. The first topic is the patient's early family life. He is asked where he came among the children of the family, and by how many years he was separated from each. What kind of person did his father seem to him to be? Did he show personal interest, did he punish, and if so did it seem just or not? Is the father still alive? If not, how did he die, and what was effect of his death upon the patient? The same questions are asked about the mother. How well did the parents get on with each other? Were there any other important adults in the patient's early home life? Who were they and what was their influence upon the patient? How did he relate to his siblings? How important was his religious training, and how much of an influence upon him does religion retain? Were there any childhood fears or nervous habits?

The next group of questions relate to the patient's education. Did he enjoy school? If so, what did he like about it; if not, for what reason? How well did he do academically? Did he take part in athletics, and how good was he at them? Did he make friends and were any of the friendships intimate? Were there any people, either among teachers or students, whom he grew to fear or especially dislike? At what age did he leave school? Did he graduate from high school? What did he do next — embark on a life of leisure, go to work or continue his studies at a university or other institution? How did he get on at the institution, academically and socially? Upon graduating, what work did he do, how did he function at it, and how satisfying did he find it? Have there been changes of employer, and if so for what reasons? How does he get on with employers, underlings and peers?

The patient's sex life is then traced from his first awareness of sexual feelings. At what age and in what context was he first aware of sexual arousal? What were the experiences that followed? Did he masturbate, and was this associated with any feelings of fear or guilt? At what age did he commence dating? When did he have his first important relationship? What attracted him to the girl, and what brought the association to a close? The same questions are asked about subsequent associations. What attracted him to his wife? How did the courtship go? Were there obstacles from the families of either party? How have they got on together over the years? How has the sexual side of the marriage been?

What are his present social relationships? Does he have difficulties with any of his friends? Does he have any particularly intimate friends? How does he get on with people with whom his association is casual?

After the anamnesis, the patient is given three inventories to fill out — the Willoughby (a short form of the Clark-Thurstone Inventory), a Fear Survey Schedule, and the Bernreuter Self-Sufficiency Scale. These inventories will be briefly discussed.

The Willoughby Schedule (Original Form Appendix 1) consists of 25 questions that are answered on a 5-point scale — (0-4). About half of the questions yield information about common areas of neurotic reactivity — mainly interpersonal, and the other half indicate degrees of general emotional sensitivity. This questionnaire is a highly significant indicator of neuroticism (Wolpe, 1958, p. 110). Decreases in the score are correlated with the patient's improvement. But it is possible for a person to have a low Willoughby score and yet be highly neurotic in areas not covered by the schedule. A revised Willoughby for self-administration is given in Appendix 2.

The Fear Survey Schedule (Appendix 3) (Wolpe & Lang, 1964) lists a large number of stimulus situations to which fear is unadaptive. The patient indicates on a 5-point scale how disturbed he becomes in each situation. This schedule is an exceedingly useful clinical instrument that frequently brings to the therapist's attention neurotic sensitivities that he would not otherwise have suspected. A list with additional items is shortly to be published (Wolpe & Lang, 1969).

The Bernreuter Self-Sufficiency Inventory (Appendix 4). This list of 60 questions is used less consistently than the foregoing two schedules. Its main relevance is to cases with serious dependency habits. It indicates the patient's probable capacity to carry out instructions with regard to self-assertion. A normal score is generally between 24 and 42. A score of less than 20 generally suggests that he will have considerable difficulty.

When there is a question of psychopathic personality and when there are ambiguous manifestations of hysteria, the introversion - extraversion scale of the Maudsley Personality Inventory or of its derivative, the Eysenck Personality Inventory, often provide decisive information.

If there is the slightest suggestion that organic disease may be playing a part in the patient's illness, a medical investigation should be undertaken. One of the strongest indications for this is the presence of episodic anxiety attacks to which no constant stimulus antecedents can be attached. Common organic causes of anxiety are hypoglycemia, including relative hypoglycemia (Salzer, 1966), and hyperthyroidism. Among less common causes are limbic lobe seizures and pheochromocytoma.

When sufficient data has been gathered, the therapeutic goals and strategies are discussed with the patient. The therapist decides to which areas of disturbance to give priority. The degree to which a neurotic habit is detrimental to the life-economy of the patient is usually a prime consideration. Thus, in a recent case, agoraphobia was treated first because of its profoundly incapacitating consequences, even though other neurotic reactions had pre-existed it and, in a sense, spawned it.

Behavior therapy is always an individual matter. Nevertheless, a few general rules may be stated with regard to the initiation of therapy — (1) The emotional climate is, as at all other times, a blend of objectivity and permissiveness. (2) The patient must be assured that his unpleasant reactions are reversible. Having been learned, they can be unlearned. The therapist can often illustrate the learning process from the patient's own history. (3) Misconceptions must be corrected as soon as possible. This applies both to socially conditioned misconceptions (e.g. "masturbation is dangerous") and iatrogenic misconceptions (e.g. "I need my symptoms"). (4) Assertive behavior (Chapter V) should be instigated at an early stage unless there are severe phobic reactions to some aspect of it, e.g. to the patient's own 'aggression' (see Case 2).

SPECIMEN FIRST INTERVIEWS

Case 1: The interview with Mrs. P. was selected because the *apparent* unifocal phobia for knives led the therapist rapidly to uncover broad areas of the patient's history. The reader should attend to the manner and content of the questioning procedure. It should particularly be noted that the therapist goes out of his way to be permissive — condoning acts and attitudes that the patient seems to believe it natural to deplore; and that he tries to establish with great precision points that he thinks may be significant for therapeutic action. In this particular case one benefit expected from therapy was obvious — the removal of the phobia.

An inexperienced therapist might have been tempted at once to proceed with systematic desensitization, but the *second* interview (not given here) led in another direction, and illustrated how unwise it is to plunge into the treatment of a case without adequate understanding of it. Exploration of factors currently controlling the fear of knives revealed that it became particularly strong when other people's children were unruly inside her house. It then emerged that she was extremely inhibited in almost all interpersonal situations, and habitually suppressed her anger for fear of disapproval. (Note that direct questioning failed to elicit the presence of suppressed anger during the first session). In keeping with all this, her Willoughby score was 66. The first therapeutic undertaking was, accordingly, *not desensitization but assertive training*. It was postulated that by developing an ability freely and appropriately to express her feelings she would remove a major stimulus antecedent of her phobia. Assertive training was rapidly effective, but though the phobia then became less troublesome, desensitization eventually had to be carried out as expected.

First Interview in a Case of Phobia for Sharp Objects (Mrs. P., aet.32).

THERAPIST: Dr. N. has written to me about you, but I want to approach your case as though I knew nothing about it at all. Of what are you complaining?

MRS. P.: I'm afraid of sharp objects, especially knives. It's been very bad in the past month.

THERAPIST: How long have you had this fear?

MRS. P.: It began 6 years ago when I was in hospital after my first child was born. Two days later, my husband brought me some peaches and a sharp knife to cut them with. I began to have a fear that I might harm the baby with it.

THERAPIST: How long had the knife been with you when it occurred to you that it might harm the baby?

MRS. P.: I don't believe I let him leave it overnight, that night; or else we left it that night and then the next day — I think you could say I told him to take it home. I can't remember exactly, I know I just didn't want it around. From that day to this I don't mind using knives as long as I'm with someone but when I'm alone with the children I just don't want them around.

THERAPIST: Can you remember in what way the thought first came into your mind that you might hurt the baby?

MRS. P.: I can't remember.

THERAPIST: Now since that time, generally speaking, has this fear been the same all along, or has it got better or worse?

MRS. P.: Well, right after we moved to Richmond about 5 months ago I felt a little bit better about it. At first when I got home from the hospital I made my husband take all the knives away from the house. I didn't want them around, so he took them to my mother's. I brought a couple back from her house when we moved to Richmond. But I couldn't — after I brought them — I couldn't use them. I couldn't keep them out where I could see them and might pick one up and, you know — use it sometime.

THERAPIST: So what do you say in general — that the fear has been much the same?

MRS. P.: It seems the same. In fact mostly I think that it's gotten worse.

THERAPIST: Is there anything — any situation — that you can associate with it getting worse?

MRS. P.: No. Only it just seems to be on my mind I guess. Ah — if you don't mind me going back to something that Dr. N. said that I just didn't want them around that it was a habit, and I mean I guess I've just been thinking about that and — its hard to admit — the children, I don't know why they make me nervous and I just am afraid that — that sometime it may get the better of me.

THERAPIST: Are the children making you more nervous — in the past month?

MRS. P.: Well, ah, you know in the summertime they stay outside; but in this kind of weather they can't get out, and, of course, they like to run and when they run in the house it does kind of get me.

THERAPIST: When you were in the hospital that time after your baby had been born, what was your general feeling about the situation?

MRS. P.: Well, I wasn't too happy in the first place because we had just built a house. I had just started to work and was working about 6 months when I got pregnant and I wasn't too happy about the whole thing then, because I liked my job and, building a house, we wanted new furniture and all — Well, I guess we neither one of us were happy about it. And then just before the baby was born I said if it's a girl, a dark headed girl with brown eyes it will be fine, but it turned out that it was blonde and a boy too. *(Laughs)*.

THERAPIST: Was that important?

MRS. P.: That it was a girl or boy?

THERAPIST: Yes. Were you just joking?

MRS. P.: Well, no I don't think I was joking, because I really didn't much want it to look like my husband and his side of the family *(Laughs)* but it turned out to be the image of his Daddy. But I think that was a selfish . . .

THERAPIST: Well, that's all right.

MRS. P.: . . . on my part. It's probably a selfish way to look at it. I wanted a dark headed girl.

THERAPIST: Well, you were expressing how you felt about the child at that time. It was just your feeling, and there's no question of right or wrong. It was your true feeling . . . Don't you like the way your husband's family looks?

MRS. P.: (*laughing*) I could never like their looks. I know they like me because of the way they act and . . .I wouldn't do anything against them.

THERAPIST: It is quite possible not to like the way some people look.

MRS. P.: I must have liked the way my husband looked or I wouldn't have married him.

THERAPIST: Then why was it important to you to have a child look like your family?

MRS. P.: Well, as I said, I think it was just selfish on my part.

THERAPIST: But, you had a preference. It is not a matter of being selfish. You had a preference.

MRS. P.: Well, I felt I had to go through having and caring for the baby and all and I felt like I sort of wanted it to look like me since I had to go through it all.

THERAPIST: Sort of reward for your trouble?

MRS. P.: That's right.

THERAPIST: Did you ever have this sort of feeling before this child was born?

MRS. P.: Never.

THERAPIST: Well, when I said that, I wasn't thinking only about this feeling about knives, but has it ever happened before that you had a feeling of wanting to smash up things, maybe, if you were cross about them?

MRS. P.: I've always been sort of, you know perfectionist, I guess you'd say, particular about my things. I had two younger sisters and I know if they meddled with any of my things it . . .I would get awfully mad about that . . . but I never wanted to hurt anybody.

THERAPIST: Would you ever want to hit them?

MRS. P.: I don't think so.

THERAPIST: Would you ever want to hit anybody who annoyed you? Or when situations worked out the way you didn't like?

MRS. P.: I don't think so. I can't remember it . . .

THERAPIST: Well, it doesn't have to be a matter of hurting anybody physically, but just a feeling of anger and expressing anger towards people. Well, now let's get your background. Where were you born?

MRS. P.: Norfolk.

THERAPIST: How many brothers and sisters?

MRS. P.: Four sisters and one brother.

THERAPIST: And where do you come?

MRS. P.: I'm in the middle. There's two sisters and a brother older and two sisters younger.

THERAPIST: Will you just tell me how much older than you your eldest sister is?

MRS. P.: She was 47 in October . . . and I've got one who will be 45 in January and my brother will be 43 in December, and then 18 months younger there's a sister, and one 2 years younger than her.

THERAPIST: Are your parents alive?

MRS. P.: Yes.

THERAPIST: What kind of person is your father, especially as you remember him in your childhood?

MRS. P.: Sweet and easy going.

THERAPIST: Did you feel he was interested in you?

MRS. P.: You mean what I did at school and like that?

THERAPIST: Was your father interested in you personally and in what you were doing?

MRS. P.: Not too much.

THERAPIST: Did he ever punish you?

MRS. P.: No.

THERAPIST: And what about your mother?

MRS. P.: Well, I could say the same about her. They were both good — you know — provided. She . . .well she was interested, did things like driving us to school. She didn't seem to be too interested in how we got along or what we did. And I failed and I made awful grades in school. She never talked to the teacher to find out if I could have done better, or anything like that. She never helped with homework or anything like that. Of course, I guess she always had too much else to do.

THERAPIST: Aside from the fact that your parents were rather similar people would you say they sort of liked each other and also behaved towards you as though they liked you?

MRS. P.: Well, they tried to see that we did right and I can remember they always took us to Sunday School and to church.

THERAPIST: Did they get on well together?

MRS. P.: Well, yes. As far as I know. They had arguments.

THERAPIST: Did they have lots of arguments?

MRS. P.: Well, no; after all they lived together forty some years.

THERAPIST: Were there any other adults who played any important part in your early home life — like grandmothers, aunts or nurses?

MRS. P.: No, I don't remember any grandmothers or aunts.

THERAPIST: How did you get on with your brother and sisters?

MRS. P.: Well, pretty good, I guess. Of course, when you are children I think you fuss and fight lots of times. Now I think we all get along good.

THERAPIST: Did you have any particular fears when you were a child?

MRS. P.: Well no, not that I know of. But when I was eight years old our house burned down. I was on my way home from school and the fire trucks passed us. It was in January and it was snowing like anything and somebody told us that our house was on fire. And there was a fear . . . it was. My parents lost most everything they had. And I know they . . .oh, 5 or 6 years after that every time I would hear a fire engine I would get so nervous if I was in school I would have to get up and leave. I wouldn't leave the school, but I would have to get out of the class — but things like that don't bother me now.

THERAPIST: Did you have any other such experiences, or any other fears at all when you were a child?

MRS. P.: No.

THERAPIST: Well now, you said that you didn't get on very well at school. Apart from the fact that your studies were difficult how did you like school?

MRS. P.: I liked it fine. I mean I just played right along.

THERAPIST: Well, did you always do badly at your classes.

MRS. P.: Yes.

THERAPIST: What about sports? How were you at them?

MRS. P.: I might have taken after father in sports. I did well.

THERAPIST: Did you make friends at school?

MRS. P.: Yes, I had plenty of friends at school.

THERAPIST: Did you have any close friends?

MRS. P.: Well, yes. There were about six or eight of us that always chummed around together, girls and . . .

THERAPIST: Were there any people at school you were afraid of? I mean either among the girls or teachers?

MRS. P.: No.

THERAPIST: How far did you go in school?

MRS. P.: I finished high school.

THERAPIST: How old were you then?

MRS. P.: Eighteen.

THERAPIST: And then what did you do?

MRS. P.: I worked for a doctor for three years.

THERAPIST: As a receptionist?

MRS. P.: I did his lab work and typing, shorthand . . .helped with his patients.

THERAPIST: Did you like that work?

MRS. P.: Yes, very much.

THERAPIST: And then what did you do?

MRS. P.: I worked for a power company for five years, as a clerk-stenographer. I liked that too.

THERAPIST: And then?

MRS. P.: Got married. I didn't work for about ten months. Then I worked for a plastic firm in Norfolk until the first child was born — as I told you.

THERAPIST: And since then?

MRS. P.: Housewife.

THERAPIST: How do you like being a housewife?

MRS. P.: Fine.

THERAPIST: Is there anything you don't like about it?

MRS. P.: That things don't stay clean when cleaned. *(Laughs)* No, I like it fine, I wouldn't go back into public work for anything. Unless I could work in a hospital, something like that. I should say something like that when my children are through school.

THERAPIST: How old were you when you first had any kind of sexual feelings?

MRS. P.: Well, I . . . *(desperate gesture)*

THERAPIST: Well. roughly — were you ten, or fifteen or twenty? More or less?

MRS. P.: Well, I can't remember. I have no idea.

THERAPIST: Well then, was it before ten?

MRS. P.: I wouldn't think so.

THERAPIST: Was it before fifteen? . .Before twenty?

MRS. P.: Well I would think it was before twenty.

THERAPIST: Say about seventeen?

MRS. P.: Well, yes, maybe.

THERAPIST: In what kind of a situation did you have your first sexual feeling? Was it out with boys, or at the movies, or what?

MRS. P.: Well, I never dated, too much. And when I was in school, well, in my class in school there just wasn't any boy. And . . .

THERAPIST: So, you started to date when you were eighteen or so, after you left school?

MRS. P.: That's right.

THERAPIST: At that stage did you go out with lots of different boys or just one at a time? Did you go to parties? What was the pattern?

MRS. P.: Well, I went around with several. I belonged to the choir at church and whenever there were things like Sunday School parties we'd usually take somebody with us.

THERAPIST: Well . . .when did you first become especially interested in anybody?

MRS. P.: Well, let's see. I started going with my husband, Charles, I guess in July of '49. And after I started going with him I never did go out with anybody else.

THERAPIST: There has been nobody else ever in whom you have been really interested?

MRS. P.: Well, when I was working at my second job, there was a boy there, but he was married, and I never did go out with him.

THERAPIST: What did you like about him?

MRS. P.: Well just everything. (*Laughs*) And, ah, well he showed me a lot of attention too. Then he quit and went to Richmond to work and I never did see him again.

THERAPIST: So you didn't have any kind of going out with him or any physical contact?

MRS. P.: I know a lot of people wouldn't believe this but it's absolutely true.

THERAPIST: Well, then you began going out with Charles?

MRS. P.: No I had already been going out with him previously, since the summer of '49, and I didn't stop work there until summer of '51.

THERAPIST: What did you like about him?

MRS. P.: My husband is just . . .the way he . . . well just everything I guess. He was nice and the thing that impressed me with him most was the way he treated his mother. He was good to his mother. His father had been dead for a few years and he was good to her, and he always phoned her, and I felt like anybody who would be that good to his mother might be a good husband.

THERAPIST: Well, when did you feel that you were ready to marry him?

MRS. P.: I don't know if I ever did feel like I was. I went with him for seven years.

THERAPIST: Well was he interested in marrying you earlier?

MRS. P.: Uh-huh. Everytime I would put it off. And I would say okay and then I would get nervous and upset and couldn't sleep and would say well, I can't go through this again. So we would put it off again, until he got fed up with that. He was working, and when he got fed up he said he was going to quit his job and go to college. And he did.

THERAPIST: He went to college?

MRS. P.: Uh-huh. From January '53 to June '56. And then he went to Tennessee and got a job at——. When he left, of course, it left me sitting at home by myself and I nearly died. I lost twenty pounds, I couldn't eat, I couldn't sleep.

THERAPIST: Well, can you tell me what the other man you mentioned had that Charles didn't have? What points were important as far as your feelings were concerned?

MRS. P.: Oh, he was good looking. But I was thinking of my husband's blonde hair and blue eyes. He had dark hair and dark eyes.

THERAPIST: When you had the prospect of marriage to Charles before you, and you felt nervous, what did you feel nervous about? Was there any particular aspect of the relationship that made you feel nervous?

MRS. P.: The whole thing I guess. I just wasn't ready to get married.

THERAPIST: In 1954 Charles went to study?

MRS. P.: January 1953. And he finished in '56.

THERAPIST: To do that he went out of town?

MRS. P.: Yeah, he went to Baltimore.

THERAPIST: So eventually you got married. When?

Mrs. P.: In August of 1956.

Therapist: At that stage were you satisfied about being married?

Mrs. P.: Well, he first of all, he called me from Tennessee and said, "If you don't marry me now," he says, "we're through. I'm leaving the country." So it was then or never, so I said "Okay." So we got married the next autumn.

Therapist: Well, how do you get along together?

Mrs. P.: We get along fine. I knew I would never marry anybody else. Well, I guess I'm just the type of person, you know, someone sort of has to say well we are going to do it now or never.

Therapist: How is the sexual side of your marriage?

Mrs. P.: Fine, I hope he'd say the same (laughs).

Therapist: At this moment I'm only interested in your side. Do you have climaxes?

Mrs. P.: Yes.

Therapist: Always?

Mrs. P.: Well, no I don't always, but I do at least part of the time.

Therapist: So you're quite happy in general about the marriage?

Mrs. P.: Well, I wouldn't be any other way.

Therapist: What do you mean by that?

Mrs. P.: Well, I mean I wouldn't be single again.

Therapist: But you have no complaints about the marriage?

Mrs. P.: No.

Therapist: How many children have you now?

Mrs. P.: I have two. The girl will be three on the 16th of this month.

Therapist: Do you like your children?

Mrs. P.: Well, I should say I do.

Therapist: Except when they make a lot of noise and get on your nerves?

Mrs. P.: Well, that's to be expected. I wonder sometimes what my mother did when there were six of us. Of course we weren't all there at the same time.

Therapist: Your children are quite well?

Mrs. P.: Yes.

Therapist: Do you like living in Richmond?

Mrs. P.: Better than I expected. I'd heard that the people were not too friendly, but I found out that they are.

Therapist: Is there anything you're not satisfied with?

Mrs. P.: Well, I would like to have a new house. We had to buy an old house and there wasn't anything to rent or to buy right when we had to move so we bought this old house and it still needs a lot done to it.

Therapist: What's your religion?

Mrs. P.: Methodist.

Therapist: Is religion important in your life?

Mrs. P.: Yes it is.

Therapist: Well, in what way?

Mrs. P.: Well, I don't think you can get along without it.

Therapist: Do you spend a lot of time with church activities?

Mrs. P.: Oh, no, no. I haven't been to church in Richmond. We have taken the children to Sunday School.

Therapist: Well, do you worry much about what God is thinking about what you're doing?

Mrs. P.: I do the best I can.

Therapist: Well, I've got enough of the important background information. I will give you one or two questionnaires to do as homework and then next time you come here we'll talk of the treatment procedures. We'll probably be doing a special kind of treatment, called desensitization. It involves deep muscle relaxation and other special procedures. That is all for now.

Case 2: This first interview portrays the therapist's insistent efforts to define the stimulus sources of the patient's anxiety reactions to certain social situations. After his initial probings in this direction, he turns to the patient's life history, but interrupts the chronicle repeatedly to follow up clues that may throw further light on the anxiety-controlling stimuli. Towards the end of the interview, although the life history has not been completed, he renews his focus on these stimuli. During this part of the exploration, there is an examination of some situations that require self-assertion, from which it emerges that anxiety towards the consequences of assertion is so great as to render futile any attempt to instigate it without prior desensitization.

First Interview in a Case of Interpersonal Anxiety (Miss G. aet.21).

THERAPIST: So your name is Carol Grant? How old are you?

MISS G.: 21.

THERAPIST: What is your complaint?

MISS G.: I am very very nervous all the time.

THERAPIST: All the time?

MISS G.: Yes, all the time.

THERAPIST: How long has this been so?

MISS G.: Since I was about fourteen.

THERAPIST: Can you remember what brought it on?

MISS G.: No, not really. I wish I could.

THERAPIST: But, are you not saying that before you were fourteen you were not nervous?

MISS G.: Well I was, but not to this extreme. I remember being . . .especially in elementary school when I would have to read something in front of the class, then I would get very nervous about that — giving speeches or anything or answering in class. That would bother me.

THERAPIST: Well, that is a special situation.

MISS G.: Yea, but now all the time. When I go out of the house, or walk out the door.

THERAPIST: Well, let's try to build up a picture. You say that in elementary school you were only nervous when you had to get up and speak in front of the class. Only then?

MISS G.: Yes.

THERAPIST: And then in high school?

MISS G.: It got worse. When we would go out with boys I would be very nervous.

THERAPIST: Do you mean that you became more nervous in front of the class?

MISS G.: I wouldn't sleep for nights worrying about giving a speech in front of class or something like that.

THERAPIST: And you also said you became nervous about going out with boys.

MISS G.: Yes. You know, I was afraid, especially if I would have a blind date I would be scared to death.

THERAPIST: Well, isn't that to some extent natural?

MISS G.: I guess so, but not to the extremes that I would go to.

THERAPIST: And if you went out with somebody you knew. What about that?

MISS G.: Well, after a while I would be a little calmer, but still nervous.

THERAPIST: And what about if you went out with girl friends?

MISS G.: Not as much. I wouldn't be quite as nervous, but still a little bit.

THERAPIST: Were there any other situations in which you developed nervousness while you were in high school?

MISS G.: No others that I can think of, just basically when I would walk out of the house everything would just bother me.

THERAPIST: Everything? Like what?

MISS G.: Well, you know I was afraid to take tests or things like that or make speeches like I said before. Just to be with people would scare me.

THERAPIST: Just being with any people?

MISS G.: Yes, it would bother me more if I was with people I didn't know too well.

THERAPIST: What about at times of vacation?

MISS G.: Vacation? I don't understand what you mean.

THERAPIST: Well, I mean you have to take tests and so on at school, but during vacation there are no tests. So would you still be nervous going out of the house?

MISS G.: A little bit. But not quite as much. Because I wouldn't be thinking of that.

THERAPIST: What year did you graduate from school?

MISS G.: 1963.

THERAPIST: And what did you do then?

MISS G.: I went to school and became a technician.

THERAPIST: What kind of technician?

MISS G.: X-ray.

THERAPIST: Do you like this work?

MISS G.: Not really. It's just because I didn't know really what else to do. I thought it would be interesting and the only reason I went into it is because I thought it was interesting, but once I got there I was very nervous about everything. It would scare me to be with patients.

THERAPIST: Patients would scare you?

MISS G.: Well, especially the sick ones. If something would happen to them.

THERAPIST: You were scared that something might happen to them?

MISS G.: Yes, like they would have an attack or something.

THERAPIST: Has this ever happened?

MISS G.: No, not really.

THERAPIST: Well, it is now about five years since you became a technician.

MISS G.: It is about four.

THERAPIST: During those four years have you become more nervous or less nervous or stayed the same?

MISS G.: Definitely more.

THERAPIST: You have been getting gradually more nervous?

MISS G.: Yes.

THERAPIST: All the time?

MISS G.: Yes. My mouth tightens up all the time.

THERAPIST: I see. Now, are there any special things that make you nervous nowadays?

MISS G.: Special things?

THERAPIST: Well, let's start off by considering your work situation.

MISS G.: Yes?

THERAPIST: You said that sick patients make you more nervous.

MISS G.: And my boss.

THERAPIST: Yes?

MISS G.: He makes me extremely nervous. I am afraid of him.

THERAPIST: Why, is he very strict?

MISS G.: Um, yes, he gives that appearance.

THERAPIST: Does he carry on? Does he scream and so on?

MISS G.: Never at me. But I am always afraid that will happen.

THERAPIST: And what about nurses?

MISS G.: Not really. I am not in too much contact with them.

THERAPIST: And who else scares you?

MISS G.: Men.

THERAPIST: Men?

MISS G.: If I go out with them.

THERAPIST: Yes. What about men who come in where you are working, like medical students?

MISS G.: Yes, they scare me too. They do.

THERAPIST: They scare you, how?

MISS G.: I am afraid to . . . I don't know. I am not afraid of them really. I am just afraid of how I'll act . . . that my nervousness will show through. And I think about it so much.

THERAPIST: Well, is it correct to say that you are sort of scared of being watched?

MISS G.: Yes. I think everybody is always watching me.

THERAPIST: Now, that is at work. What other circumstances scare you when you are away from work?

MISS G.: Just going out. I am afraid, you know, that they'll see the way I am. I am afraid to pick something up, because I am afraid that I am going to shake, and my mouth is all tightened up. I am afraid to look at people directly in the eye.

THERAPIST: Are you only afraid of looking at your escort in the eye, or afraid of anybody?

MISS G.: Anybody.

THERAPIST: So looking at a person face to face increases your nervousness?

MISS G.: Yes.

THERAPIST: Suppose that you were walking down the street and there was a bench across the road with some people waiting for a bus. Now those people would be sort of vaguely looking across the street. Would you be aware of their presence?

MISS G.: Yes, definitely.

THERAPIST: Even though they might not be particularly looking at you?

MISS G.: Yes.

THERAPIST: Now, supposing we take people away altogether. Suppose that you are just walking all by yourself, say in a park. There is no one else at all there. Are you then completely comfortable?

MISS G.: Yes.

THERAPIST: I must be quite certain of this.

MISS G.: Yes.

THERAPIST: If you are completely by yourself, are you absolutely calm and comfortable?

MISS G.: Yes, I am. The same way I am at home. I feel alright.

THERAPIST: Well, that means there are some people who can look at you and not bother you.

MISS G.: Yes, at times. But I don't know why this happens.

THERAPIST: Well, what about your mother?

MISS G.: No, it doesn't bother me at home.

THERAPIST: Your mother can look at you as much as she likes?

MISS G.: Yes. It's silly but . . .

THERAPIST: Well, that's not silly. I mean this is just the way things have developed.

MISS G.: I know.

THERAPIST: And who else can look at you without bothering you?

MISS G.: My whole family.

THERAPIST: Who is in your family?

MISS G.: My father, my mother, my sister, my grandmother.

THERAPIST: Besides these people, are there any others at all who can look at you without disturbing you?

MISS G.: No.

THERAPIST: What about a little baby?

MISS G.: No, that doesn't disturb me, and an older person who is senile or something. That doesn't bother me.

THERAPIST: What about a little boy of four?

MISS G.: No.

THERAPIST: Six?

MISS G.: No.

THERAPIST: Eight?

MISS G.: No. It's when they get older, I get nervous.

THERAPIST: Twelve?

MISS G.: Around in their teens.

THERAPIST: About twelve? They sort of begin to bother you?

MISS G.: Yes.

THERAPIST: I take it that a boy of twelve wouldn't be as bad as one of eighteen?

MISS G.: No.

THERAPIST: Let's go back to the street where you are walking and there are 3 people sitting on a bench across the road. Would it make any difference to you whether they were three men or three women?

MISS G.: No, it wouldn't. I would feel worse if I would see somebody very handsome.

THERAPIST: When you see him, even if he is not looking at you?

MISS G.: Yes, that's correct.

THERAPIST: If you go to a movie and see a very handsome film star, does that bother you?

MISS G.: No, not really, because I know he is not there looking at me.

THERAPIST: And if there is a handsome actor on the stage?

MISS G.: Yes, it would.

THERAPIST: It would bother you even though he was not looking at you?

MISS G.: Unless it is very dark and he could not see me.

THERAPIST: Well then, it is only if he can see you that you feel afraid — because you think that he might see you.

MISS G.: I think he might.

THERAPIST: Besides looking at you, what else can people do to make you nervous? You have, I think, mentioned one thing. They can be critical of you. You are scared of your boss criticizing you.

MISS G.: Any criticism gets me upset even if I know that I am right. I can't talk back and tell them that I am right in this case, I just get all choked up and feel like I am going to cry.

THERAPIST: Is there anything else that people do to upset you?

Miss G.: Well, let them just tell me I'm wrong — if I am wrong or if I'm right it still bothers me. It upsets me.

Therapist: That's a kind of criticism. Supposing people praise you?

Miss G.: That makes me feel good.

Therapist: It makes you feel good. Okay. Who is older, you or your sister?

Miss G.: I am.

Therapist: By how much?

Miss G.: Three years.

Therapist: What sort of person is your father?

Miss G.: He's on the quiet side, and both of my parents are on the nervous side. My sister, too. The whole family really.

Therapist: Was your father kind to you when you were a little girl?

Miss G.: Yes.

Therapist: And your mother?

Miss G.: Yes, she's the stronger one. I'm more like my father and my sister is more like my mother.

Therapist: In what way is your mother stronger?

Miss G.: Well, things don't bother her, at least outwardly, as much as they do my father and me. She sort of makes decisions.

Therapist: What does your father do?

Miss G.: He sells insurance.

Therapist: Did either of your parents punish you when you were young?

Miss G.: They used to hit me once in a while. My mother did. My father hardly ever did — not if I did something wrong.

Therapist: Did your mother hit you often?

Miss G.: Not that often.

Therapist: Well, did she do anything else to discipline you?

Miss G.: No, that's all. She would have little talks.

THERAPIST: Did you feel when your parents punished you that it was unreasonable?

MISS G.: Sometimes I did.

THERAPIST: Were there any other adults who played any important part in your home life — grandmothers, aunts, nurses?

MISS G.: Yes, my grandmother — she lives with us.

THERAPIST: Okay, well now — what about her? What kind of a person is she?

MISS G.: She is very good to me. I am her first grandchild, so she pays more attention to me than to my sister, but she doesn't understand a lot of things because she wasn't born in America and she did not have an education.

THERAPIST: How do you get along with your sister?

MISS G.: We used to fight an awful lot, but lately we have been getting along better than we used to, but we are not really close because she is completely different than I am.

THERAPIST: What is she like?

MISS G.: She's more talkative than I am — more outgoing. I'm on the quiet side.

THERAPIST: Did you go to school in Philadelphia, Carol?

MISS G.: Yes, I did.

THERAPIST: Did you like school?

MISS G.: Not really.

THERAPIST: What did you dislike about it?

MISS G.: I was afraid in getting up in front of the class.

THERAPIST: Yes, is that all?

MISS G.: Yes.

THERAPIST: How well did you do?

MISS G.: I was a B average.

THERAPIST: Did you take part in sport?

MISS G.: No.

THERAPIST: Did you make friends?

Miss G.: Yes, I have a lot of friends.

Therapist: Any close friends?

Miss G.: Yes, one in particular.

Therapist: You say that you don't like being an X-Ray technician. What would you like to be?

Miss G.: I would like to be a kindergarten teacher.

Therapist: A kindergarten teacher?

Miss G.: I like to be with children.

Therapist: Apart from this fear of getting up and speaking, did you have any other fears when you were small?

Miss G.: No.

Therapist: Like, maybe, insects, darkness?

Miss G.: I was afraid to take a shower because I had claustrophobia.

Therapist: When was that?

Miss G.: It was about 12 or 13. I was afraid to be closed in. Somebody locked me in a closet and I couldn't stand it. It scared me.

Therapist: How old were you when that happened?

Miss G.: I really don't remember. I guess about 10 or 11.

Therapist: After you were 12, that fear disappeared?

Miss G.: Well, I would still be afraid if someone would lock me in a closet. I am not afraid to take showers.

Therapist: Do you like going into elevators?

Miss G.: I used to be afraid, I am not anymore.

Therapist: You're quite okay now?

Miss G.: Yes, I take it everyday.

Therapist: Do you remember any experience at all when you were at school that was particularly frightening in relationship to getting up and talking in class?

Miss G.: Yes, when I was in sixth grade I had to read something in front of the class. I was holding the paper and I started shaking. And the teacher said "What's the matter?" and

I couldn't really talk. And from then on if I had to read something I'd put it down on the desk and look at it. I would still be nervous.

THERAPIST: Before this happened were you already nervous?

MISS G.: Yes.

THERAPIST: And after this, you were much worse?

MISS G.: Yes.

THERAPIST: Let me ask you how you would react to certain everyday situations. Supposing you were standing in line and somebody got in front of you, how would you feel and what would you do?

MISS G.: I wouldn't do anything but I would feel I would be ready to explode because I would think it was wrong.

THERAPIST: Yes, certainly it would be wrong.

MISS G.: But I can't say anything about it. I can't get up the nerve to say anything.

THERAPIST: And does that apply to every situation of that type?

MISS G.: Yes. There's a man who gets on the same bus and he limps and he hasn't gotten in front of me but he pushes and slides and nobody says anything to him and it really upsets me because everybody always complains but nobody says anything.

THERAPIST: Well, why would you not say something to him?

MISS G.: I would just be afraid to. He has a mean temper.

THERAPIST: Well supposing it wasn't him? Supposing you were standing in line at the Academy of Music box office and somebody you don't know got in front of you?

MISS G.: I probably still wouldn't say anything.

THERAPIST: Why not?

MISS G.: Just because I'm afraid to. I'm afraid to open my mouth.

THERAPIST: Does this have anything to do with the idea that if you were to say something, people would start looking at you?

MISS G.: Maybe.

THERAPIST: Let me try to put the question in another way. I would like you to think very carefully before you answer. Supposing you didn't care if people looked at you, would you say something?

Miss G.: I really don't know. It's just that I can't get it out. The words just won't come out.

THERAPIST: Well, all right. You realize that if somebody does a thing like that, getting in front of you, he is doing you a wrong. One of the things you are going to learn to do when you are treated here is precisely to take action about that kind of thing — to stand up for yourself and not allow people to do you wrong.

Miss G.: How do you go about planning that?

THERAPIST: Essentially what you do is to express the annoyance that you rightly feel. It is very hard at first, but if you make a special point of doing it, you find that it gets easier and easier.

Miss G.: I have tried but I can't; if the situation arises, the words just don't come out and I start stuttering.

THERAPIST: Well, I will help you. Later on, each time you come here, I will say, "Carol, did you have any situations of this sort last week?" You will say, maybe, "Yes," and I will want to know what you tried to do about it. But in the meantime, I know it is difficult for you because of the very special fear you have of being the center of attention; if you tell someone to get back in line, he would look at you and other people would look at you. And that makes it more difficult.

Miss G.: Yes.

THERAPIST: So one of the things we will have to do is to break down this fear that you have of being looked at. In order to do this, we need to know more about it. Let's use as a kind of basic situation the one we mentioned in which you are sitting on a bench across the road. Now, would it make any difference to you how wide the street was?

Miss G.: Yes — if they were closer to me I would feel worse.

THERAPIST: I see. Now I find it very useful to have some kind of quantitative way of expressing how much afraid a person would be. One way to do it is to ask you to think of the worst fear that you ever had and call that 100; and then you think of being absolutely calm, as when you are at home, and call that zero. Now, consider that the street is as wide as Broad Street (about 100 feet) and there is just one person sitting on that bench; how much anxiety would you feel? Would it be five, fifty, or twenty or what?

Miss G.: I guess around 50.

Therapist: Now supposing that the street was twice as broad as Broad St. and there is just this one person?

Miss G.: I guess about 25.

Therapist: Now, if you see two persons, would it still be 25?

Miss G.: Yes.

Therapist: It doesn't matter how many?

Miss G.: No, well if there is a whole group it's worse.

Therapist: Supposing that you are standing at one side of a football stadium that is twice as wide as Broad St., and there is one man sitting on one of the stands right across the other side; how much anxiety would that cause you?

Miss G.: Around 25.

Therapist: And if instead of being a man, it was a boy of twelve?

Miss G.: It wouldn't be as large . . . 5, 10.

Therapist: Well, if when you were standing at one side of the stadium, there was one boy of 12 sitting in the stand at the other side, you said you would have 5 or 10 degrees of anxiety. If it is a man of 25 it would be 25 degrees. With a boy about 15, would it be in between?

Miss G.: Yes.

Therapist: I see. Well I think we can take that as a basis for action. But before we can take any action we have to do something else. Let me explain something to you. You know well enough that you have anxiety where you shouldn't have it. In order to combat the anxiety, we have to use reactions inside of you which will fight the anxiety. One very convenient one is brought about by muscle relaxation. Now, you have probably never learned how to relax your muscles properly, have you?

Miss G.: No.

Therapist: Next time I will start to show you.

CHAPTER IV

Setting The
Stage For
Behavior Therapy

THE OBJECTIVE non-judgmental attitude that character-izes the gathering of information as portrayed in the previous chapter permeates every phase of behavior therapy. It is an attitude that comes easily to the dyed-in-the-wool behaviorist but is awkward for almost every-body else.

The behavior therapist takes it for granted that human behavior is subject to causal determination no less than the behavior of falling bodies or of growing plants. For example, a man pauses at crossroads, un-decided along which of two routes to proceed. The route that he eventually takes is the inevitable one, being the resultant of a balancing out of conflicting action-tendencies. The strength of each action-tendency is essentially a function of the incipient reactions evoked by impinging stimuli, internal and external, whose effects depend primarily on the character of previously established neural interconnections — that is, on pre-existing habit structures.

The general attitude of the behavior therapist to his patients accords with this deterministic outlook. He regards the patient as the product of his physical endowment and the cumulative effects of the experiences he has undergone. Each environment, each exposure to stimulation, has modified, through learning, the patient's character as a responding organism to a greater or lesser extent.

Since the patient has had no choice in becoming what he is, it is incongruous to blame him for having gone awry, or to disparage him for the continuance of his unhappy state. The behavior therapist therefore does not moralize to his patient, but on the contrary goes out of his way to dislodge any self-blame that social conditioning may have engendered and that may have been magnified by statements made by friends, relations, and previous therapists. He enables the patient to realize that his unpleasant reactions are due to emotional habits that he cannot help; that they have nothing to do with 'moral fiber' or an unwillingness to get well; that similar reactions are easily induced in animals, who remain neurotic for just as long as the experimenter chooses and that when the experimenter decides to 'cure' the neurosis, he applies to the problem methods that are determined by principles of learning. The unlearning of the experimental neurosis is completely in the control of the experimenter, and, in a parallel way, the overcoming of a human neurosis is within the control of the therapist through techniques quite similar to those used in the laboratory.[1]

[1]It is particularly difficult for those who have previously been trained psychoanalytically to align themselves with this orientation. Even those who have become intellectually disenchanted with 'dynamic' theories and practices, lapse through habit into teleological modes of thought and tend to make interpretative statements that sometimes have condemnatory overtones.

The patient thus oriented is now introduced to the practices of behavior therapy. This is done either by means of short didactic speeches, or else in the course of discussions between patient and therapist that may include other topics.

The central role of fear (anxiety) in the neurosis must be brought to the fore at an early stage. Most patients are quite aware of being hamstrung by fear. Not so many recognize it to be the essence of their disturbed reactions (as shown in Table 1); but most can accept it when the therapist points it out. The distinctive features of the origins of *neurotic* fears are brought out in statements on the following lines:

> You have realized that fear figures excessively in your life. It is necessary to have some perspective about it. It is an emotion that plays a normal part in everybody's life whenever a situation involving a real threat arises — for example, walking alone and unarmed at night in an unsavoury neighborhood, learning that one's firm is about to retrench its staff, or being confronted by a poisonous snake. Nobody would come for treatment because he experiences fear in such situations. It is a different matter when fear is aroused by experiences that contain no real threat — such as seeing an ambulance, entering a crowded room, or riding in a car — to take examples other than your own. To be fearful in such situations is obviously inappropriate, and can interfere with daily functioning in a most distressing way. It is this that we call neurotic fear; and it is the task of therapy to detach it from the stimuli or.situations that provoke it.

> Let us consider how neurotic fears originate. The process is really what common sense would lead you to expect. Let me illustrate it by the old-fashioned example of the burnt child. The child places his hand on the big, black, hot coal stove. He quickly withdraws the painful hand, tearful and fearful. His mother comforts him, but later notes that he keeps away from the stove and seems afraid

of it. Clearly, the child has developed a beneficial habit of fearing and avoiding an actually harmful object.

But in some cases the experience also has other and less favorable consequences. Suppose in the mother's bedroom there is a large black chest of drawers. The child may have become afraid of this too — purely on the basis of its *physical resemblance* to the stove — a phenomenon known in psychology as generalization. Fear of the chest of drawers is neurotic because there can be no harm in touching it. It can have several undesirable implications. In the first place the very presence of an unpleasant emotion like fear, where it is not appropriate, is objectionable. Secondly, the child is now forced to make a detour if the chest of drawers is in his path; and thirdly, he no longer has easy access to any delectable contents of the drawers, such as candy. In these features of the child's case we have the model of all neurotic fear reactions.

Your own fears were likewise acquired in the course of unpleasant experiences, some of which we touched upon in your history. The unpleasant emotions you then had became conditioned, or connected, to aspects of the situation that made an imprint on you at the time. This means that subsequent similar experiences led to the arousal of these same unpleasant feelings. Now just because these reactions could then be produced by particular stimulus-triggers as a result of the operation of a process of learning it is possible to eliminate them by the application of the principles of learning.

In animals the treatment of a neurosis is a very straightforward matter, especially when the experimenter himself has induced the neurosis. In human subjects it can be just as simple but may be complicated by various factors in the more complex organism. However, endowed with language we can unravel most webs and our very complexity gives to human behavior therapy the possibility of a large repertoire of techniques.

Other kinds of orientating information are quite often needed. Although the patient can usually distinguish quite easily between those of his anxiety reactions that are adaptive and those that are not, there can be misapprehensions, and when they appear the therapist must spare no effort to remove them. It is scarcely possible to decondition anxiety from a situation that the patient believes, however wrongly, to embody real danger. No amount of desensitizing effort is likely to make a person indifferent to handling a snake he believes to be poisonous. Misapprehensions are particularly common in fears of the 'hypochondriacal' kind. Only when the patient with recurrent pains in his chest is both assured that the pains do not signify heart disease and also shown their *actual* source, can desensitizing operations be hopefully undertaken. Rarely does 'insight' alone dispel such fears.

Some other kinds of corrective statements that commonly need to be made are typified by the following:

1. *"You are not mentally ill and there is no chance of your going insane."* The bizarreness of their symptoms causes many patients to feel they are 'cracking up', an interpretation that is 'confirmed' when other people, and particularly doctors, do not understand what they are talking about when they try to describe their symptoms. The patient's dismay is naturally much exacerbated if a psychiatrist has told him that he is, or may become, psychotic. It is often sufficient to express reassurance in an authoritatively dogmatic way; but with educated patients a good deal of evidence may have to be provided. It may have to be argued that neuroses and psychoses are not on the same continuum. Thus, however bad a neurosis becomes it is still not a psychosis. Unusually sophisticated individuals may need to be given supporting facts: that psychoses show

a clear inherited pattern not manifest in neuroses; that there is evidence of biochemical abnormality in the serum of psychotics while that of neurotics is indistinguishable from normal; and that in the course of World War II, while the incidence of neuroses gradually rose that of psychoses remained stationary. They may also be told of Eysenck's (1958) finding that neuroses and psychoses are deviations in different dimensions.

2. *"All your reactions are explicable."* Patients who from time to time are overtaken by panic states or depressions whose antecedents are not clear may come to feel chronically apprehensive: they do not know when the 'hidden forces' will strike. Careful examination of the circumstances of these severe reactions almost invariably reveals constancies; and knowing them gives great comfort to the patient — in itself removing a significant source of anxiety.

3. *"There is no virtue in confronting your fears."* Many patients, either on the basis of their moralistic training, or urged by friends or therapists feel that they should benefit by 'facing up' to the situations that evoke anxiety in them. It is usually sufficient to refer to their own experience to convince them that this is futile and even aggravating. It is penance unrewarded by blessings. They should be told how, by contrast, graduated and controlled exposures to disturbing stimuli are more likely to be therapeutically effective.

CHAPTER V

Assertive Training

THE WORD *assertive* is applied to the outward expression of practically all feelings other than anxiety. Experience has shown that such expression tends to inhibit anxiety. Assertiveness usually involves more or less aggressive behavior, but it may express friendly, affectionate, and other non-anxious feelings. Salter (1949) has called such outward expression *excitatory*, but *assertive* in a more accurately informative adjective, since anxiety, too, is a form of excitation.

THE RATIONALE OF ASSERTION

Assertive training, generally speaking, is required for patients who in interpersonal contexts have unadaptive anxiety responses that prevent them from saying or doing what is reasonable and right. If they are inhibited from doing things about which they feel strongly, the suppression of feeling may lead to a continuing inner turmoil which may produce somatic symptoms and even pathological changes in predisposed organs — psychosomatic illnesses (see p. 25). The therapist's interventions are aimed at augmenting every impulse towards the elicitation of these inhibited responses, with the expectation that each time they do, there will, reciprocally, be an inhibiting of the anxiety, resulting in some degree of weakening of the anxiety response habit (Wolpe, 1958, p. 72).

In the acting out of assertion, there is a potentiation or augmentation of the emotion at its core; and the strength this emotion thus acquires enables it to inhibit the concurrently evoked anxiety. Meanwhile, the motor act itself is reinforced by its consequences, such as the attainment of control of a social situation, reduction of anxiety, and later, the approbation of the therapist. Thus, the counterconditioning of anxiety and the operant conditioning of the motor act take place simultaneously, facilitating each other. (For a fuller discussion, see Wolpe, 1958).

Arnold (1945) marshalled the evidence at that time available of a physiological antagonism between anger and anxiety. Ax (1953) expressed doubts about this, although his own data to some extent supported it. Recent Soviet research (Simonov, 1967) has yielded unequivocal evidence of the existence of separate and reciprocally inhibitory centers for anger and anxiety in the midbrain. Both by drugs and by ablations, it is possible to do away with one of these patterns of emotional response while preserving the other.

THE INSTIGATION OF ASSERTION

Information about the patient that leads to the instigation of assertive behavior frequently emerges clearly from the clinical history. The patient may be constantly placating other people because he fears to offend them, or because he feels a moral obligation to place the interests of others before his own. He may allow people to maneuver him into situations he does not desire. He may be unable to express his legitimate wishes. The therapist must explore all areas of difficulty to determine the controlling factors — the situational and personal variables that raise anxieties and decrease the patient's ability to behave appropriately.

Other clues to the need for assertive training may be found in the Willoughby Personality Schedule (Appendix 1) — particularly if strong responses are given to the following questions: Are your feelings easily hurt? Are you shy? Does criticism hurt you badly? Are you self-conscious before superiors?

It is a useful routine to ask the patient how he behaves in a number of set situations with strangers. For some years I have presented these five:

1. What do you do if after having bought an article in a shop you walk out and find that your change is a dollar short?

2. Suppose that, arriving home after buying an article you find it slightly damaged. What will you do?

3. What do you do if somebody pushes in front of you in line (e.g. at the theatre)?

4. At a shop, while you wait for the clerk to finish with the customer ahead of you, another customer arrives and also waits. What do you do if the clerk subsequently directs his attention to that customer instead of to you?

5. You order a steak rare and it arrives well done. How do you handle the situation?

In all these situations, the individual ought to be able to stand up for himself, and is likely to feel upset when he does not. Insofar as he does not, assertive training is indicated.

A very common type of patient for whom assertive training is needed is the one whose early training has over-emphasized social obligations and made him feel that the rights of others are more important than his own. An extreme but not unusual example was a 38-year-old woman who, having been divorced, invited her sister to live with her. Though the sister turned out to be a millstone around her neck, she could not bring herself to ask her to leave. In the course of two years of conflict between the impulse to expel her sister and a conditioned fear of hurting her feelings, she had a continuously high anxiety level which led to the conditioning of further neurotic reactions.

Most patients recognize the need for appropriate assertiveness without any difficulty; but the insight alone, however clear, produces no change (see Wolpe, 1958, p. 120). An indispensable function of the therapist is to help the patient translate the insight into action. Simple direct instruction is sometimes all that is necessary. More often the patient must be gently led towards action. It is helpful to give him an example from a previous case.

My favorite example, which I have used for many years, concerns a university student who, though extremely bright, kept failing his examinations and had great trouble in forming relationships with males or females. Assertive training relative to a particular person brought about important changes in interpersonal attitudes and behavior, and diminished his neurotic anxiety. The person concerned was his stepmother, a sarcastic, domineering woman who came closer than anybody else I have ever met to the classic witch of the story books. When he came home from the university, she would attack him with statements like this: "Why can't you pass your exams like Johnny Jones next door?"

He would respond to her attacks in one of three ways. Sometimes he would try to defend himself rationally. Sometimes he would have an outburst of helpless rage. Sometimes he would just feel hurt and perhaps go to his room and sulk. While these patterns of behavior are outwardly various, they all have the same emotional wellspring — a sense of helplessness — an anxious inability to master the situation. When a person is unjustly attacked, even though he may feel anxious, he usually also feels anger and resentment at the attacker. This was the case with this student, as I easily ascertained by questioning him. From this point onward, I began to encourage the expression of the angry feelings, which in the past he had always suppressed. There was some difficulty with this, as there quite often is, but after two or three weeks of persuading he began to be able to do it. To illustrate, let me take again the context of being attacked in relation to Johnny Jones next door. If she now made this attack, he would have responded by saying, "Look here, you say this sort of thing because you are jealous of Mrs. Jones"; or "What is the real reason for your carrying on about this?" By such words expressing his anger and annoyance, he inhibited to some extent the simultaneously present anxiety. Each time he inhibited the anxiety he diminished its habit strength. In about eight weeks, he achieved complete control of his relationship with this woman; and there was generalization to other interpersonal situations.

The particular assertions required of the patient are, on the whole, an individual matter. The following is a sampling of assertive statements, expressing either hostility or commendation. The former are more numerous because they are easily the more frequently relevant to the needs of therapy.

Assertive Statements

A. "*Hostile*"

1. Would you please call me back. I can't speak to you now.
2. Please don't stand in front of me.
3. Will you kindly stop talking during the play/movie/music.
4. This is a line. Your place is at the back.
5. Do you have special privileges in this line?
6. You have kept me waiting for 20 minutes.
7. Do you mind turning down the heat?
8. It's too cold for me to go outside.
9. Please put those heavy packages in a *double* bag (at a supermarket).
10. Your behavior disgusts me.
11. I hate your duplicity.
12. I despise your intolerance/unreasonableness.
13. I can't stand your nagging.
14. If it is not inconvenient, will you pick up my parcel?
15. I'm sorry, but it won't be possible.
16. (To the stewardess on a flight that is late for a connection) Would you ask the pilot to radio ahead to my connecting flight?
17. I would rather not say.
18. Why are you late?
19. If you persist in coming late, I am going to stop making appointments with you.
20. I insist that you come to work on time.
21. How dare you speak to me like that.
22. Pardon me — I was here first.
23. I enjoy talking to you, but please be quiet while I am reading/writing/thinking/listening.

B. "*Commendatory*"

1. That's a beautiful dress/brooch, etc.
2. You look lovely, terrific, ravishing, glamorous, etc.

3. That was a clever remark.
4. What a radiant smile.
5. I like you.
6. I love you.
7. I admire your tenacity.
8. That was brilliantly worked out.

With a reasonable amount of pressure and encouragement, most patients begin to be able to assert themselves in a matter of days, or a week or two. At each interview, they report what they have done in the intervening time, and the therapist commends their successes and corrects their errors. They must be warned not to rest on their laurels, but to be alert for every opportunity for appropriate assertion. As their interpersonal anxiety decreases in consequence of their efforts, acts of assertion become easier to perform. The more they do, the more they can do. One rule must always be observed: *Never instigate an assertive act that is likely to have seriously punishing consequences for the patient.*

Some patients have great difficulty in performing any assertive acts at all. The therapist must ascertain why. He may discover a 'phobic' reaction to some aspect or implication of assertion. For example, the patient may have a strong conditioned anxiety response to perceiving himself behaving aggressively or to the idea of *having* behaved aggressively (i.e. guilt about aggression). A preliminary program of systematic desensitization to the relevant stimulus configurations is then needed (Chapter VII). Severe fear of aggression from others (which is always a *possible* response to assertion) similarly requires desensitization (see Case 2).

When no especially powerful extrinsic fears are evident, more vigorous direct efforts are made towards eliciting assertion. It may suffice simply to increase the patient's motivation by strongly contrasting the negative and unprepossessing effects of timidity with the benefits that assertion is expected to yield; or the therapist may refuse to see the patient until he can report some action. Another possibility is behavior rehearsal.

BEHAVIOR REHEARSAL

This technique (Wolpe, 1958), which has the great merit of lending itself to graduated maneuvers, was originally referred to as "behavioristic psychodrama." *Behavior rehearsal* is a more suitable label. The therapist takes the role of a person towards whom the patient has a neurotic anxiety reaction and instructs him to express his ordinarily inhibited feelings towards that person. Particular attention is given to the emotion infused into the words. The voice must be firm, and suitably modulated. The patient is made to repeat each statement again and again, being constantly corrected until the utterance is in every way satisfactory. The aim of the rehearsal is, of course, to make it possible for him to express himself with his real 'adversary' so that the anxiety the latter evokes may be reciprocally inhibited, and the motor assertive habit established.

Actually, a *good deal of deconditioning of anxiety frequently takes place during the behavior rehearsal itself.* For example, an intelligent woman of 42 had so much anxiety at the idea of inconveniencing people that she could not be persuaded to make even the most miniscule demands of anybody except her closest friends. In behavior rehearsal with her, I took the role of one of her office colleagues who lives near her, and told her to ask me for a ride home (that would only take me out of my way one block). She had difficulty even in formulating this request. I therefore gave her this sentence to use: "If you are going home after work, would you mind giving me a ride home?" Her first enunciation of this was very awkward, and she stated that doing so had evoked a good deal of anxiety (70 *suds* — see p. 118). My reply was, "I will take you with pleasure." With repetition, she articulated the sentence with greater ease and expression, while the level of her anxiety progressively fell. After a total of 8 repetitions in two sessions, she could request that ride with practically no anxiety. During subsequent sessions, the distance she was taking me out of my way was progressively increased. These 'rehearsals' enabled the patient comfortably to make reasonable requests in reality.

The ability of 'put on' behavior to bring out real therapeutic change is in accord with some observations on actors reported by Simonov (1967). Especially (but not only) when the actor has been trained by the Stanislavsky method (which requires him to try to *live* each part), he evinces autonomic responses in the direction of the emotions that he is simulating. Simonov states, "The actors were asked to pronounce certain words under various mentally reproducible conditions. . .The changes in the heart rate, recorded in the actor when he was fulfilling the task, confirm that he was actually reproducing an emotionally colored situation and was not copying intonations formerly noticed in other people. This conclusion was confirmed by comparison with the results of analyzing speech in natural situations." However, there are differences too, because if the actor is doing his part well he gets a pleasurable feeling intermixed with the anxiety or anger that he is enacting. A detailed account of this work is unfortunately available only in manuscript form (Simonov, 1962).

"LIFEMANSHIP"

There are circumstances in which direct assertion is inappropriate, but in which it is nevertheless desirable for the patient to achieve some kind of control. For example, it is not often advisable for an employee to give his employer 'a piece of his mind.' It is then necessary to use more subtle tactics. These are sometimes suggested by special knowledge of the other person's weaknesses, but there are also possibilities that may be applied to almost anybody — statements that automatically put the recipient at a disadvantage, without revealing an aggressive intent on the part of the speaker. A widely usable example is, "Is anything wrong? You don't seem to be quite your usual self today."

A large variety of clever instances of behavior of this kind appear in a series of small books by the British humorist, Stephen Potter, who refers to them as the ploys and gambits of *Lifemanship*. Although Potter's aim is humor and not psychotherapy, there is much that the psychotherapist can use. For example, Potter describes how one day he and Professor Joad were playing tennis against two Oxford University students — fine upstanding young men. A student's first service, delivered to Joad, was an ace which Joad did not get near. He then served to Potter with the same result. At the next service, Joad just managed to get the wood frame of his racket to the ball, which went flying over the net and hit the bottom of the wire netting boundary on the students' side. Then, as the student was crossing over to deliver the *coup de grace,* Joad shouted out, "Was that ball in or out?" The student replied, "I am terribly sorry, Sir, I thought it was out. Shall we have it over?" "No, no," said Joad, "it is quite all right, but in the future will you state clearly whether or not the ball is in or out." This slight suggestion of unsportsmanlike behavior was sufficiently upsetting to undermine the students' performance and make them lose the game!

Of all the methods under the rubric of behavior therapy, assertive training lends itself least to the kind of description that the reader can directly transfer to cases of his own. Little practical purpose is served by longitudinal case accounts (of which Case 10 in Chapter XIII is an example). Technical nuances are more readily conveyed by live demonstrations than by written accounts: Films and tape recordings have a very useful role. A published tape of my own that *inter alia* demonstrates assertive training, is the *Case of Mrs. Schmidt* (1964).[1]

---

[1]Published by Counsellor Recordings, Nashville, Tenn.

CHAPTER VI

Therapeutic Sexual Arousal: The Treatment Of Impotence And Frigidity

BECAUSE of the predominantly parasympathetic character of preorgasmic sexual arousal (Langley and Anderson 1895; Masters and Johnson, 1966) — it is not surprising to find that sexual arousal can be an anxiety inhibitor, and, consequently, a source of conditioned inhibition of anxiety habits. Napalkov and Karas (1957) have shown that experimental neuroses in dogs can be overcome by counterposing sexual excitation to neurotic anxiety; and clinical neuroses have been treated with considerable success on the same basis — as will be described below.

As would be expected, it is usually in connection with anxieties related to sexual stimuli that sexual arousal has therapeutic application. But its effects are not necessarily confined to these stimuli. The neurotic reactions of the dogs treated by Napalkov and Karas were conditioned to nonsexual stimuli. Similarly, sexual emotions are not infrequently instrumental in overcoming human nonsexual neuroses. But so far the effects obtained in this direction have been fortuitous. A fortunate twist in the course of a person's life may provide him with an exciting new sexual relationship that results in therapeutic consequences. The emotion then involved is, however, not purely sexual excitation — but a broad-based arousal that in many instances would be called 'love'. A case in point was an exceptionally intelligent young woman who felt herself disparaged by all other intelligent people whom she encountered, especially at social gatherings. Then she married a man with whom she had fallen deeply in love. Now, constantly suffused with amorous feelings, she found that she no longer had anxiety in social contexts. Years later, when the phase of high romance was long past, she was still free from her original anxiety. The anxiety had presumably undergone conditioned inhibition due to reciprocal inhibition at the time of romantic arousal.

As a matter of fact, a variety of nonanxious emotions are responsible for those therapeutic changes that occur without any intervention by a therapist. It is probable that the majority of neuroses that people suffer are mild, and that most of these are in time overcome by the competition of the intercurrent emotions that are aroused by life events (Wolpe, 1958, p. 198).

THE TREATMENT OF IMPOTENCE

The main deliberate use of the anxiety-inhibiting effects of erotic arousal is in the treatment of impaired sexual performance in the male, which is generally manifested as inadequacy of penile erection or premature ejaculation or both. Penile erection is a parasympathetic function. The sympathetic discharges that characterize anxiety tend both to inhibit erection and also to facilitate ejaculation, because it too is subserved by the sympathetic (Langley and Anderson, 1895). Thus, the key to the problem of impaired sexual performance is the subtraction of anxiety from the sexual encounter. Sometimes the anxiety has nonsexual antecedents, e.g. a fear of traumatization of human flesh (Wolpe, 1958, p. 152), but in the great majority of cases its stimuli are within the sexual situation.

In using the sexual response as an anxiety inhibitor, the first requirement is to ascertain at what point in the approach anxiety begins and what factors increase it. Perhaps the man begins to feel anxiety the moment he enters the bedroom, or perhaps it is when he is lying in bed in the nude with his wife. The basic idea of the treatment is explained to him. He has to obtain the cooperation of his wife. She has to know he has a problem that must be handled gently. The essence of her role is to avoid making her husband tense and anxious. She must not mock, goad or press him to achieve any particular level of performance. Though this means her enduring a good deal of frustration, she may hope to reap the reward of her patience eventually. Where the man begins to feel anxiety just lying next to his wife in bed, nothing more active should be done until the anxiety has entirely dissipated. Usually, after 2 or 3 occasions he will be able to say, "I feel perfectly comfortable, now — only sexually excited." Then, he can go on to the next stage — perhaps to turn towards her and lie facing her on his side while she remains on her back. When this can be done without anxiety, he again advances — this time, perhaps, to lying on top of her but not attempting intromission. At the next step, the penis may be approximated to the clitoris or other parts of the vulva, but still without intromission. After this he is permitted a small degree of entry, and later greater degrees, followed by small amounts of movement and then greater movement. The precondition for advancing beyond a stage is the disappearance from it of all anxiety.

The details of treatment vary from case to case. Male sex hormone is occasionally indispensable (Miller, Hubert and Hamilton, 1938); and tranquillizing drugs also have a place (see Chapter IX). A procedure that is frequently of great value was first suggested by Semans (1956). The wife is asked to manipulate the penis to a point just short of ejaculation and then to stop. After an interval, she does so again. It may be repeated several times during a session, and over several sessions. The effect is to increase the latency to ejaculation from a few seconds to half an hour or more. It is easy to see that once this has been achieved, the man is in a much better potential position to achieve successful intercourse. Semans describes his technique, which Case 3 illustrates, as follows:

> If fatigue is present in either partner, he or she should sleep for a brief period of time. After this love play is begun and progresses to mutual stimulation of the penis and clitoris. Each is instructed to inform the other of the stage of sexual excitement being experienced. When the husband feels a sensation which is, for him, premonitory to ejaculation, he informs his wife and removes her hand until the sensation disappears. Stimulation is begun again and interrupted by the husband when the premonitory sensation returns. . . .By continuing the technique described above ejaculation can eventually be postponed indefinitely. Both husband and wife are advised that if erection subsides more than temporarily, a brief sleep

or postponement of further stimulation is to be preferred to continuing their efforts at that time. Next, each is told separately, and later together, that ejaculation occurs more rapidly with the penis wet than dry. It is necessary, therefore, to use a bland cream or other means to lubricate the penis while the procedure is repeated.

Masters and Johnson (1967) describe a maneuver that can facilitate this technique. They state that when ejaculation seems inevitable it can be inhibited by the woman applying gentle pressure on the penis at the coronal sulcus, one finger pressing on the urethra and another on the dorsum.

In quite a number of cases of premature ejaculation, recovery may be obtained in a much more simple way. The couple are told to have coitus as frequently as possible. The husband is instructed to try to enjoy himself as much as possible, just letting himself go and not caring how soon he ejaculates. The wife is asked to endure the situation if she can (and of course some can not). It is quite helpful in cases like this to encourage the procural of orgasm in the wife by noncoital means — by manual and oral manipulations. A method that Semans (1962) claims is very effective is for the woman to move her clitoris rhythmically against her husband's thigh. Preliminary reorienting discussions are needed for those individuals who regard such noncoital maneuvers as reprehensible for religious or psychoanalytic reasons.

Problems of Female Collaboration

I have emphasized that a cooperative sexual partner is indispensable to the success of techniques utilizing sexual responses, and many patients have one readily available. Others are less fortunate. Sometimes one has

to wait many months before the patient has found somebody sufficiently interested in him to be willing to make
the effort, and bear the discomforts required for his
treatment. Sometimes, although the patient has a wife
or other stable partner, she is unable to participate
as needed, either because she is contemptuous of her
husband's impotence, or more often, because a long
history of disappointment and frustration has quenched
her amorous responses, and left only a heavy negativity
or a dull resentment. If she is unmoved by her husband's
prefiguration of the behavior therapy program the
therapist should arrange to speak to her himself. If
she can be persuaded to take the first steps, and if these
are early encouraged by success, the rest can be plain
sailing. In other cases there is a need to devise a schedule
of approaches to raise the woman's threshold of tolerance
of the man.

When all reasonable efforts have failed to procure
the kind of physical and affectional relationship needed
for the therapeutic program it seems entirely reasonable
to encourage the husband to seek out another woman
who may be more responsive to him. If, through her,
his potency is restored, this in itself may ultimately
lead to the reconstruction of the marriage; and even
if it does not, the man is better off biologically and
psychologically being able to have outside satisfactions
than being doomed to lifelong chastity.

Provided that reasonable safeguards are observed,
it is best for a therapeutic extramarital relationship
to be conducted with somebody in whom there is some
kind of personal interest, but when this is not possible,
paid help has to be sought. The casual 'pick up' will
not do, as she is likely to be interested only in her own
immediate pleasure. Perhaps there will some day be

a 'pool' of accredited women who will sell their services to men with sexual problems. At present there seems to be no other recourse than to seek out a regular prostitute — and it is usually no easy matter to find one who is both personally appealing and able to muster enough sympathetic interest to participate in the therapeutic program. One patient, with a 16-year history of impotence, tried about 10 prostitutes before he found a warm-hearted and considerate one with whose help his sexual anxiety was overcome and his potency restored. Others have found help more easily.

The following is a characteristic therapeutic chronicle:

CASE 3.

> Mr. I., a 36-year-old realtor had suffered from premature ejaculation ever since the beginning of his coital life at the age of 16. Ejaculation generally occurred within 15 seconds of intromission. He had married at 24. His wife, though deriving some satisfaction from digital orgasms, had become increasingly conscious of her incomplete fulfillment, and had in the past two years been showing interest in other men. About 18 months previously, Mr. I. had had about 25 consultations with a 'dynamic' psychiatrist. Though he had found the probing type of approach irritating, his general confidence had been improved by the treatment; but his sexual performance had remained unchanged. In three short-lived extramarital affairs, his sexual performance had been no better than with his wife. He usually felt that he was doing the 'chasing,' and was being accepted to some extent on sufferance.

> Mr. I.'s Willoughby score was 30, with highest loadings for humiliation, stage fright, and being hurt. He lacked assertiveness in relation to people close to him, but not at all in business affairs. A program of assertive training was seen as a secondary but very relevant therapeutic requirement.

Mrs. I., briefly interviewed, expressed great willingness to take part in a behavior therapy program. She stated that digital orgasms satisfied her physically but not emotionally. She felt that even a relatively small degree of prolongation of intromission would enable her to have coital orgasms. She regarded her marriage as very satisfactory in all other respects.

Therapy of the sexual inadequacy based upon use of sexual responses made combined use of two lines of approach: (1) graded penile stimulation by the technique of Semans (see above); and (2) gradual advances towards coitus. Mr. I. kept a detailed record of his performances, which he timed as accurately as possible with a bedside clock. The data of the early and middle stages of his record are reproduced below. Each figure refers to the *number of minutes of manual stimulation of the penis by his wife that brought him just short of ejaculation* for each successive sequence of stimulations.

First occasion (Saturday) 8, 6, 6, 6, and 3 minutes

Second occasion (Saturday) 11, 7, 3, 4 and 4 minutes

Third occasion (Sunday) 8, 6, 5, and 18 minutes.

Fourth occasion (Sunday) 17 minutes

Fifth occasion (Monday) 33 minutes. At this juncture he felt confident enough to have Mrs. I. stimulate him as he sat astride her. The time to 'pre-ejaculation' on two successive sequences was 2 minutes and 3 minutes.

Sixth occasion (Monday) lying face to face sideways the pre-ejaculatory point was reached in 10 minutes and was maintained for 20 more minutes, when Mrs. I. desisted because of fatigue.

After this occasion, Mr. I. declared that he had never before been able to reach and maintain so high a level of excitement; but this became the norm subsequently.

Seventh occasion (Monday) Same as sixth occasion but 'pre-ejaculation' was reached in 14 minutes and again maintained to a total of thirty minutes.

Eighth occasion (Tuesday) Same as sixth occasion but 'pre-ejaculation' was reached in 12 minutes and maintained to 30 minutes.

Ninth occasion (Wednesday) Penile stimulation while astride: 5, 12+, and 9+ minutes.

Tenth occasion (Wednesday) Penile stimulation while astride: 12 and 11 minutes.

Eleventh occasion (Thursday) Penile stimulation while astride: 12½, 12 and 23 minutes. After the last, Mr. I. inserted just the glans of his penis into the vagina, maintaining it there for 5 minutes. In the course of this time Mrs. I. became excited. Thereupon he withdrew and they both had orgasms digitally.

Twelfth occasion (Friday) Partial insertion (glans penis) for 20 minutes during which Mrs. I. alone moved and in this way gradually manipulated the penis deeper. At the end of the period Mr. I. withdrew as he felt ejaculation imminent.

Mr. I. now reported to the therapist that he was feeling very much less anxious than before at partial insertion of his penis. He was finding that his stimulation of his wife was the greatest factor increasing his own excitation. The next objective was to increase both depth and duration of insertion, and thereafter to add small amounts of movement. In the meantime at each meeting with the therapist the patient was receiving training in progressive relaxation.

Thirteenth occasion (Friday evening after meeting with therapist) Partial intercourse lasted 30 minutes — partial insertion 80 per cent of the time and full insertion about 20 per cent, for about a minute at a time. During this minute Mr. I. would move constantly, without feeling any danger of ejaculation, but when Mrs. I. moved 5-10 times ejaculation would become imminent.

Fourteenth occasion (Saturday) Partial intercourse as above, 23 minutes and then Mr. I. ejaculated during an attempt to reverse positions.

Fifteenth occasion (Saturday) Fifteen minutes, much the same as the thirteenth occasion.

Sixteenth occasion (Sunday) Ejaculation after four minutes.

Seventeenth occasion (Monday) Forty minutes, varying between one-quarter to half insertion of penis. Ejaculation was several times imminent, but Mr. I. averted it by relaxing each time.

Now the therapist directed Mr. I. to concentrate first on prolonging full intromission, and then gradually to introduce movement, but preventing excessive excitation by avoiding stimulation of Mrs. I. He was told always to keep well within his capacity to control. After a few minutes of this it would be permissible to go on to orgasm, concentrating then on clitoral pressure by the penis.

Eighteenth occasion (Monday) Orgasm after 15 minutes of complete insertion with small movements.

Nineteenth occasion Orgasm after 29 minutes of small movements. Mrs. I. said that she too had been on the point of orgasm.

Further sexual occasions enabled gradually increasing excursions of movement, and finally a major break through occurred after the thirteenth therapeutic interview. While Mr. I. retained his erection, Mrs. I. had four orgasms, and he ejaculated during the last of them. From this time onward there was mutually satisfactory sexual performance that gradually improved. There were 14 therapeutic interviews in all, over 5 weeks. Mr. I.'s Willoughby score at the last interview was 13.

THE RESULTS OF TREATMENT OF MALE SEXUAL INADEQUACY BY COMPETING EROTIC RESPONSES

In 31 cases reported by Wolpe and Lazarus (1966), 21 (67.7%) recovered to the extent of achieving entirely satisfactory sexual performance. Another 6 cases (19.4%) attained a level that was acceptable to their partners.

The mean time span required was 11.5 weeks and the median 8.0 weeks. Table 2 gives some details of several of my personal cases.

TABLE 2.

A SURVEY OF SOME CASES OF IMPOTENCE

TREATED BY RECIPROCAL INHIBITION OF ANXIETY

BY SEXUAL RESPONSES

Patient No.	Age	Therapeutic Time Span	Outcome and Remarks
1	31	1 week	Recovered
2	40	8 weeks	Recovered
3	46	10 weeks	Recovered
4	46	20 weeks	Recovered
5	40	4 weeks	Recovered
6	41	12 weeks (intermittent and furtive)	Much Improved
7	50	6 weeks	Recovered but no transfer to wife.
8	49	2 weeks	Recovered (major factor was removal of anxiety through wife taking contraceptive pills).
9	20	6 weeks	Recovered (major factor was resolution of fears about masculinity from psychoanalytic reading).

(Table 2—*cont.*)

Patient No.	Age	Therapeutic Time Span	Outcome and Remarks
10	49	10 weeks	Improved from almost complete erectile failure to functionally sufficient erections to make marriage possible and to satisfy and impregnate wife.
11	35	6 weeks	Markedly improved when therapist left country. Appropriate assertion towards wife major factor.
12	36	5 weeks	Recovered (Case 2)
13	44	16 weeks (infrequent opportunities)	Unimproved. No apparent sexual anxiety. Hypersensitivity of glans penis.
14	40	9 weeks	Recovered (Details in Wolpe, Eysenck 1960).
15	35	8 weeks (preceded by 12 weeks of overcoming interpersonal fears)	Improved from no erection to strong ones. Coitus improving when therapist left country.
16	18	66 weeks (very irregular opportunities at first)	Recovered
17	53	3 weeks	Recovered with new consort. Previously no benefit in 12 weeks with uncooperative consort.
18	39	12 weeks	Recovered. At first erections occurred only after testosterone injections.

THE TREATMENT OF FRIGIDITY

Frigidity is an unfortunate term inasmuch as it seems to suggest a total lack of sexual response. It would be more correct to speak of varying degrees of failure of sexual response in women, ranging from absolute frigidity (no response whatever of a sexual kind) to the inability to achieve orgasm on the part of a woman who is capable of very high sexual arousal.

Two kinds of cases must be distinguished. In 'essential' frigidity, the lack of response is in relation to all males, while in situational frigidity it is relative to a particular male who in many cases is, unfortunately, the patient's husband. The solutions required are of very different kinds.

Essential Frigidity

Some cases of essential frigidity have an organic basis. Occasionally, it appears as though a woman's sexual response system has somehow failed to develop. One encounters women who do not recall ever having known sexual arousal and give no history of distressing sexual experiences that might have led to conditioned inhibition. It must be supposed that their deficiency is constitutional, and there seems to be no available solution to the problem. In other cases, frigidity is due to some pathological condition of the vagina that makes coitus painful — usually either a very thick hymen or an inflammatory lesion. I once saw a woman who had been psychoanalyzed for the whole 4 years of her marriage for vaginal spasm that was really due to a painful ulcer. A gynecological examination should be advised in every case of frigidity in which there is the slightest possibility of physical pathology.

In the great majority of cases, essential frigidity is a matter of conditioned inhibition. Some women are either absolutely or relatively frigid due to specific early experiences that have attached negative, and usually anxious feelings to sexual stimuli. Sometimes, the relevant experiences have consisted of anti-sexual indoctrination that may have a religious basis, or may have come from a mother who herself has had unhappy or fearful sexual experiences. The patient may have been told that sex is filthy and disgusting and excusable only for the sake of having children. In other cases that originate in early life, the frigidity is the direct result of traumatic experiences related to sex. Sometimes, it is enough to have been frightened in the context of masturbation.

Frigidity that develops in adult life is usually a consequence of sexual experiences that have been unrewarding in one way or another. Generally, the patient relates that she has rarely or never achieved a satisfactory orgasm; and repeated frustration has created a growing revulsion towards sexual activity. Occasionally, one comes across a case whose frigidity has a different history. For example, a woman who had for years had a very good sexual relationship with her husband developed a vaginitis which made intercourse painful. However, because of her great affection for her husband she had gone on permitting intercourse; but it was so aversive that she had become completely frigid, with marked vaginismus. Even after the vaginitis had been treated and intercourse was no longer painful, the vaginismus had persisted so that it was impossible for her husband to gain entry. When I first saw her this state of affairs had been going on for 3 years.

The treatment of essential frigidity depends upon the basis of the individual case. Where there has been faulty indoctrination, it is necessary to remove misconceptions about sex and to reeducate the person concerning sexual activity. Having done this, one is almost inevitably still left with a negative emotional response, together with anxiety towards various aspects of the sexual situation, and the treatment of this is generally a matter of systematic desensitization. As usual in behavior therapy, the details are determined by the identified stimulus antecedents of the undesirable emotional response (see Chapter VII).

Taking as an example the case of vaginismus described above, the spasm was part of an anxiety reaction to the entry of any object into the vagina. Treatment consisted of a combination of conventional desensitization and *in vivo* desensitization. I instructed the patient to relax and to imagine, at first, a very thin rod (about ⅛ in. in diameter) being inserted a distance of ½ in. into her vagina. This produced anxiety. I continued repeating the scene until the anxiety disappeared. I then gradually increased the length of the rod's insertion, and subsequently repeated the sequence with progressively wider rods. When the width of the *imaginary* rod had reached ½ in., I arranged for the construction of a set of wax rods (bougies) that varied in diameter from ⅛ in. to 1½ in., that the patient was to use at home, starting with the insertion of the ⅛ in. bougie into her vagina, slowly, inch by inch. Thereafter, *in vivo* 'shadowing' a few widths behind the imaginary diameter was continued. When we reached about ¾ in. diameter in imagination, movement such as would occur during coitus was introduced. This was a new source of anxiety which required repeated scene presentations for its desensitization. Then, movement with the bougie was started. Increasingly rapid movement came to be comfortably tolerated. At this point, I began to encourage careful experimentation with actual coitus, which became possible very soon, without producing vaginismus or any anxiety.

A more commonplace case was that of a woman who had from puberty had an anxious revulsion against sex. She had nevertheless married, and had borne four children in six years, because being pregnant was a 'defense' against sex. She had been treated by various methods, including drugs and electro-shock treatment. Her psychiatrist, not a behavior therapist, had then decided to try systematic desensitization. This had been a fiasco, because the weakest item, the sight of naked female breasts, was far too anxiety-provoking. When he had presented this image to her it had produced such a severe anxiety reaction that it was impossible to go on with the treatment. When he referred her to me, I found it necessary to start at a much more remote point. The first scene I asked her to imagine was being at a swimming pool where there was only one male present, 50 yards away, with his bare chest exposed. This man was later brought progressively closer. Next, we utilized, first at a distance of 50 yards and then closer, a completely nude male statue in a park. A later item in the hierarchy was seeing a little nude boy of four gambolling in a swimming pool. Eventually, after many steps, she was successfully desensitized to such images as dogs fornicating, French pictures of nude males, four-letter words, and, finally, personal coital contingencies. It became possible for her to indulge in and enjoy sexual intercourse with her husband.

I recently demonstrated the treatment of a somewhat similar case to a group of Temple psychiatric residents

— a 27-year-old married woman with several interpersonal neurotic problems in addition to frigidity. I first treated the interpersonal anxieties by teaching her how to assert herself. She grasped the idea very quickly, and soon began to implement it. After the fifth session, most of our attention turned to the frigidity. Though she had worked as an actress, and though actresses are supposed to be rather free and easy sexually, she had been extremely reticent. She had often been darkly warned by her mother about the evils of sex. These warnings had been reinforced by an attempted sexual assault by a much older man about the time of puberty. After her marriage, she had found sex unpleasant and tried as much as possible to avoid it. The essence of her problem was a feeling of tense revulsion to the male sex organ. In treating this by desensitization, I started by having her imagine looking at a nude male statue in a park, from a distance of 30 feet. After coming progressively closer to the statue, she eventually imagined herself handling the stone penis with equanimity. The next series of scenes began with imagining herself at one end of her bedroom and seeing her husband's nude penis 15 feet away. As desensitization proceeded, he was brought closer and closer. Then she imagined that she quickly touched the penis. When this stopped arousing anxiety, I gradually increased the duration of contact. By about the 20th therapeutic session, she was enjoying sexual relations and having orgasms on about 50 per cent of occasions.

It is quite often helpful to employ tranquilizing drugs in deconditioning the neurotic anxieties on which frigidity is based. Brady (1966), who treated frigidity by desensitization, but used intravenous Brevital as an adjuvant to relaxation, gained the impression that his cases improved more quickly than if he had used relaxation alone. If this impression is confirmed its relevance is not likely to be confined to the special field of frigidity (see Chapter IX).

Situational Frigidity

It often turns out that a woman who complains of frigidity is not negatively conditioned to sexual stimuli in general, but not responsive to the particular man with whom she consorts. The question then is why she does not respond to him. In many cases, one finds that she simply does not care for her husband as a person. Perhaps she did once, but no longer does. She may have no specific complaints about him. When that happens, I know of nothing that can be done about it. Perhaps one day we shall have ways of making people like things that they do not like, but we do not have them now.

However, one should not admit defeat without carefully investigating the case to see whether change is possible. Sometimes one discovers something relevant and changeable in the husband's behavior. It may be that he does not show his wife reasonable consideration. Perhaps he comes home from work at irregular hours without ever telling her in advance or phoning her. Such behavior can be extremely disturbing, and if persistent may transform a woman's attitude from affection to revulsion, and her sexual pattern from passion to frigidity. One patient in whom this happened has a husband who is an 'empire builder,' busy establishing branches of his business all over the United States. He is usually out of town. When he gets home, he gives his wife scant attention, rushes out to play golf, or watches baseball or football on television. Though he protests that he loves his wife (who is in fact very attractive), all my efforts to change his behavior have failed. He has a sardonic attitude towards her, and regards her demands as childish.

It should not be concluded from the foregoing that it is by choice that a behavior therapist intercedes directly with a husband. The usual aim is for the husband to change his behavior as a result of the wife asserting herself appropriately (see Chapter V). The above-mentioned wife could not do so, for reasons that were in part realistic. An example of effective assertiveness is provided by a woman whose husband is engaged in international politics. This involves him with many people from overseas and requires his wife to prepare endless dinners and entertainments. Her response was originally extremely passive and compliant. I told her to stop behaving slavishly, and to start structuring activities in such a way as to follow the principle: "If you will do things for me I will do things for you." This almost at once made his attitude towards her more pleasant. The next step was for her to make a stand regarding their way of life: "This kind of living does not suit me. I can not have people here every night. I can not have you running up and down. We need some personal life, and I would like you to do something about it." Fortunately, he acceded to this. If he had not, she might have had to say, "If this goes on I shall leave you."

CHAPTER VII

Systematic Desensitization

INTRODUCTION

SYSTEMATIC desensitization is the breaking down of neurotic anxiety-response habits in piecemeal fashion. A physiological state inhibitory of anxiety is induced in the patient, who is then exposed to a weak anxiety arousing stimulus. The exposure is repeated until the stimulus loses completely its ability to evoke anxiety. Then progressively 'stronger' stimuli are introduced and similarly treated. This technique, which characteristically employs relaxation as the anxiety-inhibiting state, has made it possible for the first time to exert direct control over a great many neurotic habits. The therapist has been enabled to treat these habits in almost any order that he chooses, and as far as he chooses.

Employing a counteracting emotion to overcome an undesirable emotional habit *step by step,* has its precedent in an age-old method: a child is gradually accustomed to situations he fears by exposing him to small doses of what is feared in circumstances in which other emotions are also present. For example, if the child fears a visitor's black beard, he is quite likely to become reconciled to it by deconditioning events that may occur if he sits on his father's lap while the latter speaks to the visitor. He may at first intermittently glance at the beard whose anxiety-arousal occurs against a background of warm and pleasant responses to the father. The small fear arousals are presumably inhibited, and gradually, as the fear subsides, the child tolerates lengthening looks at the beard.

Besides being inadvertent agents to such spontaneous therapy, parents quite often 'instinctively' treat established fears of their children in an essentially similar way (deliberately and fairly systematically). When a child is afraid of bathing in the sea, the parent will at first take him by the hand to the very fringe of the approaching waves and lift him up when a wave approaches; then when the child has become comfortable about this he is encouraged to dip his foot into a wave, and later his ankle, and so on. Conquering his fear by degrees, the child eventually becomes able to play in the sea with pleasure. This is very much like the routine followed in primitive societies to prepare individuals to undergo ceremonial ordeals; and in our society in the training of mountaineers and trapeze artists. The first known example of the deliberate use of counteracting responses to overcome neurotic anxieties in piecemeal fashion was the use of feeding to overcome children's phobias in the work of Mary Cover Jones (1924) described in Chapter I.

THE FORMAL BASIS OF SYSTEMATIC
DESENSITIZATION

Systematic desensitization technique had its formal roots in the experimental laboratory (Wolpe, 1948, 1952, 1958). Having produced experimental neurosis in cats confined in a small cage (as described in Chapter I) by administering to them high voltage, low amperage shocks, I found that neurotic anxiety responses to the cage and related stimuli and to an auditory stimulus that had preceded the shocks, were extremely resistant to the normal process of extinction. Neither prolonged nor repeated exposure of the animals to the environment of the cage led to decrement in the intensity of the anxiety responses even though the animals were never again shocked. The animals, however hungry, could not be tempted to eat attractive food scattered in the experimental cage. However, because they also showed milder anxiety in the experimental laboratory and still less in a series of other rooms according to their degree of resemblance to the laboratory, they were offered food in these various places in descending order. When in a particular room the evocation of anxiety was not great enough to inhibit feeding, successive offerings of food were accepted with increasing readiness until all signs of anxiety receded. The room next in resemblance to the experimental laboratory could then be introduced. After several similar series of steps, eating behavior was eventually restored in the experimental cage itself, and this made possible the total elimination of all signs of anxiety there. In parallel piecemeal fashion anxiety was deconditioned from the auditory stimulus that had preceded the shocks.

While these observations led to a search for methods by which the neurotic habits of humans might also be broken down bit by bit, they did not immediately suggest the systematic desensitization technique. This emerged from a succession of further experiences. Since 1947 I had been using with considerable success a variety of techniques requiring direct behavioral changes in the life situation of the patient. The most important of these was the instigation of assertive behavior. I was greatly encouraged in the use of these techniques by the appearance of Salter's *Conditioned Reflex Therapy* (1949), and, in fact was moved by its buoyant optimism to a generalized advocacy of self-expressive behavior in all patients. But it was not clear how this could affect those neuroses in which the stimuli controlling the neurotic reactions were in no way brought into the interpersonal situations in which the assertive behavior occurred.

It soon became evident that non-interpersonal neuroses were not responding to assertive behavior training, precisely as had been expected on theoretical grounds. Conditioning theory requires that to eliminate or change a habit of reaction to a stimulus, that stimulus must be present in the deconditioning situation. Such deconditioning as occurs through acts of assertion can affect only the anxiety-response habits to stimuli that are present. If a patient has a fear of being alone, this will not be diminished by assertive behavior (if only because assertion implies the presence of another person). Certainly now and then benefit is noted in special cases in which a chain of other habits may be secondarily altered when interpersonal fear has been diminished. In general, however, assertion towards persons is irrelevant where anxiety responses are to such non-personal stimulus constellations as enclosed spaces, animals, heights, the sight of blood — in short, all classical stimuli to phobic reactions. It is also irrelevant when anxiety responses are to persons to whom direct action on the part of the patient would be inappropriate — for example, where the fear is evoked by the mere presence of particular persons, by being the center of attention, or by a feeling of 'rejection,' such as in a social situation when it seems to the patient that too little attention is being directed to him. A case which exemplified the irrelevancy of interpersonal expressiveness was that of a woman who was severely anxious at all manifestations of illness in other people. Successful schooling in expressive behavior failed to diminish her anxiety and the case was sorrowfully abandoned as a failure. At that time I knew no way to inhibit anxieties aroused by stimuli to which no relevant *action-response* could be proposed for the patient — stimuli that oppress the patient 'without *animus*' against him.

Soon afterwards, I was fortunate to come across Edmund Jacobson's *Progressive Relaxation* (1939). Here was described an anxiety-inhibiting response that did not call from the patient *any kind of motor activity towards the source of his anxiety*. I began to give relaxation training to patients for whose neuroses assertion was not applicable. However, an enormous relaxation-potential was necessary to inhibit the anxiety evoked by a major real-life phobic stimulus. I conjectured that Jacobson's patients were enabled to inhibit *high* levels of anxiety because of prolonged and assiduous training.

I began to organize programs of exposure to graduated phobic stimuli *in vivo* for patients who had acquired some facility in relaxing, usually after 6-10 sessions. But these programs were often very awkward to execute, and I therefore began to explore the possibility of making use of imaginary situations in the place of real ones. I was gratified to find that magnitudes of experienced anxiety diminished progressively at repeated presentations of imaginary situations that were weakly anxiety-arousing. Furthermore, increasingly strong imaginary stimuli could be divested in turn of their anxiety-evoking potential, and there was transfer of the deconditioning of anxiety to real situations. At first, influenced by certain of Pavlov's experiments, I presented only one stimulus of any class at a session, but cautious trials of multiple presentations revealed no disadvantages and greatly enhanced the possibilities of speeding therapy.

GENERAL STATEMENT OF DESENSITIZATION PARADIGM

The autonomic effects that accompany deep relaxation are diametrically opposed to those characteristic of anxiety. Jacobson (1939,1940) long ago showed that pulse rate and blood pressure were diminished by deep muscle relaxation. It has subsequently been shown (Drvota 1962, Clark 1963, Wolpe 1964) that skin resistance decreases and respiration becomes slower and more regular during relaxation. These effects are perceived as concomitants of the relaxation effort and not as secondary to the relaxed state of the muscles.

In the same way as in the neuroses of cats it was found that feeding can be used to counteract an anxiety response only if the latter is weak enough, so in human beings the autonomic effects of relaxation will be able to counteract only relatively weak anxiety responses. I have found again and again that a stimulus evoking a *strong* anxiety response may be presented many times to the relaxed patient without the strength of anxiety diminishing in the least. By contrast, if the anxiety response is weak, it is found that from one presentation of the stimulus to the next the amount of anxiety is diminished until at last there is none whatsoever.

The role of relaxation in the inhibition of anxiety has been experimentally demonstrated. Working independently, on spider and snake phobias respectively, Davison (1965) and Rachman (1966) have found that subjects to whom the whole desensitization sequence of procedures was applied showed significantly more improvement than either those receiving relaxation training without scene presentations or others to whom scenes were presented without relaxation.

Once a weak stimulus has ceased to arouse any anxiety it is possible to present a somewhat stronger stimulus to the fully relaxed patient and this stronger stimulus will now evoke less anxiety than it would have done before. Successive presentations will bring the amount of anxiety aroused down to zero. Stronger and stronger stimuli are thus brought within the anxiety-inhibiting capacity of the subject's relaxation. To put the matter in another way, if there are ten stimuli which in their variations along a single dimension evoke in a subject quantities of anxiety which vary from one to ten, and if through the inhibiting effects of relaxation the anxiety aroused by the stimulus evoking one unit is reduced to zero, the stimulus originally evoking two units of anxiety will be found to be evoking only one unit. This is illustrated in Fig. 1. Thus, in an acrophobic subject who has one unit of anxiety produced by looking out of a second floor window, and two units by looking out of a third floor window, reduction of the amount of anxiety from the second floor window to zero would have the effect that the amount of anxiety evoked at a third floor window would be diminished to one unit.

It must be emphasized that these decrements of response are not transient but lasting. As in the animal experiments they are indicative of decrease of strength of anxiety-response habits.

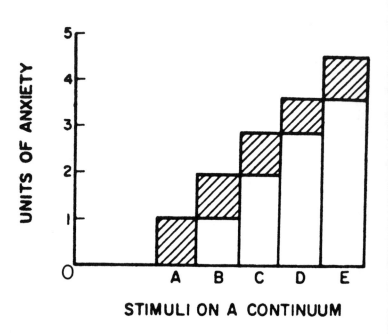

FIG. 1. Illustrating desensitization process.

When A's ability to evoke anxiety goes down from 1 unit to O, B evokes 1 unit in place of an original potential of 2 units; and when B's evocation is O, C evokes 1 unit; and so forth.

In a recent psychophysiological study (Wolpe & Fried, 1968) evidence has been provided that the galvanic skin response (Lathrop's (1964) variability measure) shows decrements during desensitization that are parallel to the decrements of anxiety that patients report. Fig. 2

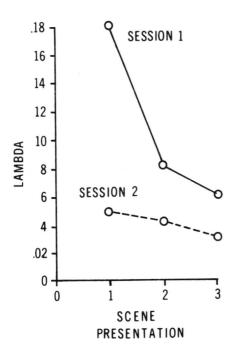

FIG. 2. Showing the lambda values for 3 presentations of the same scene during 2 successive desensitization sessions. The figure averages the readings for four different patients. Note that reactivity not only declines during each session but the decrement obtained at the end of Session 1 is maintained at the beginning of Session 2.

shows the summated changes of four patients, to each of whom hierarchical phobic scenes were presented thrice on each of two sessions. The decrease of response from one presentation to the next should be noted, as well as the 'savings' between Session 1 and Session 2.

THE TECHNIQUE OF
SYSTEMATIC DESENSITIZATION

The problems posed by the patient are carefully considered by the therapist, and if changed behavior is required in social, sexual or other life situations, this will usually be given attention first. If systematic desensitization is also indicated, it is started as soon as possible in parallel with whatever measures have been instituted in life situations. The technique involves three separate sets of operations:

1. Training in deep muscle relaxation;
2. The construction of anxiety hierarchies;
3. Counterposing relaxation and anxiety-evoking stimuli from the hierarchies.

1. Training in relaxation

The method of relaxation taught is essentially that of Jacobson (1938), but instruction is completed in the course of about six interviews, in marked contrast to Jacobson's very prolonged training schedules. The patient is asked to practice at home for two fifteen-minute periods a day.

In introducing the subject of relaxation, I tell the patient (who has usually already gained a general idea of the nature of conditioning therapy) that relaxation is just one of the methods in our armamentarium for combating anxiety. I continue as follows:

> Even the ordinary relaxing that occurs when one lies down often produces quite a noticeable calming effect. It has been found that there is a definite relationship between the extent of muscle relaxation and the production of emotional changes opposite to anxiety. I am going to teach you how to relax far beyond the usual point, and with practice you will be able to 'switch on' at will very considerable emotional effects of an 'anti-anxiety' kind.

There is no established sequence for training the various muscle groups in relaxation, but whatever sequence is adopted should be systematic. My own practice is to start with the arms because they are convenient for purposes of demonstration and easy to check on. The head region is next because the most marked anxiety-inhibiting effects are usually obtained by relaxations there.

The patient is asked to grip the arm of his chair with one hand to see whether he can distinguish any qualitative difference between the sensations produced in his forearm and those in his hand. He is told to take special note of the quality of the forearm sensation because it is caused by muscle tension in contrast to the touch and pressure sensations in the hand. He is also enjoined to note the exact location of the forearm tensions in the flexor and extensor areas. Next, the therapist grips the patient's wrist and asks him to bend his arm against this resistance, thus making him aware of the tension in his biceps. Then by instructing him to straighten his bent elbow against resistance, he calls his attention to the extensor muscles of the arm. The therapist goes on to say:

I am now going to show you the essential activity that is involved in obtaining deep relaxation. I shall again ask you to resist my pull at your wrist so as to tighten your biceps. I want you to notice very carefully the sensations in that muscle. Then I shall ask you to let go gradually as I diminish the amount of force exerted against you. Notice, as your forearm descends, that there is decreasing sensation in the biceps muscle. Notice also that the letting go is an activity, but of a negative kind — it is an 'uncontracting' of the muscle. In due course, your forearm will come to rest on the arm of the chair, and you may then think that you have gone as far as possible — that relaxation is complete. But although the biceps will indeed be partly and perhaps largely relaxed, a certain number of its fibers will still, in fact, be contracted. I shall therefore say to you, 'Go on letting go. Try to extend the activity that went on in the biceps while your forearm was coming down.' It is the act of relaxing these additional fibers that will bring about the emotional effects we want. Let's try it and see what happens.

The therapist then grips the patient's wrist a second and asks him to tense and then gradully to relax the biceps. When the forearm is close to the arm of the chair the therapist releases the wrist, allowing the patient to complete the movement on his own. He then exhorts him to "go on letting go," to "keep trying to go further and further in the negative direction," to "try to go beyond what seems to you to be the furthest point."

When the patient has indicated that he fully understands what is required, he is asked to put both hands comfortably on his lap and try to relax all the muscles of both arms for a few minutes. He is to report any new sensations that he may feel. The usual ones are tingling, numbness, or warmth, mainly in the hands.

After a few minutes the therapist palpates the relaxing muscles. With practice he learns to judge between various grosser degrees of muscle tension.

Most patients have rather limited success when they first attempt to relax, but they are assured that good relaxation is a matter of practice, and whereas initially twenty minutes of relaxation may achieve no more than partial relaxation of an arm it will eventually be possible to relax the whole body in a matter of a minute or two. However, there are some fortunate individuals who from the first attempt experience a deepening and extending relaxation, radiating, as it were, from the arms, and accompanied by general effects, like calmness, sleepiness or warmth.

I customarily begin the second lesson in relaxation by telling the patient that from the emotional point of view, the most important muscles in the body are situated in and around the head, and that we shall therefore deal with this area next. We begin with the muscles of the face, demonstrating the tensions produced by contracting the muscles of the forehead. These muscles lend themselves to a demonstration of the characteristic 'step-like' character of increasing relaxation. The therapist simultaneously raises the frowning groups of muscles in his own forehead very intensely, pointing out incidentally that an anxious expression has thus been produced. He then says: "I am going to relax these muscles in a controlled way to give you the feeling of the step-like way in which decrements of tension occur during attempts at deep relaxation, although in actual relaxing, the steps are usually much less rapid than in my demonstration." The muscles are then relaxed as stated, making an obvious step-down about every five seconds until, after about half-a-dozen steps, no further change is evident; nevertheless, it is emphasized to the patient that relaxation is continuing and that this relaxation 'beneath the surface' is the part that matters for producing the desired emotional effects. The patient is then told to contract his own forehead muscles and is given about ten minutes to relax them as far as possible. Patients frequently report spontaneously the occurrence of 'relaxation feedback' in their foreheads, which they may feel as tingling, or "a feeling of thickness, as though my skin were made of leather." These sensations are as a rule indicative of a degree of relaxation beyond the normal level of muscle tone.

This lesson usually concludes by drawing attention to the muscles in the region of the nose by getting the patient to wrinkle his nose, and to the muscles around the mouth by making him purse his lips and then smile. All these muscles are now relaxed.

At the third lesson the patient is asked to bite on his teeth, thus tensing his masseters and temporales. The position of the lips is an important indicator of relaxation of the muscles of mastication. When these are relaxed, the lips are parted by a few millimeters. The masseters cannot be relaxed if the mouth is kept resolutely closed. Of course, it does not follow that an open mouth is proof of relaxation.

At the same lesson, I usually also introduce the muscles of the tongue. These may be felt contracting in the floor of the mouth, when the patient presses the tip of his tongue firmly against the back of his lower incisor teeth. Relaxing the tongue muscles may produce such local sensations as tingling or a feeling of enlargement of that organ.

Patients who have special tensions in the neck region are now shown how to relax the pharyngeal muscles — which can be felt beforehand by the act of preparing to clear one's throat. Other muscle groups that receive attention only for special purposes, are those of the eyeball (which are first individually contracted by having the eyes turned in succession left, right, up and down), and the infrahyoid group (which the patient can be made to feel by trying to open his jaws against resistance).

The fourth lesson deals with the neck and shoulders. The main target in the neck is the posterior muscles that normally maintain the head's erect posture. Most people become aware of them merely by concentrating on sensations in the back of the neck. When they relax these muscles the head falls forward, but because in the unpracticed individual the relaxation is incomplete, stress is imposed on muscle fibres that are still contracted, and discomfort, and even pain, is frequently felt. As Jacobson has pointed out, persistent practice, while ignoring the discomfort leads to a progressive yielding of these muscles, and usually in a week or so the patient finds his neck is comfortable though his chin will press against his sternum. Those who find the discomfort of the forward leaning head too great, are instructed to practice relaxing the neck muscles with the back of the head resting against a high-backed chair.

Shoulder muscle tensions are demonstrated by the following routine. The deltoid is contracted by abducting the arm to the horizontal, the lateral neck muscles by continuing this movement up to the ear, the posthumeral and scapulo-spinal groups by moving the horizontal arm backward, and the pectorals by swinging it forward across the chest. In relaxing these muscles the patient is directed to observe their functional unity with those of the arm.

The fifth relaxation lesson deals with the muscles of the back, abdomen and thorax. The procedure in respect to the first two areas follows the usual pattern. The back muscles are contracted by backward arching of the spine. The abdominal muscles are tensed as if in anticipation of a punch in the belly; and after contracting them the patient lets them go as far as he can. The thoracic muscles, or, more accurately, the muscles of respiration, are necessarily in a different category — for total inhibition of breathing is not an achievement to try to promote! But the respiratory rhythm can often be used to augment relaxation. Attention to the musculature during a few fairly deep breaths soon reveals that while some effort is involved during inhalation, expiration is essentially a 'letting-go.' Some patients find it very helpful to coordinate relaxation of various other muscles with the automatic relaxation of the respiratory muscles that takes place with the exhalation during *normal* breathing.

In making patients aware of the muscles to be relaxed in the lower limbs it has been my custom to start with the feet, and work upwards. The flexor digitorium brevis is felt by bending the toes within the shoe; the calf muscles by placing some weight on the toe; the peroneal and anterior tibial muscles by dorsiflexing the foot; the quadriceps femoris by straightening the knee; the hamstrings by trying to bend the knee against resistance; the adductors of the thigh by adduction against hand pressure on the inner aspect of the knee; and the abductors (which include some of the gluteal muscles) by abduction against pressure.

All these muscles are the subject of the sixth lesson, and the patient should be allowed enough time for relaxing them.

2. The construction of hierarchies

An anxiety hierarchy is a list of stimuli on a common theme ranked in descending order according to the amount of anxiety they evoke. In some anxiety neuroses the rank order of the stimuli is an exceedingly difficult matter. Case 2 in Chapter XIII illustrates how intricate a matter hierarchy construction can be.

The theme, or common core, of a neurosis is usually derived from extrinsic stimulus situations disturbing to the patient — like spiders or criticisms; but sometimes the core subsists in response-produced stimuli. A variety of physically disparate stimulus situations may all induce a common response. For example, a case of claustrophobia (Wolpe, 1961) had the same kind of trapped feeling when she had irremovable nail polish on her fingers or was wearing a tight ring as when she was physically confined. Such commonality of response is the basis of secondary generalization (Hull, 1943, p. 191).

Hierarchy construction usually begins at about the same time as relaxation training, and is subject to alterations or additions at any time. It is important to note that both the gathering of data and its subsequent organizing are done in an ordinary conversational way and *not under relaxation,* since the patient's *ordinary* responses to stimuli are what the therapist needs to know.

The raw data from which the hierarchies are constructed come from four main sources: (a) the patient's history (see Chap. III); (b) responses to the Willoughby Questionnaire, which reveals anxieties mainly in certain interpersonal contexts; (c) a Fear Survey Schedule[1] (Wolpe & Lang, 1964) (see Appendix 3) and (d) special probings into all possible situations in which the patient feels unadaptive anxiety. It frequently helps to assign the patient the homework task of listing all situations, thoughts, or feelings that he finds disturbing, fearful, embarrassing, or in any other way distressing.

When all the identified sources of neurotic disturbance have been listed, the therapist classifies them into themes. Usually there is more than one theme. In most cases these are fairly obvious, but there are many exceptions. For example, a fear of going to movies, parties and other public situations may suggest a claustrophobia and yet really be a basic fear of scrutiny. Frequently, fear and avoidance of social occasions turns out to be based on fear of criticism or of rejection; or the fear may be a function of the mere physical presence of people, varying with the number to whom the patient is exposed. One patient's ostensible fear of social situations was really a conditioned anxiety response to the smell of food in public places. A good example of the importance of correct identification of relevant sources of anxiety is to be found in a previously reported case (Wolpe, 1958, p. 152) where a man's impotence turned out to be due to anxiety not related to any aspect of the sexual situation as such, but to the idea of trauma. In the context of an attempt at defloration, anxiety had been conditioned to the sexual act. In this instance the strategy of treatment was shifted by this revelation from *in vivo* use of the sexual response to systematic desensitization to tissue damage.

[1]A more extensive inventory (Wolpe & Lang, 1969) is commercially available. Knapp, San Diego.

It is not necessary for the patient actually to have experienced each situation that is to be included in a hierarchy. The question posed is, "If you were today confronted by such and such a situation, *would you expect* to be anxious?" To answer this question he has to *imagine* the situation concerned, and it is generally almost as easy to imagine a supposed event as one that has at some time occurred. The temporal setting of an imagined stimulus configuration scarcely affects the responses to it. A man with a phobia for dogs will usually have about as much anxiety at the idea of meeting a bulldog on the way home tomorrow as at recalling an actual encounter with this breed of dog.

The following list of fears from a recent patient will be used to illustrate some of the intricacies of hierarchy construction. This list is reproduced exactly as the patient presented it.

Raw List of Fears

1. High Altitudes
2. Elevators
3. Crowded Places
4. Church
5. Darkness - Movies, etc.
6. Being Alone
7. Marital Relations (pregnancy)
8. Walking any Distance
9. Death
10. Accidents
11. Fire
12. Fainting
13. Falling Back
14. Injections
15. Medications
16. Fear of the Unknown
17. Losing My Mind
18. Locked Doors
19. Amusement Park Rides
20. Steep Stairways

With the help of a little clarification from the patient the items were sorted into categories, thus:

A. Acrophobia

1. High Altitudes
19. Amusement Park Rides
20. Steep Stairways

B. *Claustrophobia*
   2. Elevators
   3. Crowded Places
   4. Church

   5. Movies (darkness factor)
   18. Locked Doors

C. *Agoraphobia*
   6. Being Alone

   8. Walking any Distance (alone)

D. *Illness and its Associations*
   12. Fainting
   13. Falling Back

   14. Injections
   15. Medication

E. *Basically Objective Fears*
   7. Marital Relations (pregnancy)
   9. Death
   10. Accidents

   11. Fire
   16. Fear of the Unknown
   17. Losing My Mind

Before considering the true hierarchical groups A-D to which desensitization is relevant, some remarks must be made about group E. The patient's fears of pregnancy, accidents, death and fire were all in contexts in which fear can be reasonable, but in her case, apprehension about these matters was somewhat more than normal. I considered that this might be a function of a generally elevated level of anxiety — as is quite often found — and would probably disappear when the major neurotic anxiety sources had been removed by therapy. Her fear of the unknown was bound up with the idea of death. Her fear of losing her mind, an inference from the bizarre and uncontrollable feelings that characterized her neurosis, was overcome by strong assurance that her condition was not related to insanity and could *never* lead to it, assurance that was reinforced by demonstrating that hyperventilation could precipitate many of her symptoms. There are some cases in whom *all* fears would belong to group E, in which instance, of course, desensitization would not be relevant; and thought-stopping (p. 226) may be the most important technique to use.

On scrutinizing the stimulus groups A-D the reader should observe that the items are very general and not sufficiently well-defined for hierarchial ranking. In fact, the items of each group are merely exemplifications that will generate stimulus situations specific enough to be ranked only after further communication between patient and therapist. But this is not very obvious. It is common for newcomers to behavior therapy to attempt to form such exemplification into hierarchies. Recently, I asked a group of 25 members of a behavior therapy class (none of whom had previously treated more than two or three patients) how they would proceed to build a hierarchy out of the five claustrophobia items of group B. The majority of them were disposed to ask the patient to rank elevators, churches, movies, etc., hierarchically, and to consider the influence of modifying factors, like size of elevator, as bounded by the limits of the hierarchical ranking. But actually these five items were grouped together under claustrophobia only because they embodied space-constriction. Further questioning of the patient showed quite clearly that claustrophobic anxiety was an inverse function of the size of the enclosing space and a direct function of duration of confinement. Desensitization, consequently, involved two hierarchical series: First, the patient was 'confined' for a constant length of time in a progressively smaller room; and, secondly, she was 'confined' in a very small room (4 ft. square) for increasing periods.

Similarly, in group A, acrophobia, each of the three items refers to a whole range of concrete situations. They do not have the specificity that would permit them to be used in desensitization; but particularizing within the areas they encompass provided a range of concrete situations evoking responses of different intensities.

Further questioning disclosed that increasing heights were increasingly fearful, starting from about 20 feet (or a second floor window); and that at all heights, motion aggravated the fear. Similarly, group D yielded a fairly extensive hierarchy some of whose items, ranked in descending order, were:

1. Feeling of being about to lose consciousness
2. Feeling of falling backwards
3. Marked dizziness
4. Feeling of lightness in head
5. Moderate dizziness
6. Smell of ether
7. Receiving an injection
8. Racing heart (anxiety increasing with rapidity of heart-beat)
9. Weak knees
10. Seeing syringe poised for an injection
11. Sight of bandages

It may be observed that the stronger stimuli (1-5) are all endogenous, and most of the weaker ones exogenous. What is common to all is the feeling of personal threat.

In other cases, besides multiplicity of hierarchies, one encounters multiple 'dimensions' within a single hierarchy. For example, in a patient having claustrophic reactions in social situations five variables controlled the intensity of the reaction. The reactions were the *stronger*:

1. the greater the number of people present.
2. the more strange the people.
3. the greater the difficulties in the way of leaving the room (both physical factors and social propriety being relevant).
4. the shorter the time since her last meal (this factor determining the measure of a fear of vomiting).

They were *weaker* if she was accompanied by

5. protective persons — husband, mother and close friend (in descending order of effectiveness).

Sometimes, the most difficult problems of hierarchy construction become evident only after attempts at desensitization have begun and it is seen that the anxiety level does not diminish after repeating presentations of the weakest scenes contained in the hierarchies, even though relaxation is manifestly good. The problem is then to seek still *weaker* scenes, whose evoked anxiety can be inhibited by the patient's relaxation. In many cases, it is obvious where to look for weaker items. For example, in a patient who had an anxiety hierarchy on the theme of loneliness, the weakest item in the original hierarchy — being at home accompanied only by her daughter — was found to evoke more anxiety than was manageable. To obtain a weaker starting point all that was needed was to add items in which she had two or more companions. But it is not always so easy, and the therapist may have to use a good deal of ingenuity to find manipulable dimensions.

For example, following an accident three years previously, a woman patient had developed severe anxiety reactions to the sight of approaching automobiles. The therapist had been led to believe that the patient noticed the first glimmerings of anxiety when a car was two blocks away, and that the anxiety increased gradually up to a distance of half a block, and then much more steeply with further approximation. This seemed to promise straightforward progress; but at the first desensitization session even an imagined distance of two blocks from the car aroused anxiety too great to be inhibited by the counteraction of relaxation. Further investigation revealed that the patient had considerable anxiety at the very prospect of even the shortest journey by car, since the whole range of threatening possibilities was already present for her the moment a journey became imminent; but she had not thought this amount of anxiety worthy of report. As in all other cases, desensitization could not begin unless the amount of 'danger' contained in scenes from the hierarchy was under control. What was required was a sharp delimitation of the implications of each situation. Accordingly, an imaginary enclosed field, two blocks square, was drawn on paper. The patient's car was 'placed' in one corner of the field and the early items of the hierarchy came to consist of a trusted person driving his car up to a stated point towards her car, and then to ever-closer agreed points as the patient progressed. The 'danger' was thus always circumscribed. This, and later steps in the treatment of the case are described in some detail in the full account of this case in Chapter XIII.

Another case in whom it was difficult to obtain sufficiently weak anxiety-evoking stimuli was a patient with a death phobia, whose items ranged in descending order from human corpses to funeral processions to dead dogs. Presentation of scenes of dead dogs produced marked and undiminishing anxiety, even when they were imagined at distances of two or three hundred yards (where they were hardly discernible). A solution was found in the use of a temporal dimension, beginning with the historically inaccurate sentence, "William the Conqueror was killed at the Battle of Hastings in 1066."

An ever-present question in constructing hierarchies is whether the items constitute a reasonably evenly-spaced progression. If items are too similar, time will be wasted; if adjacent items differ too widely in anxiety-evoking potential, progress will be halted upon moving from the lesser to the greater. The patient may even sometimes be further sensitized, i.e. conditioned to higher levels of anxiety as the result of severe anxiety being evoked. When a hierarchy is based on a directly measurable dimension such as distance, a well-spaced progression is relatively easy to obtain. However, this is not a linear function. It has been shown (Wolpe, 1963) that a simple power function is involved, whose index exceeds unity in some cases and is fractional in others. In phobias in which anxiety increases with proximity to the feared object, and also in claustrophobias, small changes of distance increase in importance with closeness of the object. The opposite applies to acrophobia and agoraphobia. Similarly where fear is a function of number of feared objects, small increments are more potent at low numerical levels. Further reference to this topic will be made later.

It is always a great advantage for a hierarchy to be in clearly quantifiable form; and the therapist should exercise every effort to achieve this. Often, it requires the utilization of a setting that is far removed from the patient's problem. For example, in a 42 year-old woman with a fear of travelling alone of 21 years' duration, it became evident that the center point of her disability was a fear of *being alone* away from home. It would certainly have been possible to deal with this in the context of traveling, but her sensitivity was extreme and aloneness would have been difficult to quantify in terms of distance. It was possible to obtain much better control of her re-actions by using an elevator as the vehicle of her separa-tion from the outside world. The weakest items of the hierarchy were set in a completely open elevator in which she ascended an increasing number of floors up to 100. Then she was 'placed' in an elevator that had a single one-foot-square window, and in this a similar sequence was followed. The same was then done in an elevator with a window whose dimensions were 9 in. x 3 in., an elevator with a 2 in. peephole, and finally a completely opaque one. Desensitization to these items was attended by a progressive increase in her capacity to travel afield precisely because distance had not figured at all in the desensitization up to this point. But now a new series was started embracing special anxiety-conditioned stimuli belonging to journeys of various kinds.

The problem of determining reasonably evenly spaced differences is much more difficult when the hierarchy does not depend upon an externally measureable independent dimension — when it depends upon secondary generalization — for example a hierarchy based on feelings of rejection. This, and many other difficulties of quantification that arise not only in doing desensitization, but in psychotherapy in general, are greatly aided by the use of a *subjective anxiety scale*. This is constructed by addressing the patient as follows: "Think of the worst anxiety you have ever experienced, or can imagine experiencing, and assign to this the number 100. Now think of the state of being absolutely calm and call this zero. Now you have a scale. On this scale how do you rate yourself at this moment?" Most patients can give a figure with little difficulty, and with practice come to be able to indicate their feelings with increasing confidence, in a way that is much more informative than the usual hazy verbal statements. The unit is called a *sud* (subjective unit of disturbance). It is possible to use the scale to ask the patient to rate the items of the hierarchy according to the amount of anxiety he would have upon exposure to them. If the differences between items are similar, and, generally speaking, not more than 5 to 10 *suds* the spacing can be regarded as satisfactory. On the other hand, if there were, for example, 40 *suds* for item number 8, and 10 *suds* for item number 9, there would be an obvious need for intervening items.

Some examples of hierarchies

1. *A cluster of hierarchies involving people*

CASE 4. Miss C. was a 24-year-old art student who came for treatment because marked anxiety at examinations had resulted in repeated failures. Investigation revealed additional phobic areas. The hierarchies are given below. All of them involve people, and none belong to the classical phobias. (Freedom from anxiety to the highest items of each of these hierarchies was achieved in 17 desensitization sessions, with complete transfer to the corresponding situations in actuality. Four months later, she passed her examinations without anxiety.)

Hierarchies[2]

A. Examination Series

1. On the way to the university on the day of an examination.
2. In the process of answering an examination paper.
3. Before the unopened doors of the examination room.
4. Awaiting the distribution of examination papers.
5. The examination paper lies face down before her.
6. The night before an examination.
7. One day before an examination.
8. Two days before an examination.
9. Three days before an examination.
10. Four days before an examination.

[2]All hierarchies are in descending order of reaction intensity.

11. Five days before an examination.
12. A week before an examination.
13. Two weeks before an examination.
14. A month before an examination.

B. *Scrutiny Series*

1. Being watched working (especially drawing) by 10 people.
2. Being watched working by six people.
3. Being watched working by three people.
4. Being watched working by one expert in the field. (Anxiety begins when the observer is ten feet away and increases as he draws closer).
5. Being watched working by a non-expert. (Anxiety begins at a distance of four feet).

C. *Devaluation Series*

1. An argument she raises in a discussion is ignored by the group.
2. She is not recognized by a person she has briefly met three times.
3. Her mother says she is selfish because she is not helping in the house. (Studying instead).
4. She is not recognized by a person she has briefly met twice.
5. Her mother calls her lazy.
6. She is not recognized by a person she has briefly met once.

D. *Discord Between Other People*

1. Her mother shouts at a servant.
2. Her young sister whines to her mother.
3. Her sister engages in a dispute with her father.
4. Her mother shouts at her sister.
5. She sees two strangers quarrel.

2. *Some variants of hierarchies on the theme of sickness and injury.*

The examples that follow are given chiefly to illustrate individual differences in the grading of reactions. In each of the cases there was fear of both external and internal stimuli, but in the first of them, the feared internal events had never actually happened. The first two cases were also agoraphobic. All three required and received training in assertive behavior in addition to desensitization.

CASE 5. Woman of 35.

External Stimuli

1. Sight of a fit.
2. Jerky movement of another's arm.
3. Sight of someone fainting.
4. An acquaintance says "That man across the street has some form of insanity."
5. The word "insanity."
6. The word "madness."
7. Insane sounding laughter.
8. An acquaintance says "That man across the street has an anxiety state."
9. The sound of screaming (the closer the more disturbing).
10. A man with a fracture lying in bed with ropes and pulleys attached to his leg.
11. A man propped up in bed short of breath because of heart disease.
12. An acquaintance says "That man across the road is an epileptic."
13. Seeing a man propped up in bed short of breath because of pneumonia.
14. A man walks by with a plaster cast on his leg.
15. A man with Parkinson's disease.
16. A man with blood running down his face from a cut.
17. A person with a facial tic.

Endogenous stimuli

1. Having a fit.
2. Fainting.
3. Tremor of her hand.

Note: None of these possibilities had ever actually been experienced by the patient.

CASE 6. Woman of 32.

External stimuli

1. The sight of physical deformity.
2. Someone in pain (the greater the evidence of pain the more disturbing).
3. The sight of bleeding.
4. The sight of somebody seriously ill (e.g. heart attack).
5. Automobile accidents.
6. Nurses in uniform.
7. Wheelchairs.
8. Hospitals.
9. Ambulances.

Endogenous stimuli

1. Tense (explosive), sensation in head.
2. Clammy feet.
3. Perspiring hands.
4. Dry mouth and inability to swallow.
5. Dizziness.
6. Rapid breathing.
7. Racing heart.
8. Tense feeling in back of neck.
9. Weakness at knees.
10. Butterflies in stomach.

CASE 7. Woman of 52.

External stimuli

1. Child with two wasted legs.
2. Man walking slowly — short of breath due to weak heart.

3. Blind man working lift.
4. Child with one wasted leg.
5. A hunchback.
6. A person groaning with pain.
7. A man with a club foot.
8. A one-armed man.
9. A one-legged man.
10. A person with a high temperature due to a relatively non-dangerous disease like influenza.

Endogenous stimuli.[3]

1. Extrasystoles
2. Shooting pains in chest and abdomen.
3. Pains in the left shoulder and back.
4. Pain on top of head.
5. Buzzing in ear.
6. Tremor of hands.
7. Numbness or pain in fingertips.
8. Shortness of breath after exertion.
9. Pain in left hand (old injury).

3. Desensitization procedure: counteracting anxiety by relaxation

The stage is now set for the conventional desensitization procedure — the patient having attained a capacity to calm himself by relaxation, and the therapist having established appropriate hierarchies. It is natural to hope for a smooth therapeutic passage, and such is often the case but there are many difficulties that may encumber the path. I shall first describe the technique and the characteristic course of the uncomplicated process of desensitization.

[3]This hierarchy was previously published in another connection in Wolpe (1958).

The assessment of a patient's ability to relax depends partly upon his reports of the degree of calmness that relaxing brings about in him, and partly upon impressions gained from observing him. By the second or third lesson, most patients report calmness, ease, tranquility or sleepiness. A few experience little or no change of feeling. It would, of course, be a boon to have objective indicators to determine degree of relaxation. Jacobson (1939, 1964) has used the electromyogram, but mainly as a corroborative measure. It is too laborious for routine use. Meanwhile, fortunately, the reports of patients usually serve as a sufficiently reliable guide to their emotional state, especially with the help of the subjective anxiety scale (see above). Quite a number of patients, especially those who have little or no current anxiety, report a positive feeling of calm after only one or two sessions of relaxation training. In some fortunate individuals there appears to be a kind of relaxation-radiation zone (usually in the arms or face); and these report a diffuse spread of relaxation to many regions with correlated growth of calmness when the radiation zone is relaxed. If the hierarchies are ready early it is my practice to start desensitization with those who can attain distinct emotional calm before concluding the relaxation training (though this is continued during subsequent interviews).

In embarking upon a desensitization program it is of course highly desirable for the patient to achieve a positive feeling of calm, i.e. a negative of anxiety; but it is *not* mandatory and one is always well satisfied with zero subjective units of disturbance *(suds)*. In a fair number who have considerable levels of current anxiety [whether or not this is pervasive ('free-floating') anxiety], it has been found that a substantial lowering of the level — say, from 50 to 15 *suds* — may afford a sufficiently low anxiety baseline for successful desensitization. Apparently, an anxiety-inhibiting 'dynamism' can inhibit small quanta of intercurrent anxiety even when it does not fully overcome current anxiety. Desensitizing effects are only rarely obtainable with levels in excess of 25 *suds;* and in some individuals a zero level is a *sine qua non.*

When relaxation is inadequate, efforts may be made to enhance it by doses of meprobamate, chlorpromazine, or codeine given an hour before the interview. Which drug to use is in essence decided by trial and error (see Chapter IX). When pervasive ('free-floating') anxiety impedes relaxation, the use of carbon dioxide-oxygen mixtures by La Verne's single inhalation technique (Chapter IX) is of the greatest value and with some patients comes to be used before every desensitization session. Inhalations are given until anxiety reaches an irreducible level — usually by the fourth inhalation. In a few patients who cannot relax but who are not anxious either, attempts at desensitization sometimes nonetheless succeed, presumably because interview-induced emotional responses inhibit the anxiety aroused by the imagined stimuli. This is a supposition that requires experimental testing.

In about ten per cent of cases, I carry out desensitization under hypnosis, employing, most often, the levitation technique described by Wolberg (1948). The patient may have been hypnotized in an exploratory way during one or more earlier interviews, but more often the first attempt at hypnosis is made at the first desensitization session. In those who are difficult to hypnotize, hypnosis is abandoned, and instructions are given merely to close the eyes and relax according to the therapist's directions. But some patients certainly relax better in a formal hypnotic state.

The first desensitization session may be introduced by saying "Let's see how well you can relax and how you react to various stimuli and images. Our main aim at all times will be to keep you as comfortable as possible."

While the patient sits or lies comfortably with his eyes closed, whether hypnotized or not, the therapist proceeds to bring about as deep as possible a state of relaxation by the use of such words as the following:

> Now, your whole body becomes progressively heavier, and all your muscles relax. Let go more and more completely. We shall give your muscles individual attention. Relax the muscles of your forehead. (*Pause 5 to 10 seconds*). Relax the muscles of your jaws and those of your tongue. (*Pause*) Relax the muscles of your eyeballs. The more you relax, the calmer you become. (*Pause*) Relax the muscles of your neck. (*Pause*) Let all the muscles of your shoulders relax. Just let yourself go. (*Pause*) Now relax your arms. (*Pause*) Relax all the muscles of your trunk. (*Pause*) Relax the muscles of your lower limbs. Let your muscles go more and more. You feel so much at ease and so very comfortable.

At the first desensitization session, which is always partly exploratory, the therapist seeks some feedback on the state of the patient. He says, "If you feel utterly calm — zero anxiety — do nothing; otherwise raise your left index finger." If the finger remains still the next stage may begin; but if it is raised the therapist ascertains the level of anxiety by further probings — "Raise the finger if more than 10 *suds*", etc. This mode of inquiry is used, because it seems to cause much less disruption of relaxation than speech usually does.

If the patient continues to have a good deal of anxiety despite his best efforts at direct relaxation, various imaginal devices may be invoked. Those most commonly used are:

1. "Imagine that on a calm summer's day you lie on your back on a soft lawn and watch the clouds move slowly overhead. Notice especially the brilliant edges of the clouds."

2. "Imagine an intense, bright spot of light about eighteen inches in front of you." (This image is due to Milton Erickson.)

3. "Imagine that near a river's bank you see a leaf moving erratically on little waves."

If, despite these efforts considerable anxiety persists, the session is now terminated. Otherwise it proceeds.

There is a routine manner of proceeding with the introduction of scenes at the first desensitization session. The observations that the therapist makes at this session frequently determine details of techniques to fit in with particular requirements of the patient.

The first scene presented is neutral in the sense that the patient is not expected to have any anxious reaction to it. I most commonly use a street scene. Sometimes it is 'safer' to have the patient imagine himself sitting in his living room, or reading a newspaper; but there is no guarantee of safety unless the subject-matter has actually been explored beforehand. At one time I used to employ a white flower against a black background as a standard control scene until one patient evinced considerable anxiety to it, because he associated it with funerals, and as it subsequently turned out, he had a neurosis about death.

There are two uses of a control scene. First, it provides information about the patient's general ability to visualize anxiety-free material. Second, it permits one to look for certain contaminating factors: the patient may have anxiety about relinquishing control of himself or anxiety about 'the unknown.' In either case, anxiety will be elicited that has nothing to do with the specific features of presented scenes.

The time-honored way of introducing scenes is illustrated below with reference to the case of Miss C. whose cluster of four hierarchies was given above (p. 117). *It is no longer the method of choice,* but still has its uses. A generally preferable method will be described subsequently. When Miss C. was well relaxed, she was addressed as follows:

> I am now going to ask you to imagine a number of scenes. You will imagine them clearly and they will generally interfere little, if at all, with your state of relaxation. If, however, at any time you feel disturbed or worried and want to draw my attention, you will be able to do so by raising your left index finger. First I want you to imagine that you are standing at a familiar street corner on a pleasant morning watching the traffic go by. You see cars, motorcycles, trucks, bicycles, people, and traffic lights; and you can hear the sounds associated with all these things. *(Pause of about 15 seconds)* Now stop imagining that scene and give all your attention once again to relaxing. If the scene you imagined disturbed you even in the slightest degree I want you to raise your left index finger *now. (Patient does not raise finger)* Now imagine that you are home studying in the evening. It is the 20th of May, exactly a month before your examination. *(Pause of 5 seconds)* Now stop imagining the scene. *(Pause of 10 seconds)* Now imagine the same scene again — a month before your examination. *(Pause of 5 seconds)* Stop imagining the scene and just think of your muscles. Let go, and enjoy your state of calm. *(Pause of 15 seconds)* Now again imagine that you are studying at home a month before your examination. *(Pause of 5 seconds)* Stop the scene, and now think of nothing but your own body. *(Pause of 5 seconds)* If you felt any disturbance whatsoever to the last scene raise your left index finger now. *(Patient raises finger)* If the amount of disturbance decreased from the first presentation to the third do nothing, other-

wise again raise your finger. *(Patient does not raise finger)* Just keep on relaxing. *(Pause of 15 seconds)* Imagine that you are sitting on a bench at a bus stop and across the road are two strange men whose voices are raised in argument. *(Pause of 10 seconds)* Stop imagining the scene and just relax. *(Pause of 10 seconds)* Now again imagine the scene of these two men arguing across the road. *(Pause of 10 seconds)* Stop the scene and relax. Now I am going to count up to 5 and you will open your eyes, feeling very calm and refreshed.

She opened her eyes, looking, as is commonly the case, a little sleepy. In reply to questions, she reported that she felt very calm and that the scenes were quite clear. She stated that in both the scene belonging to the examination series and that belonging to the quarrel series, there had been moderate anxiety at the first presentation, and less at subsequent presentations, but in neither instance had the decrease been down to zero.

It was noted that the responses of this patient were of the commonplace kind that do not presage any difficulties. Since visualization was clear, and there was evidence of decrease of anxiety with each repetition of a scene, it was predicted that we would make our way through all the hierarchies without much trouble; and the course of events bore out this prediction.

At this point it is worth remarking that even though the patient had a signal at her disposal whereby to indicate disturbance, the fact that she did not do so during a scene by no means proved that it had not disturbed her. Few patients make use of this signal when only mildly disturbed. But the provision of a signal must never be omitted, so that the patient can use it if he should happen to have a strong emotional reaction. *Exposure, and prolonged exposure in particular, to a very disturbing scene can seriously increase phobic sensitivity.*

Improved Procedure For Systematic Desensitization

The following modifications of procedure originated in the course of a psychophysiological study of systematic desensitization (Wolpe & Fried, 1968), in which it was necessary to know precisely when visualization began.

The patient is instructed to raise his index finger briefly the moment the scene is clearly imagined. The therapist then lets the scene remain for exactly as long as he wants to — usually 5-7 seconds. He terminates it, as usual, by saying "Stop the scene"; and then asks the patient to state how much it disturbed him in terms of *suds*. After a few sessions, the patient gets into the habit of stating the number of *suds* automatically upon the termination of the scene. While the use of a verbal report possibly disrupts relaxation more than the raising of a finger, the adverse effects have to date in no case seemed to be important. Any disadvantages are certainly outweighed by dispensing with the need to allow 'long enough time' to be sure that the patient has visualized the scene, and by the immediate and precise feedback regarding amount of disturbance.

Procedure at later sessions takes much the same course as at the first, but there is a tendency for the preliminaries to take less and less time. Whenever the patient is judged sufficiently relaxed, he is informed that scenes will be presented to his imagination and at early sessions reminded that if anything should disturb him unduly he may signal by raising his forefinger. If at the previous session there was a scene at whose repeated presentations anxiety diminished, but not to zero, that scene is usually the first to be presented. But if at the previous session that scene ceased to arouse any anxiety, the scene next higher in the hierarchy will then be presented. There are, however, some patients who, though having had no anxiety at all to the final scene at a session, again show a small measure of anxiety to that same scene at the session — a kind of 'spontaneous recovery' of anxiety. The scene must then be repeated until the anxiety is entirely eliminated, before ascending the hierarchy. In some patients who exhibit this feature the need for back-tracking can sometimes be eliminated by *overlearning* at the earlier session, i.e., presenting a scene 2 or 3 times more after it has ceased to arouse anxiety.

All relevant occurrences during the desensitization session are noted on a card by a concise notation. The following is the record of Miss C's first desensitization session:

> S. D. by rel. Scene 1 — corner, 2 — studying at home one month before exam. (x3), 3 — two strange men argue across road (x2). Mod. decr. sl. 2, 3.[4]

Quantitative Considerations

There is great variation in *how many themes, how many scenes from each,* and how many presentations are given at a session. Generally, up to four hierarchies are drawn upon in an individual session, and not many patients have more than four. Three or four presentations of a scene are usual, but ten or more may be needed. The total number of scenes presented is limited mainly by availability of time and by the endurance of the

[4] 'S. D. by rel.' stands for "systematic desensitization by relaxation." "Mod. decr. sl. 2, 3" means that the reactions to scenes 2 and 3 were initially moderate, decreasing to slight on repetition. The numbers in parenthesis show how many presentations were given.

The usual plan followed in assigning numerical indices to scenes is to use an integer to indicate the class of subject-matter, and letters for variations of detail. For example in Miss C's case the imaginary situation of being at home working 2 weeks before the examination was given the index 1 a, one week before the examination was 1 b, and so forth. The advantages of employing these indices are: (1) they obviate repeatedly writing out the features of scenes, (2) they make it easy to find particular scenes when one consults the record, and (3) they facilitate later research work.

patient. On the whole, both of these quantities increase as therapy goes on, and eventually almost the whole interview may be devoted to desensitization, so that whereas at an early stage eight or ten presentations are the total given at a session, at an advanced stage the number may rise to 30 or even 50. The usual duration of a desensitization session is 15 to 30 minutes. However Wolpin and Pearsall (1965) reported totally overcoming a phobia in a single session conducted continuously for 90 minutes.

While the foregoing generalizations apply to the great majority of patients, there are rare individuals who manifest marked perseveration of even the mild anxiety aroused by a single scene presentation. Yet anxiety decreases from session to session. In such individuals only one scene should be given at a session. Marked perseveration of anxiety can also occur in the usual run of patients after the presentation of an unduly disturbing scene. When this happens the session should be terminated.

The *duration* of a scene is usually of the order of 5-7 seconds but it may be varied according to several circumstances. It is quickly terminated if the patient signals anxiety by spontaneously raising his finger or if he shows any sharp reaction. Whenever the therapist has special reason to suspect that a scene may evoke a strong reaction he presents it with cautious brevity — for one or two seconds. By and large, early presentations of scenes are briefer, later ones longer. A certain number of patients require fifteen or more seconds to construct a clear image of a scene in their imagination. The character of the scene also necessarily plays a part in determining the time allowed for it. A clap of thunder takes less time than making a speech.

The *interval* between scenes also varies. It is usually between ten and twenty seconds, but if the patient has been more than slightly disturbed by the preceding scene, the interval may be extended to a minute or more, during which time the patient may be given repeated suggestions to be calm, relaxed and tranquil. Until the therapist is well acquainted with the patient's modes of reacting, he should frequently check the basal relaxation level between scenes. For this purpose the *sud* scale is invaluable.

The *number* of desensitizing sessions required depends on the number of scene presentations necessary to overcome the phobic constellations of the patient. Relevant factors are the number of such constellations, the severity of each, and the degree of generalization or involvement of related stimuli in the case of each. One patient may recover in half a dozen sessions, another may require a hundred or more. The patient with a death phobia, mentioned above, on whom a temporal dimension had to be used, also had two other phobias and required a total of about a hundred sessions. To remove the death phobia alone, a total of about 2,000 scene presentations had to be used.

The *spacing* of sessions does not seem to matter greatly. As a rule, sessions are given 2-3 times a week, but may be separated by many weeks or take place daily. Some patients, visiting from afar, receive 2 sessions a day, and occasionally as many as four. Whether sessions are massed or widely dispersed there is practically always a close correlation between the extent to which desensitization has been accomplished and the degree of diminution of anxiety responses to real stimuli in the phobic areas. Except when therapy is almost terminated and nothing remains of a phobia but a few weak reactions (that may be overcome by the competition of emotions arising spontaneously in the ordinary course of living) very little change occurs, as a rule, between sessions. In one case of severe claustrophobia a marked but incomplete degree of improvement achieved by a first series of sessions remained almost stationary during a 3½ year interval, after which further sessions led to complete elimination of the phobia. The patient mentioned above with a disabling fear of cars, who had daily sessions for a week or two every 5 weeks or so, greatly improved during the treatment phases but not at all during the intervening weeks (see Case 11).

Rate of change is neither haphazard nor purely an individual matter. At least in the case of desensitization of the classical phobias it follows consistent quantitative laws. A study of 20 phobias of 13 patients (Wolpe, 1963) was prompted by the casual observation that during desensitization the number of presentations of a scene required to bring the anxiety level down to zero is not uniform but tends to increase or decrease on the way up the hierarchy. An attempt was made to establish quantitative relations by a study of those phobias that vary along a physical dimension. It was found that in claustrophobia and those phobias in which the patient becomes more anxious with increasing proximity to the feared object, the cumulative curve relating number of scene presentations to therapeutic progress is a positively accelerating function. In agoraphobias, acrophobias, and those which anxiety depends on the number of objects, the cumulative curve is a negatively accelerating function. No exceptions were found, as may be observed by studying Figs. 3-6, each of which contains the curves of a particular group. In order to make them comparable, the curves have been subjected to percentile trans-formations. The horizontal axis shows attained percentage of criterion of recovery, and the vertical axis scene presentations as a percentage of the total number employed to overcome the whole hierarchy.

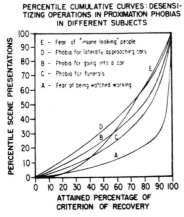

PERCENTILE CUMULATIVE CURVES: DESENSI-
TIZING OPERATIONS IN PROXIMATION PHOBIAS
IN DIFFERENT SUBJECTS

E – Fear of "insane looking" people
D – Phobia for laterally approaching cars
B – Phobia for going into a car
C – Phobia for funerals
A – Fear at being watched working

Fig. 3.

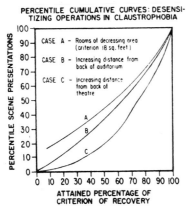

PERCENTILE CUMULATIVE CURVES: DESENSI-
TIZING OPERATIONS IN CLAUSTROPHOBIA

CASE A – Rooms of decreasing area
(criterion 18 sq. feet)

CASE B – Increasing distance from
back of auditorium

CASE C – Increasing distance
from back of
theatre

Fig. 4.

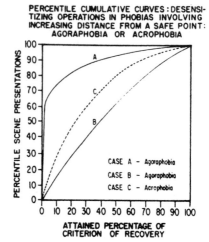

Fig. 5.

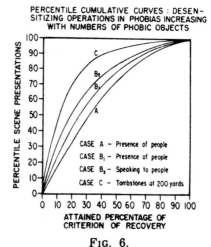

Fig. 6.

Fig. 7 illustrates that it is not the personality of the patient but the type of phobia that determines the shape of the curve. The three curves in this figure were obtained from a single patient. That displaying negative acceleration (B) delineates the desensitization of the anxiety response to an increasing number of tombstones at 200 yards. The positively accelerating curves belong respectively to proximation phobias to a dead dog (A) and to a stationary automobile (C), and are strikingly concordant.

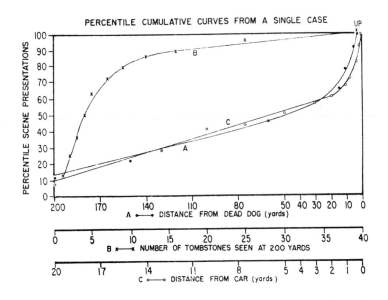

FIG. 7.

Mathematical analysis of the curves reveals that with the exception of that for agoraphobia Case A, and Curve C in Fig. 6 (which will be commented upon subsequently) they express the same kind of functional relation as has been found by Stevens (1957, 1962) in relating the physical magnitude of a stimulus to its perceived intensity — the "psycho-physical law." This is a general empirical law that the psychological (subjective) magnitude is a power function of the stimulus magnitude. This means that to make one stimulus seem twice as strong as another, the physical energy must be increased at a fixed ratio, no matter what the initial intensity level. The relationship is expressed by the formula:

$$P = kS^n,$$

where P stands for perceived intensity (psychological magnitude), S for stimulus magnitude, k is a constant, and n the exponent of the relationship. The exponent is determined empirically by the formula:

$$n = \frac{\log 0.5}{\log r},$$

where r is the ratio between the physical magnitude of a given stimulus and the physical magnitude of the stimulus that appears twice as strong as the given stimulus.

Insofar as the desensitization curves portray this kind of functional relation it may be deduced that the amount of work required for each measured unit of progress in overcoming these phobias is a function of the correlated magnitudes of the subject's pre-treatment response. The relevant indicator of response here is *autonomic response magnitude* rather than perceived magnitude. To test this presumption, it is necessary to compare the curve of directly measured autonomic magnitudes of response at different points in hierarchies *before treatment,* with the desensitization curves subsequently obtained. No direct comparison has as yet been attempted, but Lang (1967) has found that the curve correlating pulse rate change with the hierarchical position of stimulus in snake phobias is very similar to the proximation phobia curves in Fig. 2.

For several of the curves, the value of the exponent n was determined by Stevens' formula (v.s.), the value of r being derived from the point on the x axis at which $y = 50\%$ (0.5). Among the proximation phobias (Fig. 3) the exponent of the middle curve, C, is about 3.0. Among the phobias varying with numbers of phobic objects (Fig. 4) the value for Curve B_2 is 0.43. The middle curve, C, in the remoteness phobia group (Fig. 5) is almost identical with this.

As mentioned above, curve A of the remoteness group does not conform to a power function but the case was unusual in that the desensitization distances reflected in the curve ranged from 20 yards to 100 miles. It is obvious that a person's perception of difference of yards may vary in quite a dissimilar way from differences of miles. It was found upon plotting separate curves for 0-1 and for 1-100 miles that two power function curves were obtained, the first (0-1) being similar to the theoretical curve $n = 0.44$, and the second (1-100) conforming almost exactly to the theoretical curve $n = 0.26$ (Wolpe, 1963). Curve C in Fig. 4 fits an exponential function $[(P = 76.11 (1-0.85^n)]$ a good deal better than a power function, but remains close enough to the power curve $n = 0.3$ not to constitute a damaging exception to the rule.

Awareness of these quantitative relations makes it possible both to predict in general at what stages in cases of this class progress will be slowest, and, more specifically, to calculate, after treatment has proceeded long enough to provide the essential data, how much more treatment will be needed to overcome a particular phobia. Furthermore, the curves characterizing different dimensions help the therapist to decide which dimension to work with first in a multidimensional hierarchy. For example, in a woman with a dread of being seen vomiting the fear increased with numbers of witnesses and with proximity. The knowledge that the numbers curve accelerates negatively and the proximation curve positively promoted the presentation of increasing numbers at a hundred yards. This allowed the number dimension to be mastered with very little effort. Then the numerous witnesses could be gradually brought closer. If the reverse order had been adopted it would ultimately have meant working at the steep sections of both curves simultaneously.

Some Snags And Pitfalls

Sometimes, despite having carried out the preliminaries conscientiously and apparently successfully, the therapist is chagrined to find that desensitization is not proceeding according to his expectations. Either the patient experiences no decrement of anxiety to successive presentations of scenes, or reports no improvement in his reactions to real situations to correspond with progress during sessions. Human variations are so complex and subtle that even the most extensive experience can provide no absolute insurance against disappointments. What matters most is to be able to retrieve the situation. To do this the therapist must first find out what accounts for his failure. The usual reasons are of three kinds, which will be discussed in turn.

1. Difficulties of relaxation
2. Misleading or irrelevant hierarchies
3. Inadequacies of imagery

1. *Difficulties of relaxation:* The therapist may be under the impression that the patient is well relaxed when in fact he is not. A patient will often say that he feels relaxed when he is, in fact, moderately tense. This may be for various reasons. He may not yet be sufficiently aware of the internal indications of tension, or he may not think they are worth reporting, or it is so long since he has experienced a true state of calm that any substantial drop in tension *seems* like relaxation to him. The use of the quantitative subjective anxiety scale decreases the likelihood of miscommunications of this type occurring (though it does not eliminate them). No doubt continuous GSR or electromyogram recordings would help. It takes very careful questioning of the patient to reveal the true state of affairs; and then of course the therapist should intensify his efforts to improve relaxation either by further direct training or by the introduction of carbon dioxide or drugs (Chapter IX).

There are other patients who find it difficult to relax as part of a general fear of 'letting go.' Some of these patients make an effort to relax their muscles and perhaps succeed to an extent; but remain afraid. The autonomic components of the anxiety response remain unchanged, and may even increase. The solution to this difficulty varies with the case. Sometimes it is possible to achieve a basis for desensitization simply by telling the patient to get calm and comfortable in his own way, without attempting to 'let himself go.' In other cases, one may attempt prior desensitization of the fear of letting go by an *in vivo* method (Chapter VIII) and sometimes go on to attack all other anxiety constellations in the neurosis in the same way. In yet others, one may have recourse to one or other of the electrical methods of counteracting anxiety, such as 'anxiety-relief' or the recently introduced non-aversive sensory interference technique (Chapter VIII).

2. *Misleading or irrelevant hierarchies:* Even when his hierarchies have none of the faults of conception or construction that may be imputed to elementary errors, there are occasions when the therapist may find himself making no headway, and it becomes evident that the hierarchies are off the track. Sometimes he is misled by the patient's fears being frequently experienced in contexts that are the occasion for fear but not its source. For example, after a man had been treated for 20 sessions with minimal benefit for claustrophobia and agoraphobia it was found that both were based upon a central fear of dying. He was anxious when his freedom of movement was restricted or when he was far from a haven, because such situations in different degrees implied difficulty in getting help if he should collapse. During the same period another male patient with a very similar range of phobias was responding to desensitization in classical fashion — for in him the space stimuli were the true antecedents of anxiety. It pays to scrutinize the stimulus sources of anxiety carefully in advance.

There is another circumstance in which hierarchies are obtained which are not amenable to desensitization. In certain unhappily married women apparently simple phobias that have originated in the course of the marriage, turn out in reality to be fear reactions to stimulus situations related to some aspect of the marriage that evokes tension and aversion. This has recently been independently noted by Fry (1962). Such phobias may be regarded as true *symbolic* reactions, provided that the word "symbolic" is understood in the conventional terms of semantics and learning theory, and not psychoanalytically. *It is quite probable that the discovery of some cases having this unusual feature is what led Freud to the presumption that all phobias have a hidden source.*

This kind of phobia is exemplified by the case of a 34-year-old woman whose primary complaint was of a feeling of being closed in and a powerful urge to escape when engaged in conversations with adults — except interchanges on the most casual plane, such as asking the time. This reaction had begun eight years previously during the patient's first pregnancy. At the time when conditioning therapy began, no satisfactory precipitating cause of the neurosis could be discerned. She was trained in relaxation and the phobic stimuli taken at their face value. The first hierarchy to be used was based on the theme of being stared at, the patient's reactions increasing with the proximity of the starer. The scenes presented to her imagination aroused very little anxiety until a distance of 15 feet was reached — and then there was a *severe* reaction. Various other dimensions were then severally tried, including number of people at a distance, age of starer, duration of stare and intensity of illumination — in each instance with the same consequence. It was obvious that something was being missed, but this could not be identified. I was about to abandon the case in despair when the patient, whom tranquilizers had helped but little, asked "Is there *nothing* that could diminish my distress?" I replied, "At times of special stress you might try a little alcohol."

After a long pause she said "My husband doesn't let me drink." This was the first time I had heard her make an adverse remark about him; but it was the thin end of a wedge that prised open long-suppressed anger and frustration at his absolute domination over each and every one of her activities. The first pregnancy had precipitated the neurosis because it had seemed to block forever a way out of the marriage — which to the outer world and partly to herself she had represented as a great success.

The phobia now appeared to be primarily a fear of peering or prying. The impulse to get away from these situations summated with the claustrophobic feeling chronically engendered by the marriage. Thus, an unacknowledged life situation was the real basis of the phobia. Instigation to assertion with her husband now became the foremost therapeutic tactic. In case the reader should conclude that in *this* case psychoanalysis would have been the treatment of choice, it must be said that the patient had recently undergone psychoanalysis for two years without any success. The crucial aspects of the marital situation had not emerged during its course, in which, it appears, major attention was focused on oedipal attitudes and the like. The more circumstantial tenets of psychoanalytic theory often prove to be a strait-jacket that prohibits the full exploration of a patient's reactive possibilities.

3. *Inadequacies of imagery:* Most patients are able to project themselves into imagined anxiety-evoking situations in a way that evokes something of the reality of the situations and a corresponding amount of anxiety. I have found this to be the case in about 90 per cent of both South

African and American patients. In England, however, the percentage may be considerably lower, according to my personal impression and recent comments by Meyer (1963). It may be that traditional English training that encourages underplaying manifestations of feeling also impairs the ability to associate emotion with imagery.

There are those patients who are unable to conjure up either visual or auditory images — at any rate in response to the requirements of the therapist. Far more commonly, the trouble is that while images can be formed they have no sense of reality for the patient. Occasionally, action taken by the therapist leads to the difficulty being overcome. The action is of various kinds — providing much verbal detail of the situation to be imagined, inducing a 'deep' trance in good hypnotic subjects, or getting the patient to describe what he imagines. Darwin (1968) has found that in speech-anxious subjects significantly more rapid progress is made during desensitization if the patient describes the scenes instead of merely imagining them. Often, such efforts are without avail; and therapeutic change is then dependent upon the use of real stimuli.

Occasional patients visualize satisfactorily until an advanced point in the hierarchy and then detach themselves from the imagined situations, viewing them from the standpoint of a disinterested spectator. An example is Case 13 in Chapter XIII. He had a cleanliness compulsion of an extreme form, based upon a fear of contamination with his own urine. When transfer from the imaginary to the real situations ceased to occur, his relaxation was counterposed to real stimuli instead. On this basis the onslaught on his neurosis was brought to final victory.

RESULTS OF SYSTEMATIC DESENSITIZATION

It is useful to know how successful one may expect to be in applying desensitization to appropriate cases, while realizing separate evaluation entails the risk of fostering the erroneous idea that it is a method *sui generis* instead of merely a particular application of a principle. The only published statistical study to date, that by Wolpe (1962), used as its subject matter 39 patients whose case records were extracted in random fashion from the therapist's files by a casual visitor. Many of these patients also had other neurotic habits that were treated by different methods deemed more appropriate.

The details of the study are tabulated in Table 3, in which outcome of treatment is indicated on a 5 point scale ranging from 4-plus to zero. A 4-plus rating means complete or almost complete freedom from phobic reactions to all situations in the area of the phobia *encountered in actuality*. A 3-plus rating means an improvement of response such that the phobia is judged by the patient to have lost at least 80 per cent of its original strength. A zero rating indicates that there is no definite change. It will be noted that only 4-plus, 3-plus and zero ratings were applicable to the patients in this series.

Table 4 summarizes the data given in Table 3. There were 68 anxiety response habits among the 39 patients, of whom 19 had multiple hierarchies. The treatment was judged effective in 35 patients. Forty-five of the anxiety-response habits were apparently eliminated (4-plus rating) and 17 more markedly ameliorated (3-plus rating), making 90 per cent in all. It is probable that many of the latter group would have reached a 4-plus level had there been additional sessions. In cases 16 and 29 progress had diminished when sessions were discontinued, but not in any of the others.

TABLE 3.

BASIC CASE DATA

Patient Sex, Age	No. of Sessions	Hierarchy Theme	Outcome	Comments
(1) F.50	62	(a) Claustrophobia	++++	
		(b) Illness and hospitals	++++	
		(c) Death and its trappings	++++	
		(d) Storms	+++	
		(e) Quarrels	++++	
(2) M.40	6	(a) Guilt	++++	
		(b) Devaluation	++++	
(3) F.24	17	(a) Examinations	++++	See case 4
		(b) Being scrutinized	++++	
		(c) Devaluation	++++	
		(d) Discord between others	++++	
(4) M.24	5	(a) Snakelike shapes	++++	
(5) M.21	24	(a) Being watched	++++	
		(b) Suffering of others	++++	
		(c) "Jealousy" reaction	++++	
		(d) Disapproval	++++	
(6) M.28	5	Crowds	+++	
(7) F.21	5	Criticism	++++	
(8) F.52	21	(a) Being center of attention	O	No disturbance during scenes. Was in fact not imagining self in situation
		(b) Superstitions	O	
(9) F.25	9	Suffering and death of others	+++	
(10) M.22	17	Tissue damage in others	++++	
(11) M.37	13	Actual or implied criticism	++++	

(Table 3. Continued)

Patient Sex, Age	No. of Sessions	Hierarchy Theme	Outcome	Comments
(12) F.31	15	Being watched working	+++	
(13) F.40	16	(a) "Suffering" and eeriness (b) Being devalued (c) Failing to come up to expectations	++++ ++++ ++++	This case has been reported in detail (Wolpe, 1959)
(14) M.36	10	(a) Bright light (b) Palpitations	++++ ++++	
(15) M.43	9	Wounds and corpses	+++	
(16) M.27	51	(a) Being watched, especially at work (b) Being criticized	+++ ++++	No anxiety while being watched at work. Anxious at times while playing cards.
(17) M.33	8	Being watched at golf	+++	
(18) M.33	8	Talking before audience (stutterer)	O	No imagined scene was ever disturbing
(19) M.40	7	Authority figures	++++	
(20) M.23	4	Claustrophobia	++++	
(21) F.23	6	(a) Agoraphobia (b) Fear of falling	O O	Later successfully treated by conditioned motor response method

(Table 3. Continued)

Patient Sex, Age	No. of Sessions	Hierarchy Theme	Outcome	Comments
(22) M.46	19	(a) Being in limelight (b) Blood and death	+++ ++++	
(23) F.40	20	Social embarrassment	++++	
(24) F.28	9	Agoraphobia	O	
(25) F.48	7	Rejection	+++	
(26) M.28	13	(a) Disapproval (b) Rejection	+++ ++++	
(27) M.11	6	Authority figures	++++	
(28) M.26	217	(a) Claustrophobia (b) Criticism (numerous aspects) (c) Trappings of death	++++ +++ +++	Finally overcome completely by use of 'flooding'
(29) F.20	5	Agoraphobia	++++	
(30) M.68	23	(a) Agoraphobia (b) Masturbation	++++ ++++	
(31) F.36	5	Being in limelight	++++	
(32) M.26	17	(a) Illness and death (b) Own symptoms	+++ +++	
(33) F.44	9	(a) Being watched (b) Elevators	++++ ++++	

(Table 3. continued)

Patient Sex, Age	No. of Sessions	Hierarchy Theme	Outcome	Comments
(34) F.47	17	Intromission into vagina	+++	
(35) M.37	5	(a) Disapproval	++++	
		(b) Rejection	++++	
(36) F.32	25	Sexual stimuli	++++	
(37) M.36	21	(a) Agoraphobia	++++	
		(b) Disapproval	++++	
		(c) Being watched	++++	
(28) M.18	6	(a) Disapproval	+++	
		(b) Sexual stimuli	++++	Instrumental in overcoming impotence
(39) F.48	20	(a) Rejection	++++	Stutter markedly improved
		(d) Crudeness of others	++++	

TABLE 4.

SUMMARY OF DATA OF TABLE 3

Patients	39
Number of patients responding to desensitization treatment	35
Number of hierarchies	68
Hierarchies overcome	45 ⎫ 91%
Hierarchies markedly improved	17 ⎭
Hierarchies unimproved	6 9%
Total number of desensitization sessions	762
Mean session expenditure per hierarchy	11.2
Mean session expenditure per successfully treated hierarchy	12.3
Median number of sessions per patient	10.0

Among the failures, Cases 8 and 18 were unable to imagine themselves within situations; Case 22 could not confine her imagining to the stated scene and repeatedly exposed herself to excessively disturbing images. She was the patient who was later treated with complete success by the conditioned motor response method outlined on p. 160. Case 25 had interpersonal reactions that led to erratic responses and, having experienced no benefit, sought therapy elsewhere.

The mean number of sessions per phobia was 11.2; the median number of sessions given to patients 10:0. It should be noted that a desensitization session usually takes up only part of a ¾ hr. interview period, and in cases that also have non-phobic neurotic problems there may be other interviews in which a desensitization session does not occur, and these are not included in this tally.

CHAPTER VIII

Variants Of
Systematic Desensitization

THE GREAT ADVANTAGE of having a principle to utilize is that it provides one with the potentiality of practical options. If conventional systematic desensitization proves to be unsuitable in a particular case or class of cases, attempts can hopefully be made to implement, in other ways, the principle of reciprocally inhibiting small 'doses' of anxiety at a time. Even where conventional desensitization is quite successful, it is worth experimenting with new elaborations of the principle because of the possibility of their being more efficient or economical.

Several variations of technique are described in this chapter. So far, some of them have been held in reserve to be tried when conventional desensitization cannot be successfully carried out. Others have been the subject of controlled experiments that show them to be superior to conventional desensitization at least in respect to the kinds of neurotic fears figuring in the experiments.

The desensitization variants can be divided into three categories: 1. technical variations of the conventional consulting-room procedure; 2. alternative counter-anxiety responses for use with imaginal stimuli; and 3. methods involving the use of exteroceptive sources of anxiety.

TECHNICAL VARIATIONS OF CONVENTIONAL CONSULTING-ROOM PROCEDURE

While retaining the essence of systematic desensitization — the presentation of graded imaginal stimuli to a relaxed patient — one may modify the technical arrangements so as to reduce the amount of time the therapist has to spend with his patients. This has so far been done in two ways. One way is have part of the procedure automated so that it takes place without the physical presence of the therapist. The second way consists of desensitizing patients with similar neurotic fears in groups.

(a) Mechanical aids to systematic desensitization

Lang (1966) was the first to demonstrate that desensitization could be successfully accomplished by a machine. Phobias for snakes were overcome by the use of two tape recorders, one carrying hierarchy items and the other relaxation instructions. The patient controlled buttons to obtain relaxation, repetition, change, or cessation of scene. Taking a cue from Lang's observations, Migler and Wolpe (1967) used a single specially modified tape recorder to treat a patient who was severely disturbed by inferred disapproval and derision, especially when he was speaking to a group. The patient himself recorded both the hierarchy items and the relaxation instructions under supervision. He then took the tape recorder home and completely desensitized himself in seven sessions. He has now been free from his fear for two years.

The following technical details are reproduced with minor modifications from Migler and Wolpe (1967). One may use either a Wollensak T-1600 tape recorder or a Uher Universal 5000, each of which has two necessary features. First, it has a pause switch by which the tape motions can be instantly stopped. This switch is connected to a microswitch which the patient can hold in his hand and, as desired, stop the tape motion at any time, for any duration. Second, the recorder has two metal sensing strips on each side of the recording heads. When a metal foil which has been placed on the tape makes contact with the two sensing strips on the *right* side an internal circuit is closed and the tape recorder automatically switches from *playback* to *rewind*. These two strips are, for our purpose, bypassed by the tape and a pushbutton wired in parallel with them, so that now momentary depression of the pushbutton switches the recorder from *playback* to *rewind*. The second pair of sensing guides, to the *left* of the recording heads, functions to stop the rewinding and return to *playback* when another specially placed metal foil reaches these guides. This is not altered. The pushbutton and the microswitch are held together by adhesive tape, to make a combined remote control unit that the patient can hold in his hand. Depression of the microswitch (hereafter called the *pause switch)* stops the playback for as long as it is depressed. Momentary depression of the pushbutton (hereafter called the *repeat button)* produces the following sequential effects; the tape recorder stops playback and switches to rewind; rewinding continues until a metal foil is detected by the sensing guides to the left of the recording head; and when rewinding has stopped playback begins again.

In preparing the tape for desensitization Migler & Wolpe used the patient's voice throughout. The following were the operations:

1. Relaxation instructions were taped — "Relax your calves, thighs, forearms, upper arms, shoulders, neck, jaws, forehead, etc." (In using this section of the tape the patient was instructed to press the pause switch after each anatomical part was named and concentrate on that part until it felt free of muscular tension, then to release the pause switch and let the tape continue).

2. A metal foil was attached to the tape at the end of these relaxation instructions.

3. Just beyond the metal foil, (and before the first scene) were a few brief relaxation instructions: "Relax your arms, legs, stomach, chest, neck, and all your facial muscles. Now pause until you feel relaxed." (The patient was instructed to press the pause switch at this point until he felt relaxed).

4. Following these relaxation instructions, the tape contained instructions to visualize the first scene in the hierarchy: — "Now imagine *(first scene)*". Pause. (The patient was instructed to press the pause switch at this point until the visualization was clear, and then to let the tape continue).

5. Ten seconds of recorded silence followed the instruction to pause, permitting ten seconds of clear visualization. The silence was terminated by the words, "Stop visualizing it. Press the repeat button if that scene disturbed you at all." (If the patient felt any negative emotional response to the scene he was to press the repeat button, which would rewind the tape back to the metal foil (step 2 above) so that the brief relaxation instructions, the scene, and the remainder of the

sequence would recur. If the repeat button was not pressed, the tape recorder continued to the next metal foil, which, like the first, was followed by relaxation instructions; but after these came scene 2 of the hierarchy — and so forth).

More recently simpler uses of the recorded voice have been proposed. Dr. Michael Kahn of the University of Texas has devised a recording that the patient can use at home. It contains instructions for scene presentations with silences after the instructions into which the patient inserts his own hierarchical scenes as directed beforehand by the therapist. Relaxation instructions precede each scene, and the recording is worded in such a way that the patient can repeat a particular scene as many times as necessary. The only patient on whom I have until now used this recording did well with it, overcoming a fear of being looked at that had precluded desensitization in my office.

A Trenton psychiatrist, Dr. Richard Rubin, has for some time been advising patients to acquire their own tape recorders for recording and playing back hierarchy items interspersed with relaxation instructions. Repetitions of a scene are sometimes rather awkward to handle, but the procedure can be facilitated by appropriate spacing of items or by the help of a member of the patient's household. Rubin states that many of his patients have effectively desensitized themselves by the use of this equipment.

(b) Group desensitization

If several patients suffer from the same phobia, it might be expected that having been trained to relax, they could be desensitized simultaneously even if the 'slopes' of their hierarchies (p. 112) were not identical, provided that the therapist ensured that each scene had ceased to evoke anxiety in every patient before proceeding to the next scene. Lazarus (1961) originally put this idea into practice in the context of a comparative study. He treated subjects with claustrophobia, acrophobia, and sexual phobias, by group desensitization; and control groups by a Sullivanian type of group therapy. Having separated the patients into matched pairs he randomly allocated one member of each pair to a desensitization group and the other to a Sullivanian group. Each group contained about 5 patients. After 21 sessions, 72 per cent of the patients in the desensitization groups were judged recovered, and only 12 per cent of those in the Sullivanian groups. It is worthy of note that each of the recovered subjects in the Sullivanian groups was a member of a sub-group that received relaxation training (without desensitization) in addition to the group therapy. A mean expenditure of something like four sessions per patient per phobia is obviously a striking economy. Even greater economy — an average of less than 2 hours of therapists's time per client — was achieved by Paul & Shannon (1966) in the treatment of severe "social evaluative" anxiety in college students, manifested by fear and disablement in public-speaking situations. At a two-year follow-up (Paul, 1968) found that improvement had been maintained or increased.

It is possible that Paul and Shannon's patients were more rapidly desensitized because exteroceptive stimuli from the other members of the group were a facilitative factor in overcoming their fear of exposure to people. This possibility seems in a small way to be supported by an experience of my own. In 1966, during a series of behavior therapy seminars, I invited all with fears of public speaking to submit to group desensitization in front of the rest of the class of 30. Eight volunteered.

The treatment sessions — each lasting 15 minutes — took place at the end of a two-hour seminar. The group sat before me in the front row of the lecture room. The first session was devoted to relaxation training, with which they were already familiar, and which some of them had already been practicing. At subsequent sessions imaginary scenes of speaking in public were presented to the group. The first scene was speaking to an audience of three. After 5 desensitization sessions, all five of the subjects who went through with the therapy were able to imagine themselves speaking to a group of 50 without anxiety. Evidence of transfer to the real situation was subsequently obtained from 2 of the participants. One of them reported giving a lecture to a group of 75 without any anxiety at all. Since the total time spent on the group therapy was 90 minutes, if we consider only the five subjects who completed the course, we obtain a mean therapist time expenditure per patient per phobia of 18 minutes! While it is obviously not possible to make any confident deductions from this somewhat casual experiment, it does suggest that therapeutic change may have been accelerated by the subjects' awareness of sitting in a group while desensitization in imagination was being carried out. This agrees with other evidence of the superiority of *in vivo* over imaginal stimuli (see below).

ALTERNATIVE COUNTER-ANXIETY RESPONSES FOR USE WITH IMAGINAL STIMULI

One alternative to relaxation is also frequently an inadvertent facilitator of the effects of relaxation — therapist-evoked counter-anxiety emotional responses. These, arising spontaneously in many patients in the therapist's office, are probably the basis of the non-specific therapeutic effects observed in all forms of psychotherapy (Wolpe, 1958, p. 193). They are also the apparent basis of those cases of successful desensitization in which scenes are presented without relaxation; and, in addition probably play a leading part in desensitization *in vivo* (see below). Under the present heading, however, we shall be concerned with those modes of anxiety-inhibition that the therapist can deliberately induce.

(a) External inhibition

The possibility of utilizing this phenomenon (Pavlov, 1927, p. 46) became apparent to me a few years ago while observing Dr. William M. Philpott of Takoma Park, Md. performing a rather elaborate procedure to eliminate conditioned anxiety with the aid of mild electric shocks. Some controlled experiments that I shortly afterwards organized at the University of Virginia indicated that a simple technique embodying external inhibition could produce all the effects demonstrated by Philpott.

Shorn of redundancies, the technique is as follows. Encircling the patient's forearm are two gauze strips, 1½ in. wide, one just above the wrist and the other about three inches higher. Each strip is held in place by a stainless steel alligator clip connected to the source of current — a 90-volt dry cell whose output is controlled by a 50,000 ohm variable resistor. Pulses are delivered by the therapist's pressing on a soft pushbutton switch for about half-a-second. The level of current correct for the patient is that which is strongly felt *without being aversive*. In some cases a very weak pulse suffices; in others no therapeutic effects occur until the electrical stimulus is strong enough to produce vigorous contraction of the forearm muscles. (It has frequently been noted that if the patient has pervasive anxiety, 8 to 10 pulses per minute will gradually reduce it, so that in 20 or 30 minutes it may be brought down from 60 *suds* or more to zero).

Once the appropriate level of shock has been established, the desensitizing procedure is begun. First, the weakest item in the hierarchy is presented *alone* once or twice to the patient's imagination in order to determine how many *suds* it evokes. The patient is then asked to imagine the scene and to signal by raising his index finger when it is well-defined. At this point, the therapist administers two shocks of the predetermined strength separated by about a second. After about five seconds the patient is instructed again to imagine the scene, signaling as before. After a series of 5 to 20 scenes, a check is made on the status of his reaction to the scene by presenting it without any shock.

An early case to be treated by this method was a woman whose many-faceted neurosis had been largely overcome by the usual behavior therapy methods. An important remaining neurotic problem was a phobia for driving alone. Originally, she had been unable to drive up her own driveway without feeling anxious. With conventional desensitization she had progressed steadily, though slowly, until she was able to drive three-quarters of a mile without any discomfort. But, a disturbing incident half-a-mile from home had set her back to that distance. Rather than resume the desensitization that had been so tedious, I decided to try external inhibition. Mild stimulation proved to be completely ineffective; but shocks strong enough to cause muscle contraction, while she visualized herself at that critical place half a mile from home led to decreasing anxiety. With 20 repetitions of the scene the anxiety decreased to zero. The procedure was then repeated for the ¾ mile point.

When she later tested herself at that point, she found herself completely free from anxiety. Continuing this method, the patient made much more rapid progress than she had previously done with conventional desensitization.

(b) Desensitization based on inhibition of anxiety by a conditioned motor response

This technique, though first reported 14 years ago (Wolpe 1954) has been used very little. It may turn out to be essentially a matter of external inhibition as described above. Experimentation is needed to determine whether the motor response contributes anything to change. Nevertheless, it has a very credible experimental basis. It was suggested by an observation by Mowrer and Viek (1948) that when animals are enabled to learn a definite motor response to electrical stimulation, upon repetition of the stimulation they gradually develop conditioned inhibition of the autonomic responses that are evoked at the same time. In the clinical setting, the patient with an anxiety hierarchy is asked to imagine a scene in the usual way and to signal when the image is clear. The therapist then passes a fairly mild shock into the forearm, in response to which the patient flexes his arm. In an extreme case of agoraphobia that was successfully treated by this method and is elsewhere described in detail (Wolpe, 1958, p. 174), it was found that 15 to 25 flexions were generally needed to bring down to zero the anxiety response to a disturbing scene.

(c) Emotive imagery

This is the name of a procedure first described by Lazarus and Abramovitz (1962) in which hierarchical stimuli are presented to the patient in an imaginary situation in which other elements evoke responses antagonistic to anxiety. These responses thus take the place of relaxation as the source of inhibition of anxiety.

One of their cases was a 12 year old boy who greatly feared darkness. In the room he shared with his brother, a light constantly shone at night next to his bed. He was especially afraid in the bathroom, which he only used if accompanied by another member of the household. Attempts at relaxation training had failed. The child had a passion for two radio serials, "Superman" and "Captain Silver". He was asked to imagine that Superman and Captain Silver had appointed him their agent. Lazarus and Abramovitz describe subsequent developments as follows:

> The therapist said, "Now I want you to close your eyes and imagine that you are sitting in the dining-room with your mother and father. It is night time. Suddenly, you receive a signal on the wrist radio that Superman has given you. You quickly run into the lounge because your mission must be kept a secret. There is only a little light coming into the lounge from the passage. Now pretend that you are all alone in the lounge waiting for Superman and Captain Silver to visit you. Think about this very clearly. If the idea makes you feel afraid, lift up your right hand."

An on-going scene was terminated as soon as there was any indication of anxiety. When an image had aroused anxiety, it would either be repeated in a more challengingly assertive manner, or altered slightly so as to appear less threatening. At the end of the third session, the child was able to picture himself alone in the bathroom with all the lights turned off, awaiting a communication from Superman. There was complete transfer to the real situation. A follow-up 11 months later revealed that the gains had been maintained.

The technique has also been used with adults. For example, a man with a claustrophobia that was especially related to theatres and restaurants was instructed to imagine himself seated in a theatre (at the aisle in the back row, initially) watching a striptease. The sexual arousal inhibited the weak anxiety response and was thus the basis for part of the deconditioning of the latter. However, because it is usually difficult to control the strength of the juxtaposed emotions, the applicability of this technique to adults appears to be limited.

DESENSITIZATION USING EXTEROCEPTIVE STIMULI TO ANXIETY

An *exteroceptive* stimulus is one that comes from outside the body of the responding organism, by contrast with an endogenous stimulus that originates within the organism — e.g. a visceral sensation or a mental image. The exteroceptive stimuli that are employed in desensitization are either actual feared objects or pictorial representations of them (Goldberg and D'Zurilla, 1968). The former have, till now, been by far the more widely used. A variety of counter-anxiety responses have been involved, as will be indicated. The procedures fall into two main classes — (a) *in vivo* desensitization in which exteroceptive stimuli are presented to the patient in graded amounts on the general lines of conventional desensitization, and (b) *modelling* in which the patient observes a fearless subject make increasingly intimate contact with a feared object.

(a) *In vivo* desensitization

It has often been a practical policy to ask patients to try exposing themselves in reality to situations to which they have just been desensitized in imagination.

For example, a person with a fear of driving is asked to go out driving up to the last desensitized point. I used to regard this as a consolidating maneuver and a means of getting 'feedback'. Recently, a controlled study by Garfield, Darwin, Singer and McBrearty, (1967) gave evidence that it positively accelerates desensitization.

Desensitization *in vivo* has its chief indication as the prime method in the 10 or 15 per cent of patients in whom imaginal stimuli are useless for desensitization because they do not arouse emotional responses similar to those produced by the real situation. Cooke (1966) found that in snake phobias desensitization proceeded with the same speed, whether imagined or real stimuli were used.

The successful use of real life graduated exposures in an institutional setting was reported by Terhune (1949) working empirically and without awareness of the learning principles involved. The first account of *in vivo* therapy directly based on the desensitization paradigm was in connection with two agoraphobic cases treated by Meyer (1957). It was followed in 1960 by Freeman and Kendrick's report of the overcoming of a cat phobia by getting the patient to handle pieces of material progressively similar to cat fur, exposing her to pictures of cats, then a toy kitten, followed by a real kitten, and eventually grown cats. A phobia for earthworms was treated in a similar way by Murphy (1964). More recently, Goldberg and D'Zurilla (1968) have overcome fears of receiving injections by the use of slide projections of the stages of activity involved in an injection; and Dengrove (1968) has used moving film to overcome phobias for bridges.

Desensitization *in vivo* is usually quite a straight-forward affair, though inevitably less convenient than conventional desensitization. It often suffices to depend, as the above mentioned therapists have done, on interpersonal and other 'natural' stimuli to evoke anxiety-inhibiting emotional responses; but relaxation (e.g. Case 13, Chapter XIII) or other deliberate measures (e.g. anxiety-relief conditioning — see p. 165) may be needed. The procedure usually takes the form of graded exposures of the patient to real fear-evoking stimuli while the therapist is present in the double role of guide and anxiety-inhibitor. For example, a woman whose anxiety level was related to distance from a 'reliable' person, was brought by her husband to meet me in a public park in the quiet of the early morning. In the course of about 10 meetings, I effected increasingly distant separations.

The stimulus requirements are not always so obvious. Special 'dramatic' or technical arrangements sometimes have to be contrived. For example, in treating a patient whose fear of public speaking was based on a fear of humiliation, I first had him intentionally give wrong answers to simple arithmetical problems. The anxiety this at first produced faded away with repetition. I then gave him more difficult problems, some of which he really could not answer correctly; and then had him stumble in his own field — at each stage deriding his errors. Additional witnesses were later introduced, one by one, to watch the sequence of failures. As he was enabled to endure this progression of 'humiliations' without anxiety his public-speaking fear declined.

CASE 8

    A case that called for technical inventiveness was a young woman who was practically confined to her home by a fear that she would die if her heart beat too fast. She was admitted to a hospital; and when conventional desensitization had proved to be inapplicable, I arranged the following series of procedures in collaboration with Dr. John S. Jameson: (1) the induction of tachycardia by stepping on and off a stool an increasing number of times; (2) intravenous injections of increasing doses — up to 1 cc — of epinephrine hydrochloride 1:1000; (3) epinephrine with "feedback" from an oscilloscope that grossly exaggerated the tachycardia; (4) inhalations of amyl nitrate (3 cc capsules crushed in a handkerchief); and (5) locking her up for increasing periods up to 2 hours in an isolated room in the basement of the hospital. Following these measures the patient was greatly improved, though not 'cured.' She has been working regularly for the past 18 months, making an occasional telephone call to boost her confidence.

Case 9

It is interesting to record a case in which desensitization *in vivo* occurred in the first place inadvertently and was later deliberately continued. The patient who had an 11-year-long fear of confinement in social situations was being treated as a demonstration case in front of 20 members of a Behavior Therapy Institute I conducted in Holland in August, 1966. Having been trained in relaxation and with his hierarchies prepared, at his 4th interview he was asked to visualize several scenes of being in a movie house in circumstances of varying difficulty of egress; but none of them evoked the slightest anxiety. I then told him that it would be necessary for us to work with real stimuli. He replied, "Something interesting has already happened, Doctor. During my first session here I was very nervous in the group, but every day my nervousness has decreased; and today I don't feel nervous at all."

As it happened, the next day 160 psychologists were expected to attend the Institute, and I decided to make use of them in continuing the treatment. Accordingly, the next day, in a large lecture hall, I had the patient at first sit with me on the platform while the original 20 Institute members sat in the forward rows of seats. The patient reporting no anxiety, I signalled (as prearranged) for 20 other people to enter the hall. When they did so, he reported anxiety and was instructed to relax. After a minute he stated that he felt comfortable, and then another 20 people were permitted to enter. Again anxiety appeared and was relaxed away. The same procedure was followed until all 160 members were seated. The patient spent the remainder of the afternoon seated comfortably in the front row of the audience. Subsequently, further *in vivo* operations were arranged — such as jamming him in the front row of spectators at a tennis tournament — resulting in marked improvement of his neurosis.

Anxiety-relief conditioning: This counter-anxiety measure (Wolpe, 1958, p. 180) is unique in having to date been used exclusively *in vivo*. Essentially, it depends on the direct conditioning of an anxiety-inhibiting response to a neutral stimulus word ("calm") by administering an uncomfortable continuous faradic shock to the patient who has previously been instructed to say the word aloud when he strongly desires the shock to stop. The termination of the shock produces a feeling of relief, which, upon repetition often becomes conditioned to the word "calm". This happens only in individuals who experience some degree of emotional disturbance (and not only sensory discomfort) in response to shock. In these people, the feeling of relief when the shock stops may be quite strong. It may be made stronger and the conditioning may be facilitated by the administration of drugs that augment sympathetic responses (e.g. amphetamines) (Eysenck, 1963). If, subsequently, the patient utters the word "calm" subvocally in disturbing life situations, his anxiety level may be sharply reduced; and conditioned inhibition of the anxiety habit may result.

Lazarus has described a modification of this technique in which the avoidance of severe shock is made the basis of anxiety relief conditioning (Wolpe & Lazarus, 1966, p. 150). By the use of this modification he overcame in 3 weeks a very severe neurosis of about 12 years' duration whose major features were agoraphobia, and anxiety in social situations.

(b) Modelling

This recent innovation shows signs of being a significant practical advance. In the first study reported (Bandura, Grusec and Menlove, 1967), young children very fearful of dogs were assigned to one of four treatment conditions. In eight brief sessions, one group observed a fearless peer-model exhibit progressively more fear-arousing interactions with a dog. The modelled approach-behavior was presented within a highly positive party context, designed to counteract anxiety reactions. After the jovial party was well under way, a fearless 4-year-old boy entered the room leading a dog, and performed pre-arranged sequences of interactions with the dog for approximately three minutes during each session. The fear-provoking properties of the modelled displays were gradually increased from session to session by simultaneously varying the physical restraints on the dog, the directness and intimacy of the approach responses, and the duration of interaction between the model and the dog. A second group of children observed the same graduated performances, but outside the party context. A third group of children observed the dog in the positive context but with the model absent. A fourth group participated in the positive activities but was never exposed to either the dog or the modelled displays. Children's phobic behavior was measured separately toward two different dogs following completion of the treatment program and again a month later. The two groups of children who had observed the peer model interact nonanxiously with the dog displayed significantly greater approach behavior toward both the experimental and an unfamiliar animal than children in the dog exposure or the control conditions, who did not differ from each other. The party context added only slightly to the favorable outcomes of modelling. While 67 per cent of children receiving the modelling treatment were eventually able to remain alone in the room confined with the dog, this was attained by relatively few children in the two control conditions.

A study by Bandura, Blanchard and Ritter (1968) compared the effects on snake-fearful adults under four conditions. The *first group* observed a graduated film depicting young children, adolescents and adults engaging in progressively more fear-provoking interactions with a large king snake. They were taught to induce and to maintain anxiety-inhibiting relaxation throughout the period of exposure. The rate of presentation of modelling stimuli was regulated by the client through a projector equipped with remote control starting and reversing devices. Clients were instructed, whenever a particular modelled performance proved anxiety-provoking, to reverse the film to the beginning of the aversive sequence, and to reinduce deep relaxation. They then reviewed the threatening scene repeatedly until it was completely neutralized before proceeding to the next item in the hierarchy. The *second group* of clients received a form of treatment in which, after observing intimate snake-interaction behavior repeatedly modelled by the therapist, they were aided through demonstration to perform progressively closer approaches to a snake. The *third group* received conventional desensitization. As in the other conditions, the treatment was continued until the clients' anxiety reactions were totally extinguished, or the maximum time allotment of six hours of treatment (not counting relaxation training) was completed. A *control group* received before-and-after assessments without any intervening treatment. The final assessments showed that live modelling combined with guided participation was the most effective treatment, eliminating the snake phobia in 92 per cent of subjects. The desensitization and symbolic modelling groups also showed substantial change; while the control group was unchanged. A one – month follow-up assessment revealed that the beneficial changes were maintained and had transferred to real – life situations. Ritter (1968) found a similar superiority for modelling combined with guided participation in snake-phobic *children*.

The mechanism by which the guided participation group achieves more rapid changes is not entirely clear. Bandura (1968) suggests that what is added is "positive reinforcement of a sense of capability through success". This proposition is not easy to test. It seems at least as plausible that the guided participation amounts to an *in vivo* desensitization that augments the effects of symbolic desensitization, in conformity with the findings of Garfield, *et. al.* (1967).

CHAPTER IX

The Use Of
Drugs In
Behavior Therapy

SYMPTOMATIC USES

WHEN A PERSON suffers more or less continuously from considerable anxiety or related emotional disturbance it is usually desirable and often possible to obtain amelioration by the use of a drug or combination of drugs. Many people resort to such means on their own, the most usual agent being, of course, alcohol. It is less common than is generally believed for anxiety to be *entirely* removed by drugs in the usual doses. It does not, however, seem that their use is ever inimical to the achievement of the fundamental changes at which behavior therapy aims; and there is little doubt that in some cases they actively promote such changes. The hazard of addiction is small when the duration of drug treatment is limited. Usually, as the neurotic reactions are deconditioned the dosages required for symptomatic relief become less, so that it is often possible to discontinue medication altogether a good while before the conclusion of therapy.

As every experienced clinician knows, it is trial and error that ultimately decides what drug will be effective in an individual case. Meprobamate, 400-800 mg., three or four times a day, Dexamyl (100 mg. of amobarbital combined with 5 mg. of dextroamphetamine sulphate) one or two tablets morning and midday, and Librium (chlordiazepoxide) 10-30 mg. three times a day, are all useful, and it has been my practice to give them preference, though not necessarily in the order given. If there is depression, Dexamyl will usually be tried first. When none of the foregoing drugs succeeds, any of a considerable number of others may be tried — phenothiazine derivatives [e.g., chlorpromazine (Thorazine), trifluoperazine (Stelazine), thioridazine (Mellaril)], ethchlorvynol (Placidyl), the diphenyl methane derivative Atarax or Doriden, or Placidyl. To these may be added various antidepressants such as Parnate and Nardil, on the strength of Sargant and Dally's report (1962) of their efficacy in relieving the symptoms of many cases of neurosis. A recent addition to our armamentarium is the beta-adrenergic blocking agent propanolol (Granville-Grossman and Turner, 1966).

These drugs need not be administered routinely. They may be given intermittently to overcome the anxieties evoked by specific situations. For example, a patient who has a fear of 'public scrutiny' may take a tranquilizing preparation an hour before making a speech, and one who has a fear of flying may do the same before a journey by air. Many patients discover that they can protect themselves against special anxiety sources in this way.

Symptomatic control of specific syndromes by drugs has also been reported. Imipramine (Tofranil), an antidepressant, has controlled enuresis (Destounis 1963) and encopresis (Abraham 1963). Systematic use of the drug can achieve what Drooby (1964) has called a "reliable truce" with certain disabilities when attempts at reconditioning are impracticable or unsuccessful. Drooby found that enuresis ceased completely or almost completely in a matter of days in every one of 45 children to whom he administered imipramine (25 mg.) two or three times a day according to age. The treatment was not curative; for when the drug was withheld enuresis recurred. When the effects of withdrawing the drug were tested after a year of use, 30 per cent of the subjects remained free from enuresis — the same proportion as in a control group. Nevertheless, if a child and his parents can be spared the misery of enuresis without impeding the development of whatever processes lead to recovery with the passage of time, it is obviously worthwhile to employ these drugs. This is all the more justified when circumstances preclude the use of deconditioning procedures.

Drooby (1964a) has also successfully used imipramine and other drugs such as Mellaril, Valium, and Nardil (v.s.) (each sometimes in combination with ergotamine) to curb anxiety and delay ejaculation in cases of premature ejaculation. A few reports confirming his experience have been published by others (e.g., Singh 1963). Sometimes the repeated successful performance of sexual intercourse under the influence of these drugs enables the patient later to perform satisfactorily without them (see below). It is similarly possible to achieve a 'truce' with stuttering, as shown, for example, in the "good" or "very good" effects of meprobamate in 13 out of 18 patients treated by Maxwell and Paterson (1958).

In many female patients, especially those at the menopause or approaching it, emotional reactions may be accentuated (if not caused) by hormonal factors. In most of these cases exacerbation of symptoms occurs in the week before menstruation and may continue throughout the menstrual period. Marked amelioration may be obtained by the administration of female sex hormone preparations. In most cases it suffices to employ the same preparations and dosages as are used for contraceptive purposes, e.g. Ovulen, Anovlar, Enovid, or Ortho-novum (Guttmacher, 1961). One is sometimes surprised to find that the improvement in symptoms is not confined to any particular phase of the cycle, but extends to the whole of it. Some cases in whom 'contraceptive pill' medication is not particularly successful reportedly respond well to large doses of progesterone by intramuscular injection (Dalton 1964), who states that oral synthetic progestogens are not a satisfactory substitute.

An interesting new possibility for symptomatic treatment has emerged from the observation of Pitts and McClure (1967) that in patients with anxiety neuroses anxiety attacks can be produced by intravenous infusions of lactate ion, and that the anxiety symptoms can be largely prevented by the' addition of small amounts of calcium ion in the form of calcium chloride. This suggests that the oral administration of calcium chloride might be tried for controlling anxiety symptoms.

ADJUVANT USES OF DRUGS

Various drugs have been used to facilitate anxiety reduction when all efforts at active relaxation have failed to produce sufficient calmness to carry out systematic desensitization. The drugs are mainly called for when there is a very high on-going anxiety level, but sometimes when the patient is a poor relaxer and the on-going anxiety is due to specific external stimuli or thought-contents, a drug, such as one of the tranquilizers named above, may be taken an hour or so before the interview. But where the anxiety is of the pervasive 'free-floating' type, (i.e., anxiety that is apparently conditioned to pervasive aspects of stimulation, such as space, time, bodily sensations, etc.) (Wolpe, 1958) by far the most satisfactory measure is to administer to the patient one to four, single, full-capacity inhalations of a mixture of carbon dioxide and oxygen.

Carbon dioxide-oxygen

The technique that is used is not the original one of Meduna, in which the patient inhales a mixture of 30% carbon dioxide and 70% oxygen until he loses consciousness, but that of LaVerne (1953), in which a stronger mixture is inhaled, one breath at a time. The mixture that has become standard consists of 65% carbon dioxide and 35% oxygen; but a cylinder of 40% carbon dioxide and 60% oxygen should be available for those patients for whom the higher concentration is found to be irritating or excessively drastic in its effects; and also a cylinder of 100% carbon dioxide for refractory cases.

The therapist first ascertains the level of the patient's anxiety in terms of subjective units of disturbance *(suds)* (see p. 116). He then tells the patient what he proposes to do and what the probable effects will be. The exact manner of presentation varies, but a fairly typical speech is the following:

> It is now clear that your efforts at relaxing do not decrease your anxiety very much. We sometimes find that we can get a good deal of help from inhaling a mixture of carbon dioxide and oxygen. Carbon dioxide stimulates the breathing — and as a matter of fact, it is frequently used to revive patients under anesthesia. Now, in these cylinders, there is a concentration of carbon dioxide that

is much higher than that which you normally have in your lungs. When I have filled the bag, I am going to ask you to inhale the gas mixture through this mask one breath at a time. After a delay of a few seconds, you will begin to notice certain symptoms which are unusual but not really unpleasant. You will notice that you become short of breath, that your heart quickens, your face flushes and your extremities tingle. You may become rather dizzy, and possibly also have some other sensations. These reactions will reach a peak in about five seconds, and subside in another five seconds or so.

Now this is what I want you to do. Take the mask in your hand. Watch as I fill the bag with the mixture of gases. *(Pause while the bag is filled).* In a few seconds I am going to ask you to do the following things. First, empty your lungs; exhale as far as you can. Then apply the mask over your nose and chin quite firmly. After this press the button on top of the mask, which releases the gas; and, mainly through your mouth, breathe in until you have about half-filled your lungs with the gas. Then remove the mask from your face.

In some cases it is found that even half-filling the lungs with the gas mixture produces a substantial respiratory reaction; in others little or no effect is produced; in still others the reaction is small and insufficient. It is usually desirable not to fill the lungs completely the first time — especially when there is any reason to believe that the patient may be disturbed by the unusual sensations brought on by the gas. It is always *very important* to inquire beforehand whether the patient has any fears of suffocation or of anesthetics. In the case of those that do, a very slow and careful approach should be made to this method of treatment, devoting to an 'habituation program' a few minutes of each of several successive sessions. At first the patient may be asked to do nothing more than handle the mask; then he may sniff it cautiously while the gas mixture flows through the open valve; then he may take a short sniff out of the full bag; and thereafter increasingly deep breaths until he eventually inhales fully. A few individuals are so distressed by the sensations produced that it never becomes possible for carbon dioxide to be profitably employed on them.

Unless the mixture produces a marked respiratory reaction it is unusual to find any significant lowering of the level of anxiety. When even a full capacity inhalation fails to elicit hyperventilation, the requisite response can often be obtained by asking the patient to hold his breath for as long as he can after inhaling, by giving two or more inhalations in succession, or by using a higher concentration of carbon dioxide, even as much as 100 per cent.

After each inhalation the therapist solicits the patient to state the level of his anxiety, and notes the effects by the convenient notation illustrated in the following example:

"Carbon dioxide-oxygen (x5) 60 —   45 —   35 — 25 — 20 — 20 (*suds*)." (cf. p. 127)

This means that four inhalations brought subjective anxiety down from 60 to 20 and that a fifth inhalation had no effect. The failure of the score to go lower was an indication for terminating administrations of the gas mixture. While a level of 20 is not ideal, it is self-evident that the patient's efforts at relaxation are far more likely to reduce his anxiety to zero from that level than from 60 *suds*.

The mechanism of the anxiety-reducing effects of carbon dioxide-oxygen mixtures is not known. It was originally suggested (Wolpe, 1958) that it might be based upon reciprocal inhibition of anxiety by either the responses produced by the gas, by the post-inhalation state of relaxation, or possibly by both. One thing that seems reasonably certain is that the effect is not a direct pharmacological one dependent upon the presence of carbon dioxide in the body; for any surfeit of the gas is dissipated in a matter of minutes (Gellhorn, 1967); yet one or two inhalations sometimes removes pervasive anxiety for weeks or months, and usually for at least a good many hours. Only a conditioning hypothesis appears to be consonant with this. An extremely cogent fact in support of conditioning is that exposure to a specific anxiety-evoking stimulus situation seems always to be prerequisite to re-establishing the pervasive anxiety that has been removed by the inhalations; and it is only if for a particular patient such exposure is rare, that he is free from pervasive anxiety for long periods. Leukel and Quinton (1964) have shown that the acquisition of avoidance conditioning in rats is impaired by the administration of carbon dioxide. The sooner the gas is given after the conditioning, the greater the negative effect.

Granted that carbon dioxide has its effects due to a learning process, it would be both interesting and of practical importance to know precisely how. The first step is to determine what components of the procedure produce these effects. A controlled study by Slater & Leavy (1966) indicates that neither the act of inhaling gas from anaesthetic equipment nor the deep respiratory movements such as carbon dioxide induces, are relevant. An experiment by Weinreb (1966) in which strong stimulation by sniffing aromatic spirits of ammonia failed to reduce patients' anxiety significantly, speaks against the possibility that the effects of carbon dioxide are due to a special kind of suggestion associated with a strong sensory experience.

Much more experimental work needs to be done. At the moment it seems likely that carbon dioxide works by eliciting a powerful anxiety-inhibiting excitation. If so, it is possible that this could also be employed for specific deconditioning. Philpott (1967) claims that he has done this successfully by presenting hierarchical stimuli while the patient inhales the gas at a low level, maintaining a moderate degree of hyperventilation for several seconds.

Methahexitone sodium

This short-acting barbiturate, that goes under the trade names of Brietal and Brevital, is regarded by some of its users (e.g. Friedman, 1966 and Friedman and Silverstone, 1967) as a primary anxiety-inhibiting agent. Others, like Reed (1966) and Brady (1966) regard it as essentially an adjuvant to relaxation, and always include relaxation instructions when using it. It is an open question which of these views is the correct one; but as long as there is any doubt it seems reasonable to include relaxation when using this drug.

Brady (1966) describes with great clarity his use of Brevital in cases of frigidity. After an introductory explanation, he has the patient relax comfortably in a reclining chair and starts the injection of a 1 per cent solution.

> During the 2-4 minutes required for the drug to have its maximum effect, suggestions of calm and relaxation are given such as might be used to include hypnosis. When a deeply relaxed state is attained, the patient is instructed to imagine the first or weakest scene in the hierarchy. For example, "Now I want you to imagine as vividly as possible that you and your husband are seated in the living room, fully clothed, and he is kissing you affectionately on the lips. Visualize this scene — imagine yourself there — what you might hear and what you might see. You remain calm and relaxed." The patient is permitted to visualize this scene for about two minutes and is then

instructed to stop thinking of this scene and simply relax. After a minute of rest the same scene is again
suggested for about 3 minutes. After another rest period,
and assuming that no anxiety is evident, the next scene
in the hierarchy is suggested and so forth. . . . Brevital
is cleared from the body at such a rapid rate that usually
the relaxant and sedative effect of the drug is appre-
ciably diminished after 4-5 minutes. Hence, an additional
amount is usually required after this time. During a
typical session a total of 50 to 70 mg. are administered.
After the last suggested scene is terminated, the patient
is allowed to remain recumbent in the chair for about 10
minutes.

Four of his five cases were greatly improved in
a mean of 11.5 sessions. Follow-ups did not reveal relapse
or new symptoms.

Male sex hormone

From time to time reports appear in the literature
on the beneficial use of male sex hormone in the treatment of cases of impotence (e.g., Miller, Hubert and
Hamilton, 1938). In the course of 20 years of
psychotherapeutic practice, I have twice succeeded in
augmenting a very low sexual drive in males by daily
injections of testosterone to an extent that sexual performance became possible and subsequently continued
satisfactorily without further use of hormone.
Presumably, the sexual response was conditioned to
contiguous stimuli.

THE USE OF DRUGS
FOR SPECIFIC DECONDITIONING

From various reports published during the last half
century, both in Russia (e.g. Pavlov, 1941) and in the
United States (Dworkin, Raginsky and Bourne, 1937;

Masserman and Yum, 1946), it is evident that lasting recovery or improvement may be procured in neurotic animals by keeping them under the influence of such sedative drugs as bromides, barbiturates, or alcohol for long periods. It would appear, although it is not always specifically stated in the reports, that at various times while under the influence of the drugs, the animals were exposed to the stimuli conditioned to the neurotic reaction. But none of these experimenters deliberately and systematically brought the stimuli into play as part of a therapeutic design.

This was done for the first time in an experimental study by Miller, Murphy and Mirsky (1957). Using electric shock as the unconditioned stimulus, they conditioned 4 groups of rats to perform an avoidance response at the presentation of a buzzer. For the purpose of studying extinction of the avoidance response under different conditions, the animals in two of the groups received injections of saline, and those of the other two groups, injections of chlorpromazine on each of four consecutive days. One of the two saline-injected groups (Group I) and one of the two chlorpromazine injected groups (Group II) received 15 unreinforced presentations of the buzzer on each of the four days, while the animals of the other two groups were simply returned to the living cage after receiving their injections. During these four days Group II animals made far fewer avoidance responses (less than 5 per cent of trials) than Group I (more than 70 per cent of trials). On the fifth and subsequent days, when all groups were given unreinforced trials without receiving any further injections, Group II manifested a much lower percentage of avoidance responses than any of the other groups. Whereas the other groups showed an average of about 60 per cent avoidance responses, Group II showed only about 20 per cent; and in eleven of the fifteen animals that comprised the group the level did not go above that observed during the four days under the influence of the drug. That this lasting therapeutic effect was related to the autonomic action of the chlorpromazine and not to the supression of motor responses, was indicated by repeating the experiment with phenobarbital in a dosage that had previously been equated with chlorpromazine in terms of motor retardation effects. In the animals given phenobarbital the level of avoidance responses after stopping the drug was not diminished. It is crucial to note that chlorpromazine has lasting effects only if, in the authors' words, "the opportunity for relearning is afforded during the administration of the agent."

It is reasonable to assume that reciprocal inhibition was the mechanism of this relearning. The animals were, through earlier conditioning, capable of responding also to stimuli in the environment besides the buzzer; but without the 'protection' of the chlorpromazine the avoidance response to the buzzer was overwhelmingly strong. In animals who had been given chlorpromazine any remnant of the avoidance response (and concomitant anxiety) could presumably have been reciprocally inhibited by whatever responses were being produced by other stimuli in the environment. Obviously this explanation calls for systematic study; but some support for it is given by Berkun's observation (1957) that animals in whom *weak* anxiety — cum — avoidance responses have been conditioned, can overcome these responses by mere exposure, first to situations similar to those associated with the original conditioning, and then to the original situation.

It is obvious that to the extent that the paradigm of the Miller, Murphy and Mirsky experiment could be extended to human clinical neuroses great therapeutic economy could be achieved. The crucial therapeutic events take place in life and the therapist need only check occasionally, and usually quite briefly. But astonishing as it must seem, no systematic investigation has been undertaken in the course of a whole decade. Promising indications have emerged from experimental treatment of individual cases, as well as from some incidental observations in a study by Winkelman (1955). Winkelman gave his patients chlorpromazine for 6 months or more in doses sufficient to obtain marked diminution of neurotic symptoms, and then gradually withdrew the drug. He found that improvement persisted for at least 6 months after the withdrawal in 35 per cent of the patients. Unfortunately, there was no control study to show what would have happened to patients given a placebo instead of chlorpromazine. We should also have liked other information of great interest — for example, whether more lasting effects would have resulted from maintaining the original dosage for the full period of treatment.

In the past 12 years, I have seen several patients who responded well to such drugs as chlorpromazine, meprobamate, or codeine, and who after consistently taking the drug before exposure to disturbing situations found themselves later not having the expected disturbance when exposed without the drug. To achieve this result the drug must be taken consistently for a period of weeks or months so that no significant anxiety is ever produced by exposure to the relevant situations. For example, I found that the severe classroom anxiety experienced by a student was markedly ameliorated by meprobamate. After I had kept him on an adequate dosage of the drug on every school day for 6 weeks, I gave him a drug-free test-day on which he felt his anxiety to be diminished by 40 per cent. A second test after an additional 6 weeks showed a further 30 per cent decrement of the anxiety — an overall improvement of about 70 per cent. Among phobias in which I have achieved complete recovery by this method, I may mention a fear of physical deformities for which codeine was the drug used, a barber's chair phobia (cf. Erwin 1963) using meprobamate and alcohol, and a fairly mild airplane phobia that was overcome by the use of alcohol on three flights of about an hour's duration each.

There have been several reports by others of success-ful treatment by this method. Reference was made above to the lasting effects that sometimes follow when premature ejaculation is controlled by anxiety-inhibiting drugs (e.g. Drooby 1964a). Similarly, among the cases of stuttering treated by meprobamate in the Maxwell and Paterson study (1958) mentioned above, was that of a 25-year-old butcher who was eventually able to dispense with the drug and still maintain marked speech improvement. It has recently become apparent that chlordiazepoxide (Librium) and its relatives, Valium and Serax, may have a special value in treatment of this kind, because unlike meprobamate their tranquilizing effects increase with increasing dosage, and without much in the way of adverse accompaniments as a rule. Librium and Valium sometimes produce drowsiness in high dosage but Serax apparently does not (Berger, 1968). My own interest in the potentialities of this group of drugs was aroused by Miller (1967) who had achieved striking effects in four phobic cases. In his first two cases — a woman with a fear of eating in public and a man with agoraphobia — doses of 50 and 75 mg. respectively were needed. Miller states, "The medication was taken only for the purpose of desensitization and never on a routine basis. The patients 'planned' a phobic exposure, took the medication and waited until it began to exert its effect and then exposed themselves to the phobic situation (in real life, not in fantasy). The course of the therapy was four weeks in one case and six weeks in the other." Both patients were completely free of their phobias without the use of any medication when followed up six months after the treatment.

The first case with whom I systematically employed Librium in this way was a physician in whom a year previously a severe emotional reaction to noise had been conditioned, when he had been exposed to insistent hammering while trying to sleep in a hotel. The sensitivity had generalized to other noises, and the most distressful had become the sound of automobile horns because, no doubt, of their frequent occurrence. He improved moderately on the employment of behavior therapy measures such as relaxation and a masking procedure involving white noise. He was then instructed to determine the dose of Librium that could entirely block his emotional response to noise, and to take this dose (which was 30 mg.) in every circumstance in which he could anticipate being exposed to any considerable amount of honking. This schedule led to very marked improvement without the drug in the course of four months.

One point that must be underlined is that the effectiveness of such programs almost certainly depends upon insuring that high anxiety-evocation never occurs; for, whenever it does, it may be expected to recondition a substantial degree of anxiety and lose hard-won ground. On the other hand, not every drug that inhibits anxiety will do. The site of action is critical. No lasting effects can be expected of peripherally acting drugs like propanolol (Suzman, 1968) nor, perhaps, of barbiturates (Miller, Murphy & Mirsky, 1957).

CHAPTER X

Procedures Involving
Strong Anxiety
Evocation

CONTRASTING with the desensitization strategies that utilize stimuli to weak neurotic responses, is a group of treatments that involve very strong responses. The oldest of these is *abreaction,* in which memories of distressful events are the stimuli to the strong responses. More recent treatments employ strong responses evoked either by exposure to real disturbing situations or by devised imaginal situations and are collectively known as *emotional flooding* techniques.

The flooding techniques belong very properly to behavior therapy, and will therefore be considered first. They originated (probably erroneously — p. 186) on the paradigm of experimental extinction. They can be instituted at will, and their components can be quantitatively varied. The therapist, therefore, can control the therapeutic event by controlling the stimulus input. Abreaction, on the other hand, is not strictly a behavior therapy technique, because all that the therapist can do is to try to create conditions for triggering its occurrence. When it occurs, both its content and its outcome are unpredictable. More often than not, it is not therapeutic. Even when the therapist can influence the stimulus input he shoots in the dark because he does not know how to influence the process beneficially. But the fact that abreaction can be dramatically beneficial entitles it to our consideration and to our efforts to elucidate the factors that control it.

EMOTIONAL FLOODING

The first account of a case successfully treated by this kind of procedure is, I believe, due to E. R. Guthrie. For years I was under the impression that it was included in *The Psychology of Human Learning* (1935). But a recent search has failed to discover it either in that book or in *The Psychology of Human Conflict* (1935). The patient concerned was an adolescent girl with a phobia for automobiles. She was placed by force at the back of a car in which she was continuously driven for 4 hours. Her fear soon reached panic proportions and then gradually subsided. At the end of the ride she was quite comfortable, and henceforth was free from her phobia. More recent attempts at flooding therapy have been described by Malleson (1959), Frankl (1960), and Stampfl (1964).

Malleson described treating several cases by exposing them to intense anxiety. One was an Indian student who was very afraid of examinations. He was made to experience his fear as fully as possible.

> He was asked to tell of the awful consequences that he felt would follow his failure — derision from his colleagues in India, disappointment from his family, financial loss. Then he was to try to imagine these things happening; try

to imagine the fingers of scorn pointed at him, his wife and mother in tears. At first, as he followed the instructions, his sobbings increased. But soon his trembling ceased. As the effort needed to maintain a vivid imagining increased, the emotion he could summon began to ebb. Within half an hour he was calm. Before leaving I instructed him in repeating the exercise of experiencing his fears. Every time he felt a little wave of spontaneous alarm he was not to push it aside, but was to enhance it, to augment it, to try to experience it more profoundly and more vividly. If he did not spontaneously feel fear, every 20 or 30 minutes he was to make a special effort to try and do so, however difficult and ludicrous it might seem. I arranged to see him twice a day over the next 2 days until his examination.

He was an intelligent man, and an assiduous patient. He practised the exercises methodically, and by the time of the examination he reported himself as almost totally unable to feel frightened. He had, as it were, exhausted the affect in the whole situation. He passed his examination without apparent difficulty.

Intense anxiety evocation has been employed therapeutically by existentialist psychiatrists like Frankl (1960) and Gerz (1966) under the name, *paradoxical intention*. Of course, in using it, they are not guided by the idea of experimental extinction or any other learning mechanism, but by the expectation that "if the patient were to try intentionally to bring on these symptoms he would not only find difficulty in doing so, but also change his attitude towards his neurosis." Whatever their theorizing, there is no essential difference between their practical procedures and Malleson's, described above. In a good many cases treatments are given repeatedly over several months. One of Gerz's cases was a 29-year-old woman who had fears of heights, of being alone, of eating in a restaurant in case she vomited, and of going into supermarkets, subways and cars. She was instructed to try to bring about whatever she was afraid would happen to her. She was to try to vomit while dining out with her husband and friends and create the greatest possible mess. She was to drive to markets, hairdressers and banks "trying to get as panicky as possible." In six weeks she had lost her fears in her home situation, and shortly therafter drove all by herself to Gerz's office, about five miles from her home. Four months later, she drove with her husband to New York City, a hundred miles from her home, across the George Washington Bridge, back through the Lincoln Tunnel, and attended a goodbye party on the lower deck of an ocean liner. Gerz states that two years later she was free of symptoms.

Stampfl has employed the same essential tactics, but using mainly the patient's imagination, and calling his method *implosive therapy*. In his early unpublished writings to which London (1964) has made extensive reference, Stampfl expressed the view that if the anxious patient were exposed intensively to the conditioned anxiety-producing stimulus situations, and anxiety was not reinforced (presumably by an unconditioned stimulus) the anxiety response would extinguish. The essence of implosive therapy, then, was to arrange for the frightening stimulus to be presented in circumstances from which the subject could not escape. Continuous exposure to this stimulus was expected to cause it to lose all power to elicit anxiety. Stampfl advocated using every resource to frighten the patient for as long as possible at each sitting, by the general means of persuading him to imagine himself realistically in the situations which the therapist described in great detail, painting the most vivid horrors possible.

Although later accounts (e.g. Stampfl and Levis, 1967) have continued to feature the foregoing tactics, they advocate the use of weak stimuli in the first place.

They state, "The hypothesized cues which are believed to be low in the Avoidance Serial Cue Hierarchy (that is, cues that have low anxiety loadings) are presented first." This incorporation of a gradual approach would seem to be inconsistent with Stampfl's central thesis. This is how Stampfl and Levis (1967) write of their main procedure:

> Once the implosive procedure is begun, every effort is made to encourage the patient to 'lose himself' in the part that he is playing and 'live' the scenes with genuine emotion and affect . . . . The scenes which contained the hypothesized cues are described at first by the therapist. The more involved and dramatic the therapist becomes in describing the scenes, the more realistic the presentation, and the easier it is for the patient to participate. At each stage of the crisis an attempt is made by the therapist to obtain a maximal level of anxiety evocation from the patient. When a high-level anxiety is achieved, the patient is held on this level until some sign of spontaneous reduction in the anxiety-inducing value of the cues appears (extinction). The process is repeated, and again, at the first sign of spontaneous reduction of fear, new variations are introduced to elicit an intense anxiety response. This procedure is continued until a significant diminution of anxiety has resulted . . . . Between sessions the patient is instructed to reenact in his imagination the scenes which were presented during the treatment session.

One rather surprising feature of the work of these authors is that while professing to base their methods upon Mowrerian learning theory, they uncritically assume the validity of psychoanalytic theorizing, and derive some of their scene material from it. Stampfl and Levis (1968) state that "castration dangers and Oedipal time conflicts are not foreign to the implosive therapy approach in that they are hypothesized to be a product of primary or secondary aversive conditioning events." Some of the scenes based upon psychoanalytic assumptions do lead to anxiety reduction and thus successful therapy. From this they erroneously deduce that such material has special relevance. The truth is that any of a variety of scenes containing the same essential stimulus material might be expected to produce equivalent effects.

Existentialists (e.g. Gerz, 1966) and implosive therapists (e.g. Levis and Carrera, 1967) give the impression that their emotional flooding techniques are widely applicable and highly successful. There are *prima facie* grounds for reservation about this optimism in the case of Levis and Carrera's study because they measure success indirectly on the basis of changes in the Minnesota Multiphasic Personality Inventory. Gerz, on the other hand, uses the direct clinical criterion of change in presenting complaints. He states that in six years 29 phobic patients were treated of whom 22 recovered and 5 showed "considerable improvement". One wonders whether some kind of selection was exercised — whether, for example, cases that showed an unfavorable reaction at an early stage were dropped from consideration. Why else, one may ask, were such a small number of cases given this treatment in the course of so long a period?

My own experience with flooding techniques makes this a particularly important question. I have found that some patients do strikingly well, others are unaffected, and some suffer exacerbations of their phobias. Because of the last possibility, I have been exceedingly reluctant to make free use of flooding, leaving it as a final recourse to be taken only after every other measure has failed.

There are also good experimental grounds for caution. So far, nobody has cured an experimental neurosis simply by exposing the animal for long periods (hours or days) to the stimuli to which anxiety has been conditioned. This fact makes it exceedingly unlikely that experimental extinction can be the mechanism of the favorable effects of flooding when they do occur. Two contrasting clinical reports strengthen this conclusion. In snake phobias Wolpin and Raines (1966) obtained good results by 5-10 minute periods of flooding, whereas Rachman failed entirely with 100 two-minute floodings (over 10 sessions) with spider phobias. If extinction had been at work, Rachman should have done much better. Other processes must be relevant; but as long as we have not identified them, flooding procedures are a gamble we take at the patient's risk.

Here are brief accounts of two of the cases that I have treated by flooding, one by the use of imaginal stimuli, and one *in vivo*.

Imaginal stimuli were employed with Dr. E., a dentist who had had an extraordinarily severe and widespread neurosis, that had in most respects responded very well to varied and sometimes prolonged applications of the commoner behavior therapy techniques, such as assertive training and systematic desensitization. But two disabling neurotic constellations remained — an inability to give dental injections because of a fear of the patient dying in the chair, and an extravagant fear of ridicule. Since attempts to desensitize Dr. E. to these were making insufferably slow progress, I decided to try flooding. Under light hypnosis he was asked to imagine giving a patient a mandibular block, then withdrawing the syringe, standing back and seeing the patient slump forward, dead. Dr. E. became profoundly disturbed, sweating, weeping and wringing his hands. After a minute or so, I terminated the scene and told him to relax. Two or three minutes later, the same scene, presented again, evoked a similar but weaker reaction. The sequence was given three more times, at the last of which no further reaction was observed. Dr. E. said that he felt he had been through a wringer — exhausted, but at ease. At the next session, the fear of ridicule was introduced. Dr. E. imagined that he was walking down the middle of a brilliantly lighted ballroom with people on both sides pointing their fingers at him and laughing derisively. At the fifth flooding session, it was clear that nothing remained to be treated. Four years later, at an interview with Dr. E., it was evident that his recovery had been fully maintained.

In vivo flooding is exemplified by the case of Mrs. C., a woman with agoraphobia so severe that she was unable to go on her own more than two blocks by car without anxiety. Attempts at systematic desensitization had failed — apparently because she was unable to imagine scenes realistically. After other measures had also proved ineffective, I decided to persuade her to expose herself to flooding, which had to be *in vivo* because of the demonstrated inadequacy of her imagination. After resisting strenuously for some weeks, she agreed to take the plunge. Plans were made for her husband to place her, unaccompanied, on a commercial aircraft one hour's flight away from the airport at which I was to wait to meet her. When Mrs. C. in due course alighted from the plane, she walked towards me smiling. She had felt increasing anxiety for the first fifteen minutes of the flight, and then gradual subsidence of it. During the second half of the journey she had been perfectly comfortable. This single experience resulted in a great increase in her range of comfortable situations away from home. She was now able, without anxiety, to drive her car alone three or four miles from home and to make unaccompanied trips by plane without any anxiety. Plans to build upon this improvement by further flooding were foiled by problems of distance.

The following is one of several patients made worse by attempts to 'flood' them. Dr. K. was a physician who, following a horrifying encounter with a mental hospital patient that need not be detailed here, had developed a severe phobia for insane people and insane behavior. He was in military service, and soon after he began to consult me was offered a transfer to a psychiatric hospital. I encouraged this, in the hope that the phobia might be overcome by flooding. Following my advice, he exposed himself continuously to the presence of schizophrenic patients, sometimes for hours at a stretch. Far from decreasing, his reactions to such patients grew progressively worse, and, in addition, he was assailed by a rising level of pervasive anxiety. By the end of the second day he was so extremely anxious that he had to be relocated to a general hospital. He had become much more sensitive than ever before to 'insane stimuli'. He was now a far more difficult case than when I had first seen him; and far more effort was needed to overcome his neurosis by desensitization.

Clearly, there are individual differences that determine who will be amenable to flooding methods, and who will be harmed by them. To make a person worse, like Dr. K., is such a dreadful experience that it does not seem justified to expose anybody to the possibility of it except in desperation. We very much need to know how flooding works when it succeeds. One possibility is that it is due to conditioned inhibition based upon transmarginal inhibition (Pavlov, 1927; Gray, 1964). This could conceivably be associated with the counteranxiety rebound that is sometimes observed after a large amount of epinephrine has been discharged into the bloodstream (Rothballer, 1959). If so, we shall need to be able to differentiate those individuals in whom this rebound occurs from those in whom it does not. At the very least, we need to have some way of distinguishing empirically those whom flooding may benefit from those whose neuroses it may be expected to exacerbate. In collaboration with Dr. Alan Goldstein, I am about to commence experiments on neurotic cats to see whether we can find a way to make flooding therapeutically effective in them.

ABREACTION

An abreaction may be defined as the re-evocation, with strong emotional accompaniment, of a fearful past experience. Some abreactions are followed by therapeutic changes, while others are not, and may even leave the patient worse off than before. If we could induce abreaction at will and also predict which individuals would respond favorably, we should be able to expedite therapy in many cases. At present the induction of abreaction is unreliable and its effects so unpredictable that I do not attempt to bring it about unless I have failed to make satisfactory progress with the usual procedures whose effects can be controlled and whose mechanisms are understood. It would seem, however, that in some neurotic patients the unadaptive emotional responses were originally conditioned to intricate stimulus compounds that current stimulus situations cannot adequately replace; and then abreaction may be well-nigh indispensable (Wolpe, 1958, p. 198).

The therapeutic efficacy of abreaction, judging from Grinker and Spiegel's experiences (1945) with war neuroses, bears no relation to the previous *accessibility* to recall of the abreacted experience. The one apparent essential is for it to take place in a protected setting such as the psychotherapeutic relationship affords (Grinker and Spiegel, 1945). This observation was the basis for the suggestion (Wolpe, 1958, p. 196) that the therapeutic effects obtained during abreaction might be a special case of the non-specific effects that occur in a proportion of cases receiving any form of psychotherapy. In other words, abreaction succeeds when anxiety is inhibited by other emotional responses that the therapeutic situation induces in the patient.

Abreactions take place in a variety of circumstances. Sometimes they arise unbidden, during history-taking or during attempts at systematic desensitization. A truck driver had, following an accident, a marked phobia for driving (in addition to considerable pervasive anxiety). After training in relaxation and the construction of a hierarchy on the theme of driving, he was asked, during his first desensitization session, to imagine himself sitting at the wheel of a car that was stationary and whose engine was not running. He suddenly began to verbalize the details of the accident, broke into a sweat and became very agitated. After about a minute, when the reaction subsided, he was asked to open his eyes. When he did so he appeared tired but relieved, and said that he was no longer afraid to drive a truck. The test of reality proved him right.

Another example of unscheduled abreaction occurred in a 50-year-old lawyer who had been vaguely tense for decades, and who had come for treatment mainly because of increasing insomnia. During instruction in assertive behavior, he began to talk of his childhood, and mentioned that though his family had been very poor he would never take anything from other people. He recounted an incident at school when, being a good athlete, he had taken part in a race and had been the only contestant without spiked shoes. He had proudly refused to accept a pair as a hand-out from the school. He became very tearful during this narration. At the next interview, a week later, he said that he was feeling better and that the average duration of his sleep had gone up from four to six hours per night. At this interview he abreacted at telling the story of a friend in the Army towards whom he had been aggressive and who had been killed within a month. Further abreactions were subsequently deliberately induced in relation to this story under hypnosis. Each of these abreactions, though weaker than the first one, was followed by improvement. With the addition of assertive training and desensitization to receiving praise and favors, an apparently complete recovery was obtained in a total of 15 sessions.

If the therapist wishes to bring about an abreaction, there are several courses open to him. He may endeavor either with or without hypnosis to plunge the patient into re-experiencing some past situation *known* to be highly disturbing. He may also try to gain access to unknown material by asking the hypnotized patient to fantasize an unpleasant or fearful event out of the past. An impressive case of successful hypnotic abreaction of a war neurosis after 20 years was recently described by Leahy and Martin (1967). It is sometimes worth trying the "age-regression" technique in which the patient imagines himself back in past ages of his life, starting relatively recently and then going back year by year. I have used this technique very occasionally, but have not seen the dramatic effects reported by others.

The most practical way of pursuing an abreaction involves drugs. The first drug to gain widespread interest for this purpose was pentobarbital (Pentothal) whose use in this manner was introduced by Horsley (1936), and used widely during World War II. At that time, and for a few years following, I occasionally used it in the hope of obtaining beneficial abreactions; but though abreactions did occur fairly often — sometimes very vivid and exciting ones — in not a single case did I find marked and lasting benefit. Perhaps drugs that *elevate* arousal are more likely to lead to therapeutic abreactions. The most effective and hopeful of these are probably di-ethyl ether (in its excitatory phase) and lysergic acid diethylamide. The amphetamines (notably Methedrine) can also produce abreactions, but it has not been evident from the literature that these yield any lastingly beneficial after-effects; and sometimes (as has been my own experience) sensitization may afterwards be found to have been increased. Possibly, because these drugs favor responses of the sympathetic division of the autonomic nervous system, they actually militate against the therapeutic counterconditioning that we have presumed to be the basis of abreaction.

For a full description of the technique of obtaining excitatory abreaction with ether, the reader should consult the original accounts by Palmer (1944) and by Shorvon and Sargant (1947). While the patient lies on his back on a couch the therapist talks to him informally about events that preceded the incident on which it is hoped the patient will abreact. The ether-soaked mask is held a few inches from the face, and then rather rapidly approximated. In a matter of minutes the patient becomes excited, and in a successful case begins to recite the events that led to the precipitation of his neurosis. He is encouraged to "cry, shout and struggle"; and it is very desirable to have an assistant at hand to restrain excessive movement. Shorvon and Slater express the consensus when they state that one is much more likely to produce emotional release in an individual suffering from a recent traumatic neurosis than in one with a long-standing illness. But even with recent cases, as they also point out, there are many failures. An interesting case was recently described by Little and James (1964), in which a neurosis originating in battle 18 years previously was progressively overcome in 5 sessions of ether abreactions. During the course of these, the patient pieced together the tremendously disturbing sequence of events that had precipitated the neurosis, beginning with his shooting of two young German soldiers while the three of them were in a ditch taking shelter from artillery shells.

Lysergic acid diethylamide (LSD 25) is a drug that may have great abreactive potentialities if its effects can be brought under control. It was introduced into psychiatry because of its ability to promote vivid imagery and strong emotional responses. Beneficial abreactions have frequently been reported (e.g. Sandison, 1954) but can not be relied on.

Costello (1964) was the first to attempt to turn the effects of the drug to use in accordance with conditioning principles. He reported rapid recoveries in three cases. He gives the patient 400 mg. of LSD in water by mouth — a higher dose than usual, claiming that experience with the drug has suggested that higher doses make it almost impossible for the patient to fight the drug effect, thus producing better therapeutic results while the patient goes through the first stage described by Blewett and Chwelos (1959) — consisting mainly of perceptual disturbance and symptoms like palpitations and nausea. He gives reassurance and soothing music. This seems to make more acceptable the second stage of confusion due to the flooding of consciousness with ideas and visual images which supervenes in an hour

or two. Costello's description of the sequence of events
in his first case (a woman with a 16-year history of claustrophobia with religious undertones) from Stage 2 on-
wards may be quoted:

> When she reported that she was getting vivid visual
> images, part of Offenbach's Gaite Parisienne was played
> followed closely by some spirituals sung by Mahalia Jack-
> son. During the Mahalia Jackson record the patient be-
> came quite agitated. The volume was turned down and
> the patient was told to face whatever ideas, thoughts or
> pictures were presenting themselves to her. She was told
> that life was a beautiful though sometimes awesome pat-
> tern which we spoiled by turning away from it. Thus stage
> 4 of the experience, ordering of the perceptions, was sug-
> gested to the patient. The   patient at this point stretched
> out her hand for me to hold and she held my hand tight-
> ly. After a short period of a few seconds she loosened
> her hold on my hand, became very relaxed and said, "And
> I was afraid". I agreed there was nothing whatsoever to
> be afraid of and once again put the Gaite Parisienne rec-
> ord on. The patient almost immediately began to laugh.
> Then she said "sex", laughed more and then said, "I was
> going to be a nun". This was followed by more laughter.
> The Mahalia Jackson record was then played and the pa-
> tient lay on the settee looking extremely relaxed. For the
> rest of the session, until 3:00 p.m., the patient listened to
> music, drank coffee occasionally and talked a little about
> her family, their holidays, her husband's hunting, etc. At
> no time was her camp experience or her phobic condition
> discussed. At 3:00 p.m. the patient was given 100 mg.
> Sparine intramuscularly . . . .
>
> On the third day the patient was asked to visit me, and
> at this time reported that she felt very relaxed. She had
> forgotten a lot of the experience but told me: "There were
> so many things at the same time — my mother . . .
> and then a boy at high school — he wanted to touch me
> but I would not dream of it . . . and the priest, and
> then my mother back again and wanting to be a nun . . .
> all so fast." The following Sunday the patient went to
> church, sat in the middle row and "felt so comfortable".

> Six months later the patient was interviewed again and reported that she had completely recovered from her claustrophobia, that she was going to more places with her husband, and that she was generally much happier.

What is unusual about Costello's handling of this case and of the others he describes is that he deliberately attempts to displace the emotional reactions of anxiety and distress by joy and tranquility *in the continued presence of the anxiety-evoking stimuli*. Presumably the anxiety could thus be reciprocally inhibited, and the general context of high emotional arousal would make it possible for the anxiety-response habit to be largely or entirely eliminated in the course of even a single session.

My own limited experience with Costello's technique has been disappointing. None of the three cases on whom I tried it three years ago made the hoped-for improvement although two of them showed emotional responses during treatment not unlike those of Costello's cases.

CHAPTER XI

Aversion Therapy

AVERSION therapy or avoidance therapy is, in broad, a mode of application of the reciprocal inhibition principle to deconditioning motor habits or thinking habits. Thus, its uses are largely in the treatment of obsessions, compulsions, fetishes and habits of attraction to inappropriate objects, e.g. sex objects of the same sex. It also has some value in the control of drug addictions, but, as will be pointed out, in a way that is not based on fundamental knowledge of drug habits.

Aversion therapy is not often the behavioral treatment of first choice, except perhaps in certain cases of drug addiction. Usually, the compulsive or other behavior to which aversion therapy might be applied is found to have a basis in neurotic anxiety, which should, as a rule, be deconditioned first. If this is done, the compulsive behavior may disappear, having required no special attention. On the other hand, even when aversion therapy succeeds in removing a compulsion, deconditioning of anxiety is still likely to be needed. The continued presence of the neurotic anxiety can provide a basis for 'symptom substitution.' As an example — some years ago I was consulted about a woman whose compulsive eating had been overcome by aversion therapy and who had thereafter become severely depressed. Her neurotic anxiety habits had not been removed, and the depression was the evident result of her having been deprived of her anxiety-reducing activity of eating.

The essence of aversion therapy is to present, in the context of an undesired response, the stimulus to a strong avoidance response, the most typical stimulus being strong electric shock. In eliciting the strong avoidance response, the shock is likely to inhibit the undesirable response. Whenever it does so, there will be a diminution next time in the evocation of the latter response by the stimulus that evoked it. In other words, a measure of conditioned inhibition of that response will be established — a weakening of the habit — of the bond between the response and its stimulus. At the same time, that stimulus is likely to be to some extent conditioned to the response constellation which the shock evoked.

The foregoing is summarized in Fig. 8, showing the experimental paradigm on which all aversive therapeutic procedures are based. An animal is placed in a cage that has an electrifiable grid. Food is repeatedly dropped audibly into a food box within easy reach. With repetition the animal acquires the habit of approaching the food box at the sound of the food dropping into it. Appropriate autonomic responses, of course, accompany the approach — salivation, increased gastric motility, etc. Now, one day, as the animal is approaching the food box, we pass a shock into his feet through the grid on the floor of the cage. The shock triggers a much more powerful response than the conditioned approach. It produces 'pain,' anxiety, and motor withdrawal. There are

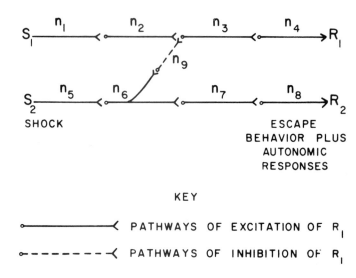

FIG. 8. When S_1 and S_2 are presented simultaneously and S_2 is relatively strong, R_2 is elicited, and R_1 inhibited by impulses from the inhibitory neurone, n_9. At the same time, S_1 is conditioned to R_2 (pathway not shown).

inhibitory arrangements in the central nervous system that prevent the simultaneous activation of two incompatible responses — (Gellhorn, 1967). One response occurs, and the other is inhibited. Each time this happens the habit patterns related to the stimuli involved are changed to some extent. Some habit inhibition of the inhibited response develops in relation to its antecedent stimulus, and at the same time some degree of conditioning of that stimulus to the responses to the shock. After several repetitions of the maneuver, the sound of food dropping into the food box evokes exclusively an anxiety-and-avoidance response in place of the approach response.

In the above experiment, it is an unconditioned stimulus that is the source of inhibition of the approach response. The same effect can be achieved with a *conditioned* aversive stimulus. This was clearly demonstrated some years ago (Wolpe, 1952) in cats in whom the sound of a buzzer had been conditioned to evoke anxiety. Attractive food was dropped in front of the animal under a particular table in a laboratory. As he approached, the buzzer was sounded. He stopped abruptly, showing mydriasis and other autonomic responses. After several repetitions of the procedure, it was noted that the animal at all times avoided the area under the table whether food was there or not.

Wherever learning occurs, we expect to find a reinforcing state of affairs (Hull, 1943); and this should be particularly obvious when strong reactions partake in the learning. In both of the foregoing experiments, the aversive stimulus (e.g. buzzer) obviously produced an excitation, which declined when the stimulus ceased — so that there was a *drive reduction* to reinforce the attachment of the anxiety responses to whatever stimuli were acting on the animal.

The first formal usage of aversive therapy was described by Kantorovich (1929) who gave alcoholic patients painful electric shocks in relation to the sight, smell, and taste of alcohol. In 1935, L. W. Max reported overcoming a homosexual's fetish by administering very strong shocks to the patient in the presence of the fetishistic object. Unfortunately, a promised detailed account of this historic case was never published. Nevertheless, his report served to guide my own first attempt, in South Africa, to treat a patient on this paradigm (Wolpe, 1954). The patient was a 32-year-old spinster who, among other neurotic reactions, was preoccupied with warding off impulses to indulge in 'eating sprees,' impulses which invariably, in a day or two, proved irresistible. Her cravings involved two kinds of 'forbidden' food — doughnuts and similar sweet foods, and salty foods. The former were disallowed because they made her fat (and she had a particular horror of obesity), and the latter because she had rheumatic heart disease and had several times been in cardiac failure — so that it was necessary for her to be on a salt-limited diet. She would try to avoid these foods by various stratagems, such as not keeping them in her apartment, and getting her African servant to lock her in the apartment when he went off at night. But at times her impulse was absolutely overpowering, and she would go out, buy food, and eat. As she went on gorging she would have a rising feeling of disgust at what she had done, that would culminate in a helpless and frantic state of prostration.

I had her make a list of all the items of food that figured in her obsession. I then attached electrodes to her forearm, told her to close her eyes and to signal by a hand movement when she had clearly formed the mental image of a selected food. At the very beginning of each signal, I passed a very severe faradic shock into her forearm. Ten shocks were given at a session. After two sessions she found that thinking of these foods at any time conjured up an image of the shock equipment, which produced anxiety. With further treatment, thoughts of the foods progressively decreased. After five sessions, she felt free of their burden for the first time in sixteen years. Life appeared bright with hope. She began to enjoy company and bought clothes, a thing she had not done for years. Unfortunately, a few weeks later she died of heart failure.

In recent years, aversion therapy has been applied to the treatment of an increasing number of neurotic conditions, e.g. fetishism (Raymond, 1956), homosexuality (Freund, 1960; James, 1962; Feldman & MacCulloch, 1965), transvestism (Glynn and Harper 1958; Blakemore, 1965) — and to the addictions — alcoholism, drug addiction, and smoking (McGuire and Vallance, 1964; Getze, 1968). A number of the procedures used are described below.

DESCRIPTION OF TECHNIQUES

Electrical Stimulation

An important advantage of electrical stimulation is that it can be administered at precise time intervals to the behavior to be modified. Depending upon the circumstances of the case, one may administer the shock either in relation to the actual objects or situations that form the basis of the obsessional or other undesirable behavior, or in relation to imaginary or pictorial representations of the objects or situations. The preferred source of aversive stimulation is either faradic current or alternating current because these can if necessary be kept at steady levels for prolonged periods. The electrodes are usually attached to the patient's forearm.[1] The baseline shock setting is determined by gradually increasing the current to a point where the patient

[1]The most satisfactory electrode is the concentric electrode (Tursky, 1965) which greatly minimizes the risk of burning the skin. Wet electrodes of saline-soaked gauze are also quite satisfactory. Ordinary electrocardiographic silver electrodes may be used if necessary.

reports it to be distinctly unpleasant. The starting point for aversive trials is then usually a current 25-50 per cent stronger.

The method of use of electrical stimulation varies in its details but always follows the general lines of the case of obsessional eating described above. It must always be administered in the presence of the stimulus to which a change of response is desired whether the stimulus appears in imagination, *in vivo,* or pictorially.

A recent use of *real stimuli* has been in the treatment of compulsive gambling by Barker and Miller (1968). One of their patients, aged 34, had been gambling steadily on 'fruit machines' for 12 years. One of these machines was borrowed from an inn and installed in the hospital. Shocks of about 70 volts were administered to the patient's forearm. "While standing gambling continuously for 3 hours (his usual practice), he withstood a minimum of 150 shocks delivered by a third party at random to all stages of his gambling procedure from insertion of the discs to the 'pay-out.' He received 672 shocks altogether, designed to produce a tolerable degree of discomfort during 12 hours' 'gambling treatment,' although he lost all desire to gamble after only 6 hours. He did not resume gambling for 18 months but then relapsed once following a period of stress. Six hours' booster treatment, using the same technique, has prevented further gambling for 6 months (to date)."

The best-known example of aversion therapy in the context of *pictorial* stimuli is Feldman and MacCulloch's (1965) treatment of homosexuality. But, as will be seen, aversion is in this case only the first part of a double maneuver. The patient is asked to examine a number of slides of males both clothed and nude and to rank them in a hierarchy of attractiveness. This hierarchy is later worked through in *ascending* order. The patient also makes up a hierarchy of female slides to be worked through in descending order, i.e. the most attractive first. Having determined a level of shock that the patient finds very unpleasant, they proceed as follows:

> . . . The patient is told that he will see a male picture and that several seconds later he might receive a shock. He is also told that he can turn off the slide by pressing a switch, with which he is provided, whenever he wishes to do so, and that the moment the slide leaves the screen the shock will also be turned off. Finally he is told that he will never be shocked when the screen is blank. It is made clear to him that he should leave the slide on the screen for as long as he finds it sexually attractive. The first slide is then presented. The patient has the choice of switching it off or leaving it on the screen. Should he switch it off within eight seconds he is not shocked and this is termed an avoidance response. Should he fail to turn it off within 8 seconds, he receives a shock. If the shock strength is not sufficiently high to cause him to switch it off immediately, it is increased until he does so. In practice this had hardly ever been necessary. The moment a patient performs the switching off response the slide is removed and the shock is terminated. This is termed an escape trial. In addition to switching off, the patient is told to say 'No' as soon as he wishes the slide to be removed. It is hoped that a further increment of habit strength will accrue to the avoidance habit by means of this further avoidance response. The usual course of events is: several trials in all of which escape responses are made; a sequence of trials in some of which the patient escapes, and some of which he avoids; a sequence of trials in which the patient avoids every time. . . . . When the patient both, (1) reports that his previous attraction to the slide has been replaced by indifference or even actual dislike; and, (2) attempts to switch off within one to two seconds of the slide appearing; we proceed to the next slide and repeat the process.

In addition to conditioning avoidance to male stimuli, they attempt to reduce anxiety toward females by introducing a female slide at the moment of the removal of the male slide. Thus, anxiety-relief (see p. 161) is associated with the introduction of the female image. The patient is also permitted to request the return of the female slide after it has been removed. The situation is such that the absence of a female slide means that a male slide, by now associated with shock and hence anxiety-provoking, may reappear. Hence, the patient gradually becomes motivated to request the return of the female slide. However, this request is met in an entirely random manner, sometimes being granted and sometimes not, so that the patient cannot predict what will be the result of his attempting to switch off the male slide, nor of his asking for the return of the female slide. The whole situation is designed to lead to the acquisition of two responses: attempt to avoid males, and attempts to approach females.

In a follow-up survey of 25 of their successfully treated patients, Feldman & MacCulloch (1967) found that 52 per cent had remained totally heterosexual for a period of 1 year.

Although this is certainly a gratifying finding, it does not, for the reasons given at the beginning of this chapter, justify the use of aversion as the primary treatment of homosexuality. The interpersonal anxiety which is the basis of many cases is not likely to be deconditioned by aversion therapy, and will usually continue to be a problem after the homosexuality as such has been overcome. In other cases, aversion therapy will fail because of interpersonal anxiety. For both of these reasons it is highly advisable for the anxiety to be deconditioned before anything else. The homosexuality may then be found to give place to heterosexuality without direct measures of any kind needing to be used — as described by Stevenson and Wolpe (1960), one of whose cases is presented *in extenso* in Chapter XIII (Case 12).

A new aversive technique that apparently works on a punishment paradigm was recently introduced by Leonard Feingold (1966) of Haverford State Hospital. His first patient was a girl of 11 who persistently kept her mouth open and thus made it unfeasible for her dentist to perform certain necessary procedures.The girl and her parents were instructed to bring him a record of each occasion on which her mouth was noticed to be open. Then, when she came to see him she was given as many strong shocks to the leg as there were recorded occasions of open mouth. The number of shocks needed decreased from 48 to zero in the course of 12 sessions, after which the mouth remained closed in a normal way, and the delighted dentist was able to proceed with his work. About a year-and-a-half ago I applied the same technique to a high school junior who despite high intelligence was getting low grades because of inability to sit down to work in the evening. He was asked to record his evening study performance and told that he would receive a severe shock for each half-hour between 7 and 11 p.m. during which, in the course of the week, he did not work. At the end of the first week, he received four shocks, at the end of the second, three; and after that no more were necessary. His report of improved work habits has been supported by his mother's report of a rise in grades from C to A minus during the past 18 months. It is presumed that the technique owed its efficacy to the conditioning of anxiety to the *idea* of not working.

The advent of small portable shock equipment (e.g. McGuire and Vallance, 1964) has made it possible to extend aversive therapy to the life situation of the patient. To do this is indispensable where target behavior cannot be evoked to order in the consulting room. For example, there are obsessions that are aroused only in particular life situations that the patient may not be able to conjure up satisfactorily in imagination. Again, in the treatment of alcoholism and other drug addictions, it has been customary to use aversive stimulation only in connection with the sight, smell and taste of the drug. No attempt has ordinarily been made to combat the often irresistible feelings of craving that arise endogenously. In any case there is no way of producing the craving at will in the consulting room. Such problems are amenable to the use of portable shock apparatus.

For example, a physician who had 5 years previously started taking Demerol to alleviate emotional distress, had in the past 3 years begun to notice the increasing incidence of a craving for the drug even in the absence of any stress. This endogenous impulse had gradually become the dominating reason for indulgence. Increasingly often, now about once a week, it would be irresistible. He would then take 1000 to 1500 milligrams of the drug. On the day following he would feel revolted and shamed, but in following days the craving would again grow. He was given a portable shocker to take home and instructed to give himself a severe shock whenever he felt a desire for the drug. On three occasions he gave himself 4, 3, and 2, severe shocks respectively. After this the apparatus broke down, but for a period of 12 weeks the patient felt only minor cravings that he could easily control (Wolpe, 1965). This single experiment seems striking enough to justify more extensive trials by psychiatrists who deal frequently with problems of drug addiction. It may be that permanent suppression of craving can be procured, but even reliably repeatable suppressions lasting several months would be a boon.

By what possible mechanism may the intrusion of electric stimulation when craving is present diminish the likelihood of recurrence of craving? We do not know the precise physiological responses that underlie the feeling of craving for a drug; but, whatever they are, they presumably have other bodily states of affairs as their antecedents — though perhaps extrinsic antecedents may one day be found. It may be possible to produce conditioned inhibition of these responses — even without identifying them physiologically — if they can be inhibited by the simultaneous evocation of an incompatible response — in accordance with the reciprocal inhibition principle. Strong electric stimulation is apparently capable of procuring response inhibition, but research is needed to reveal to what extent habit decrement follows in this very special case.

Aversion Therapy by Drugs

The treatment of alcoholism by an aversion method based on the nauseating effects of drugs was introduced many years ago by Voegtlin & Lemere (1942), and has been the subject of subsequent reports, e.g. Lemere and Voegtlin (1950). The treatment consists of giving the patient some nausea-producing drug, such as tartar emetic, emetine, apomorphine, or gold chloride, and then insisting that he drink a favored alcoholic beverage. The combination of alcohol and emetic is given daily for a week to ten days and the procedure then tested by giving the patient alcohol alone. If there is sufficient conditioning the very sight of alcohol will produce nausea. Typically, the patient is given two ten-ounce glasses of warm saline solution containing 0.1 gram of emetine and 1 gram of sodium chloride to 20 ounces of water. This is just sufficient salt to mask the bitter taste of the oral emetine. Immediately after this, he is given a hypodermic injection of 30 milligrams of emetine hydrochloride to produce emesis, 15 milligrams of pilocarpine hydrochloride for diaphoresis, and 15 milligrams of ephedrine sulphate for 'support.'

The alcoholic beverage, e.g. whiskey, is held in front of the patient's nose and he is made to smell deeply. He is then requested to sip the beverage and taste it thoroughly, swishing it around in his mouth and then swallowing it so that the maximum distastefulness is elicited. Another drink is poured and the same procedure repeated. Nausea should begin immediately after this second drink if the timing has been right — as it must be if the treatment is to have its maximum effect.

Voegtlin and Lemere (1950) reported that 38 per cent of 4,096 patients remained abstinent for 5 years or longer and 23 per cent for 10 years or longer after their first treatment. The method is, however, extremely time-consuming, tedious and messy and requires long-term accessibility of the patients. Trying it out in private practice in 1949, I found it so difficult and unrewarding that I gave it up in a few months. An institutional setting is certainly more suitable.

Drug-induced aversion for a behavioral problem was first employed by Raymond (1956) in a 33 year-old man who had been arrested for acting out destructive fetishes towards perambulators (baby carriages) and handbags (pocket-books). The fetishistic acts gave him a pleasurable erotic sensation. For purposes of treatment, "a collection of handbags, perambulators and colored illustrations was obtained and these were shown to the patient after he had received an injection of apomorphine and just before nausea was produced." Treatment was given two-hourly, day and night; no food was allowed, and at night amphetamine was used to keep him awake.

At the end of the first week, treatment was temporarily suspended and the patient was allowed home to attend to his affairs. Returning eight days later to continue the treatment, he reported jubilantly that he had for the first time been able to have intercourse with his wife without use of the old fantasies. His wife said that she had noticed a change in his attitude to her, but was unable to define it. Treatment was recommenced and continued as before, save that emetine hydrochloride was used whenever the emetic effect of apomorphine became less pronounced than its sedative effect. After several more days' treatment he said that the sight of the objects made him sick. Six months later it was suggested that he have a booster course of treatment to which he agreed, although he did not consider it necessary. Nineteen months after the beginning of therapy, he stated that he no longer required the old fantasies to enable him to have sexual intercourse, nor did he masturbate with these fantasies. His wife said that she no longer worried about him and that their sexual relations had greatly improved. The patient had been promoted to a more responsible job and had had no further trouble with the police.

Another chemically-induced aversive technique, that acts indirectly, by producing a fear-arousing physiological state, is associated with the use of curare-like drugs, e.g. Scoline (succinylcholine) (Sanderson, Campbell and Laverty, 1963). These drugs, given in sufficient dosage, produce a temporary respiratory paralysis which, added to the patient's inability to speak or move in any way, is "a most terrifying experience" If alcohol is presented to the patient just at the height of his terror, a conditioned response of fear and aversion to the drug may be established.

The technique is as follows. The subject is placed on a stretcher and connected to a respirator and to a polygraph which includes muscle tension and respiration among its measures. A 20 mg. dose of Scoline is gradually injected. As soon as there is evidence of respiratory failure, the physician holds the bottle of alcohol to the lips of the subject and deposits a few drops into his mouth. During the period of apnea the patient is made to breathe by the respirator. As soon as there are signs of natural breathing being restored, the alcohol is removed.

Of twelve subjects that Sanderson *et al* report as "Series II," six were known to be abstinent several weeks later. However, the beneficial effects often do not appear to last. Twelve cases were treated in this way by Farrar, Powell and Martin (1968) and only two were abstinent at a one-year follow-up.

There is a general comment to be made about all these aversion treatments of alcoholism. At best, they result in the patient 'recovering' on the condition that he no longer partakes of any alcohol at all. This does not amount to a restoration to normality. A cured patient would be one who could take a drink like anybody else. Such a result will remain beyond our reach until we know more about the processes that are involved in the formation of the chemical habits that we call addictions.

Covert Sensitization

This is the label Cautela (1966, 1967) has applied to his technique of establishing an aversive response to a chosen stimulus by imaginally induced nauseation. This has been successful in a variety of contexts, particularly obesity, homosexuality and alcoholism. In the last-named condition, Ashem and Donner (1968) have recently noted that six out of fifteen alcoholics were abstinent six months after this treatment in contrast to none in an untreated control group — supporting to some extent a very rosy uncontrolled report by Anant (1967). Cautela (1967) gives the following exposition of his instructions in relation to an obese patient whom he wishes to make desist from eating apple pie. The patient is relaxed and his eyes are shut.

> I want you to imagine you've just had your main meal and you are about to eat your dessert, which is apple pie. As you are about to reach for the fork, you get a funny feeling in the pit of your stomach. You start to feel queasy, nauseous and sick all over. As you touch the fork, you can feel food particles inching up your throat. You're just about to vomit. As you put the fork into the pie, the food comes up into your mouth. You try to keep your mouth closed because you are afraid that you'll spit the food out all over the place. You bring the piece of pie to your mouth. As you're about to open your mouth, you puke; you vomit all over your hands, the fork, over the pie. It goes all over the table, over the other peoples' food. Your eyes are watering. Snot and mucous are all over your mouth and nose. Your hands feel sticky. There is an awful smell. As you look at this mess you just can't help but vomit again and again until just watery stuff is coming out. Everybody is looking at you with shocked expressions. You turn away from the food and immediately start to feel better. You run out of the room, and as you run out, you feel better and better. You wash and clean yourself up, and it feels wonderful.

For further examples of the therapeutic use of this and other kinds of aversion-evoking imagery the reader is referred to Gold and Neufeld (1965) who used repulsive male images to overcome a 16-year-old boy's habit of soliciting men in public toilets; to Davison (1967) who used covert desensitization as part of his means to eliminate a sadistic fantasy and to Kolvin (1967) who used it to treat a fetish and an addiction to the sniffing of gasoline.

Other Aversive Stimuli

Anything that is unpleasant is a potential source of aversive conditioning. Philpott (1967) has claimed to overcome obsessional thinking by getting his patient to hold her breath as long as possible each time an obsessional thought obtruded itself. Lublin (1968) has described two aversive techniques for the smoking habit. One consists of puffing stale warm cigarette smoke from a machine into the face of the subject while he is smoking his own cigarette. In the other, the subject has to puff regularly at a cigarette, in time to the ticking of a metronome, inhaling every 6 seconds on the first cigarette and then puffing without inhaling every 3 seconds on a second cigarette. (This, of course, is similar to a familiar method that parents have for generations employed to make young children desist from smoking). They state that both methods are very aversive, hardly any subject ever finishing a whole cigarette. Of 36 patients whom they gave an average of 6 half-hour sessions, 16 stopped smoking completely and all are reported to have stayed off cigarettes, some for as long as a year.

About 10 years ago I treated two cases of obesity by approximating a vile-smelling solution of asafetida to their nostrils while they were handling, smelling and tasting attractive items of food. (Both of these patients also received reciprocal inhibition therapy for interpersonal anxieties to which they responded well). Temporary control of over-eating was achieved in one, and lasting control in the other who to this day has a sylph-like figure. Kennedy and Foreyt (1968) have described a very similar procedure using more sophisticated equipment to deliver noxious butyric acid gas.

The reader who wishes to inquire more fully into the theoretical and experimental aspects of aversion therapy should consult the important papers of Church (1964), Solomon (1964), Azrin and Holtz (1966) and Rachman and Teasdale (1968). Azrin and Holtz have distilled the following practical guidelines from numerous experimental studies:

1. The punishing stimulus should be arranged in such a manner that no unauthorized escape is possible.

2. The punishing stimulus should be as intense as possible.

3. The frequency of punishment should be as high as possible; ideally the punishing stimulus should be given for every response.

4. The punishing stimulus should be delivered immediately after the response.

5. The punishing stimulus should not be increased gradually but introduced at maximum intensity.

6. Extended periods of punishment should be avoided, especially where low intensities of punishment are concerned, since a recovery effect may thereby occur. Where mild intensities of punishment are used, it is best to use them for only a brief period of time.

7. Great care should be taken to see that the delivery of the punishing stimulus is not differentially associated with the delivery of reinforcement. Otherwise, the punishing stimulus would be made a signal or discriminative stimulus that a period of extinction is in progress.

8. The degree of motivation to emit the punished response should be reduced.

9. The frequency of positive reinforcement for the punished response should similarly be reduced.

10. An alternative response should be available which will not be punished but which will produce the same or greater reinforcement as the punished response. For example, punishment of criminal behavior can be expected to be more effective if non-criminal behavior which will result in the same advantages as the criminal behavior is available.

11. If no alternative response is available, the subject should have access to a different situation in which he obtains the same reinforcement without being punished.

12. If it is not possible to deliver the punishing stimulus itself after a response, then an effective method of punishment is still available. A conditioned stimulus may be associated with the aversive stimulus and this conditioned stimulus may be delivered following a response to achieve conditioned punishment.

13. A reduction of positive reinforcement may be used as punishment when the use of physical punishment is not possible for practical, legal or moral reasons.

CHAPTER XII

Operant Conditioning Methods

THE PHYSIOLOGICAL basis of learning (conditioning) is the establishment of functional connections between neurons (Wolpe, 1958). There is no reason to believe that there is more than one *kind* of learning. Variation depends on the identity of interconnected neuronal sequences. Thus, the distinction between respondent and operant conditioning is not in the nature of the conditioning, but in the fact that in the former 'nonvoluntary', especially autonomic, behavior is predominantly involved; whereas in the latter the behavior is either motor or ideomotor. It is because neurotic behavior is usually primarily a matter of autonomic conditioning that operant techniques have not been prominent in the treatment of *neuroses*.

The conditioning of operants is certainly more clearly relatable to reinforcing events, and more clearly "under the control of its consequences" (e.g. reward or non-reward) than autonomic responses appear to be. The difference, however, is not a hard-and-fast one. There is impressive evidence that autonomic responses can be brought under the control of reward contingencies (Kimmel, 1967; Miller and DiCara, 1968; Lang, 1968).

Six operant techniques are distinguishable: positive reinforcement, extinction, differential reinforcement response-shaping, punishment, and negative reinforcement. The last two of these have, as far as behavior therapy is concerned, been dealt with in Chapter XI. Differential reinforcement is a selective combination of positive reinforcement and extinction. Shaping is, in essence, a special case of positive reinforcement. For a detailed exposition see Azrin and Ayllon (1968); for briefer accounts introducing collections of cases, Ullman & Krasner (1965); Franks (1965); Ulrich, Stachnik & Mabry (1966). We shall consider positive reinforcement and extinction.

POSITIVE REINFORCEMENT

This is the process of establishing a habit by arranging for reward to follow all or many of the evocations of a response. Any state of affairs that, following a response, serves to increase the rate of responding may be called a positive reinforcer. Thus, food, water, sex, money, domination, approval or affection are all operational reinforcers when they increase the rate (or likelihood) of a response — as they will under the appropriate conditions of hunger, etc.

Examples of the habit-building power of positive reinforcement are legion, ranging from pecking habits in pigeons to the most complex rituals of mankind. In the field of therapeutic behavior change, it has already been noted (Chapter V) that the motor behavior of assertion is reinforced by such consequences as the achievement of interpersonal domination, and the approval of the therapist; but the context there is a complex one. Simple examples are easy to find in relation to commonplace behavior problems of children. A child habitually screams to get what he wants, and getting what he wants (sooner or later) maintains the habit of screaming. Now the child is told, "You will never get it (e.g. a toy) if you scream. You will get it if you say quietly, Please, may I have it?" If he asks as directed, he is at once rewarded, which immediately increases the likelihood of his asking in this new way again. Consistently rewarding the new behavior results in its displacing the old.

The therapeutic potentialities of positive reinforcement have been strikingly demonstrated in recent years, but so far mainly in schizophrenics; though it must at once be stated that 'cure' of the psychosis is neither obtained nor claimed, but only change in particular habits. This is not surprising, since a variety of evidence, genetic (Kallman, 1953) and other, suggests that schizophrenia is a matter of biochemistry.

One of the clever treatment schedules devised by Ayllon (1963) is worth presenting at length. The patient was a 47-year-old schizophrenic woman who had been in a state hospital for nine years. Among other strange habits she always wore an excessive amount of clothing — about 25 pounds. In order to treat this, a scale was placed at the entrance to the dining room. The requirement for entering (to receive food reinforcement) was a predetermined weight.

> Initially, she was given an allowance of 23 lbs. over her current body weight. This allowance represented a 2 lb. reduction from her usual clothing weight. When the patient exceeded the weight requirement, the nurse stated in a matter-of-fact manner, "Sorry, you weigh too much, you'll have to weigh less." Failure to meet the required weight resulted in the patient missing the meal at which she was being weighed. Sometimes, in an effort to meet the requirement, the patient discarded more clothing than

she was required. When this occurred the requirement was adjusted at the next weighing time to correspond to the limit set by the patient on the preceding occasion.

At the start of this experiment, the patient missed a few meals because she failed to meet the weight requirement, but soon thereafter she gradually discarded her superfluous clothing. First, she left behind odd items she had carried in her arms, such as bundles, cups and handbags. Next she took off the elaborate headgear and assorted 'capes' or shawls she had worn over her shoulders. Although she had worn 18 pairs of stockings at one time, she eventually shed these also.

At the end of the experiment, the patient's clothing weighed a normal 3 pounds and subsequently remained stable at this level. One result of dressing normally was participation in small social events at the hospital. Another was that her parents took her out for the first time in nine years.

Anorexia nervosa is one of the few conditions classified as neurotic in which positive reinforcement has been successfully used as the main method. While at the University of Virginia School of Medicine, I was involved to an extent in the treatment of two cases, one of which has been reported in detail by Bachrach, Erwin, and Mohr (1965). This was a 37-year-old woman whose weight had fallen to 47 pounds in the face of various medical treatments. For the purposes of the operant conditioning program she was transferred from her attractive hospital room to a barren one, furnished only with a bed, nightstand and chair. Each of the three authors had one meal a day with her. The reinforcement schedule involved *verbal reinforcement* of movements associated with eating.

When the patient lifted her fork to move toward spearing a piece of food the experimenter would talk to her about something in which she might have an interest. The required response was then successively raised to lifting the food toward her mouth, chewing, and so forth. The same scheduled increase in required response was applied to the amount of food consumed. At first, any portion of the meal that was consumed would be a basis for a postprandial reinforcement (a radio, TV set, or phonograph would be brought in by the nurse at a signal from the experimenter); if she did not touch any of the food before her, nothing would be left until the next meal. More and more of the meal had to be consumed in order to be reinforced until she eventually was required to eat everything on the plate.

After two months, when she had gained 14 pounds, she was discharged to out-patient treatment, and positive reinforcement treatment was continued at home with the cooperation of her family. Eighteen months later her weight was 88 pounds.

Exploratory applications of operant conditioning techniques to delinquent behavior (Schwitzgebel and Kolb, 1964; Burchard and Tyler, 1965) have yielded encouraging results. The former authors treated 40 adolescent delinquents by reinforcement procedures. A three-year follow-up study of 20 of them revealed a significant reduction in the frequency and severity of crime in comparison with a matched-pair control group. Burchard and Tyler produced a marked decrease in the "destructive and disruptive behavior" of a 13-year-old delinquent boy by systematically isolating him when he performed in an anti-social way and by rewarding socially acceptable behavior.

Thomas (1968) has listed a number of conditions that relate to the effectiveness of positive reinforcement.

1. The response to be reinforced must first be emitted otherwise reinforcement is impossible.

2. Reinforcement must not be delayed; in general, the more immediate the reinforcement, the better.

3. Reinforcement of every desired response emitted is most effective for establishing behavior.

4. Not reinforcing every desired response during response establishment, while less effective in achieving immediate high rates of responding, is generally more effective in producing responses that endure after reinforcement is terminated.

5. The stimuli suitable to reinforce one individual's behavior may not be the most appropriate for another. Recent research suggests that one important clue to what the reinforcing conditions are in the profile is simply the rank order of activities in which a person engages in his free time (see Premack, 1965; Homme, 1965).

Thought-Stopping

The most likely basis of this procedure is the establishment of an inhibitory habit by positive reinforcement. Perseverating trains of thought that are unrealistic, unproductive, and anxiety-arousing are a common clinical problem. If chronic, they are called *obsessions*. Many are only episodic. One man, for example, had constantly brooded upon the possibility of a fire breaking out in one of his warehouses, ever since a friend of his had suffered a severe financial loss.

A thought-stopping program begins by asking the patient to close his eyes and to verbalize a typical futile thought-sequence. During the verbalization the therapist suddenly shouts "Stop!" and then draws attention to the fact that the thoughts actually do stop. This is repeated several times, and then the patient is urged to test the efficacy of the procedure by interrupting his unadaptive thoughts by saying "Stop!" subvocally. He is warned that the thoughts will return; but every time they do he must interrupt them again. The main effort later comes to be directed at learning to stifle each unwanted thought at birth. The moment it threatens to appear the patient quickly inhibits it by concentrating on something else. The thoughts in many cases return less and less readily and eventually cease to be a problem.

Modifications of the method are sometimes successful with patients with whom the standard procedure fails. A fairly uncomfortable faradic shock accompanying the "Stop" signal may successfully disrupt the negative thought sequence. Alternatively, the patient may be asked to keep his mind on pleasant thoughts and to press a button which activates a buzzer as soon as any disturbing thought intrudes. Upon the buzzer sounding the therapist instantly shouts "Stop!" There is frequently a progressive decline in buzzer-pressing, which may be steep, e.g. from 20 per minute to once every two minutes in the course of a 15-minute treatment period.

Some years ago, I took advantage of an opportunity to observe the effects of this procedure on myself. I had been involved in a legal dispute that was finally settled at a meeting of principals and lawyers. Later that day, reflecting upon the proceedings, I became very disturbed at realizing that I had handled an important interchange ineptly. Dwelling continuously on the matter, I became increasingly distressed. I decided to try thought-stopping. I found this a very difficult matter, for the thoughts were seemingly borne along by the anxiety that they themselves had stirred up; but I worked at it assiduously, and after an hour noticed that the general anxiety level was distinctly lower. After two more hours, I was no longer troubled by these thoughts. Even when my anxiety was high, it seemed that the successful exclusion of a thought slightly diminished it; but when the anxiety was low this effect was quite clear.

On the basis of this personal experience, supported to some extent by the testimony of patients, I suggest that a habit of thought-inhibition is reinforced by the anxiety-reducing consequence of each successful effort at thought-inhibition. The suggestion could easily be tested by psychophysiological monitoring.

Thought-stopping was introduced by J. G. Taylor in 1955 (see Wolpe, 1958); but unknown to him, it had already been advocated by a largely forgotten writer, Alexander Bain (1928). Taylor (1963) has also described the application of the idea to the treatment of a case of compulsive eyebrow-plucking of 31 years' duration. The habit was overcome in ten days.

EXTINCTION

Extinction is the progressive weakening of a response which is repeatedly evoked without reinforcement. This generally means that the reinforcer is omitted.

One the earliest clinical examples of a type of extinction program that is increasingly being used is a case of Ayllon and Michael (1959). The patient was a woman who, for a period of two years, had been entering the nurses' office on an average of 16 times a day.

> The nurses had resigned themselves to this activity on the grounds that such efforts as pushing her back bodily onto the ward had failed in the past and because the patient had been classified as mentally defective and therefore "too dumb" to understand.
>
> In order to extinguish the problem behavior in question, the nurses were informed simply that during the program the patient must not be given any reinforcement (attention) for entering the nurses' office. It was found

that as soon as the extinction schedule was introduced, there was a gradual and continuing diminution of entries to the nurses' office. The average frequency was down to two entries per day by the seventh week of extinction, at which time the program was terminated.

The behavior towards which an extinction program is directed diminishes at varying rates. As Thomas (1968) points out, resistance to extinction is often high in clinical cases because the operant responses have been sustained for long periods by intermittent reinforcement. For this reason, it is important that the cessation of reinforcement be abrupt and complete.

A massed practice type of extinction program was introduced by Dunlap (1932), who called it "negative practice." He described overcoming such habits as the repeated typing of errors, tics, and stuttering by persuading the subject to repeat the undesired act a great many times. The method has come to be mainly used in the treatment of tics (e.g. Yates, 1958; Jones, 1960; Rafi, 1962; Walton, 1964). In using this method it is important to ensure that the undesirable response is evoked to the point of exhaustion — so that a high degree of reactive inhibition is produced. Otherwise the tic may actually be reinforced, especially if it is not asymptotic to begin with. In any event, it is a tedious, time-consuming method. Kondas (1965) has reported that much more rapid change can be obtained if negative practice is combined with "anxiety-relief" conditioning (p. 165). While the patient repeats the tic, an unpleasant electric current is continuously applied; and it is switched off simultaneously with cessation of the tic sequence.

CHAPTER XIII

Some Complex Cases

A NEUROSIS may be complex in one or more of several
ways (Wolpe, 1964):

1. Multiple families of stimuli may be conditioned to
neurotic reactions.

2. The reactions may include unadaptiveness in important areas of social behavior (e.g., sexual deviations,
'character neuroses').

3. The neurosis may have somatic consequences (e.g.,
asthma, neurodermatitis).

4. The neurosis may include obsessional behavior.

5. There may be pervasive anxiety in addition to that
associated with specific stimuli.

The extended case summaries that make up this
chapter are intended to illustrate how complex cases
are handled by a behavior therapist. At all times,
stimulus-response relations perceived by the therapist
determine his strategies. New information frequently
leads to change of direction.

CASE 10

Anxiety with Frequent Urination, Nausea, and Diarrhea; Obsession About Wife's Premarital Loss of Virginity

Mr. B. was a 31-year-old advertising salesman who four years previously had begun to notice himself increasingly anxious in social and business situations from which it was difficult to get away. Within a few months, even five minutes in the office of a client would produce considerable anxiety accompanied by a strong desire to urinate. If he went out and relieved himself, the urge would return after a further five minutes, and so on. The only circumstances that could be associated with the onset of Mr. B.'s neurosis, were the unsettlement of having moved to a new house in a new town, and his concern at the unexpected break-up of the marriage of close friends whom he had regarded as ideally mated. His only previous neurotic phase had been a brief one that had occurred upon moving to a new school at the age of 16.* The Fear Survey Schedule revealed very high anxiety to the following stimulus classes: strange places, failure, strangers, bats, journeys especially by train, being criticized, surgical operations, rejection, planes, being disapproved of, losing control, looking foolish, and fainting.

Mr. B.'s early history was quite conventional. A feature of interest was a strong religious training with marked emphasis on "the good and the bad". Churchgoing had played a prominent part in his childhood and adolescence. In his middle teens he had come to resent it but without rebelling outwardly. He had done well in school and got on well with both classmates and

---

*This, of course, could have conditioned anxiety to 'new places'.

teachers. He had been trained in journal advertising but was now engaged in advertising salesmanship which he greatly liked.

As regards his sexual history, Mr. B. had been stimulated by erotic pictures at the age of ten. At thirteen, he had begun to masturbate but without fear or guilt. Dating and petting began at fourteen, and at eighteen he had met his wife who attracted him by her intelligence, good looks, and responsiveness to his jokes. The courtship was broken by Mr. B. after she had revealed that she had had an affair two years earlier. On reflection, he had condoned the episode, and at the age of twenty married her. The relationship had turned out to be a very congenial one, and sexually very satisfying to both; but Mr. B. was never really able to divest himself of the idea that he had been "dealt a dirty card".

At the second session, Mr. B. described how embarrassing and incapacitating he found his neurotic anxiety and the associated urge to urinate. Anxiety was greater in the presence of unfamiliar people and if there was no easy access to a toilet. Other factors that increased it were the importance of the occasion and the importance of the other person. On the whole, there was more anxiety in anticipation of a meeting than at the meeting itself.[1] Since it was evident that a desensitization program needed to be undertaken, relaxation training was started at this interview.

At his next session, five days later, Mr. B. reported that he had practiced relaxing, and that by means of it had been able to desist from urinating while at home for a period of six-and-a-half hours despite quite a strong

[1]The therapeutic implication of this last observation will become apparent later.

urge. Relaxation training was now extended, and the general desensitization strategy worked out. It was apparent that the duration of an interview was an important factor determining the strength of Mr. B.'s anxiety. It was therefore decided to treat an 'interview' hierarchy, using a time dimension for the sake of its quantifiability. I started the desensitization by having him imagine himself scheduled to a very brief meeting (of two minutes' duration) with the manager of an important firm. In spite of the fact that relaxation training had at this point involved only a limited part of his musculature, it was decided to begin desensitization at this session because this already produced considerable calmness. The first scene was presented to him as follows: "Imagine that you have just entered the office of a manager who has a rule that no representative is permitted to spend more than two minutes in his office." By the third presentation this scene produced no more anxiety; and scenes of meetings of four minutes and six minutes were then in succession presented.

In subsequent interviews the duration of these meetings was progressively extended, until by the ninth he could imagine being with an executive for sixty minutes without anxiety. He now found himself much better at real meetings and social situations. While visiting relatives, he had urinated only three times in five hours. However, anticipatory anxiety was almost as bad as it had ever been. There was some measure of it several hours before a prospective meeting, but it became much more noticeable half to one hour beforehand, and then increased rather steeply. At this ninth interview, desensitization of anticipatory anxiety was started. Anxiety decreased to zero in two to three presentations of each of the following scenes:

1. In his office, 60 minutes before visiting a client.

2. In his office, 30 minutes before visiting a client and preparing to leave.

3. Twenty minutes before visiting a client, entering his car to allow ample time.

4. In his car on the way to a client 10 minutes before the appointed time.

5. Emerging from his car at the premises of the client's office, with 8 minutes in hand.

6. Entering the waiting room of the client's office 6 minutes before the appointed time.

7. Announcing himself to the client's secretary 5 minutes before the appointed time.

At his tenth interview, a week later, Mr. B. reported considerably less anxiety in relation to anticipated business meetings. He had for the first time in many months taken his wife to a downtown restaurant. On the 25-minute ride to that restaurant he had not, as in the past, had to stop to relieve himself in a rest room. At first slightly anxious in the restaurant, he had become almost entirely calm after the first 10 minutes. Desensitization to the anticipation of interviews was continued to the point that he could calmly imagine himself in the client's waiting room 2 minutes before he was to be called in. This hierarchy was finally disposed of at the next session. At this point, Mr. B. spontaneously reported that he felt far greater confidence in all respects. He had been going out to get new business — at first feeling some strain, but later increasingly comfortably. He had spent one-and-a-half hours with one new and imposing manager of an important new client firm, with hardly any anxiety either beforehand or during the interview. He was no longer bothered at going into strange places because it no longer mattered whether or not he knew where the toilet was. For the same reason, he had ceased to fear using trains, airliners, buses and other public transportation.

Attention was now turned to Mr. B.'s difficulty in asserting himself with strangers. Assertive behavior was instigated. To facilitate it he was desensitized to one relevant situation — telling a waiter "This food is bad". Anxiety disappeared at the second presentation of this. Two weeks later, at his fourteenth interview, Mr. B. stated that he was expressing himself where required with increasing ease. For example, he had immediately and effectively spoken up at a drugstore when another customer was taken ahead of him out of turn. He had become more and more comfortable making business calls, citing as an example a one-and-three-quarter hour interview with a particular executive. He commented that 3 months earlier he would in the course of so long a period have had to go out to urinate about 20 times. However, he still had to push himself to do some of the things he had become inured to avoiding.

From this point onward, the main focus of therapy was his problem about his wife's premarital affair. First, it was mutually agreed after reference to Kinsey and others, that Mr. B's reactions were irrational. Then, an attempt was made to employ a kind of emotive imagery (p. 159) that was suggested by a discussion with Akhter Ahsen (1965) who bases some quite interesting operations that he calls "eidetic psychotherapy" upon an extremely fanciful conceptual system. The central practical idea is to ask the patient to imagine himself behaving in a new way in a past real situation, that has been emotionally distressful. The idea was employed in the present case by having Mr. B. project himself back to the time of his wife's affair and imagine that while she was amorously engaged with her lover in a hotel, he was in the next room. He was to force the connecting door open and beat up the paramour. In doing this, it was supposed that angry emotions would be counterposed to the anxiety that this image ordinarily evoked. Mr. B. was enjoined to practice this imaginary sequence 50 to 100 times a day. He felt himself making progressive improvement for about two weeks, when he stated that his obsession was about 20 per cent less in incidence and 40 per cent less in emotional intensity. But continuing the drill for a further four weeks yielded no further benefit. After the second week he was also asked to practice imagining attacking Mrs. B. in the pre-marital amorous situation, but the only effect of this was to make him feel hostile towards her generally.

I decided, therefore, to tackle the problem by systematic desensitization. In order to desensitize Mr. B. to this long-past situation, I employed images from a fictitious film supposed to have been taken of his wife's premarital amorous activities by a hidden camera in her family's living room. Relaxed and with his eyes closed, Mr. B. was asked to imagine that his wife was sitting on a couch with her lover who kissed her and then put his hand on one of her breasts over her dress for exactly five seconds. He felt no anxiety at this. A fair amount of anxiety was evoked by the next scene in which the duration of contact was made 8 seconds; but at the third presentation of this scene anxiety disapeared. Two presentations were required to remove anxiety from imagining the hand over the breast for 10 seconds, and five presentations were required for 20 seconds.

At the following session, six weeks later, Mr. B. again felt anxiety to the twenty second hand contact, but it disappeared at the third presentation. Two weeks later, he reported that his feelings toward his wife were more detached and that he was thinking of her less. In general, his thoughts were turning away from the past towards the present and future. Further scenes were presented, increasing the duration of the lover's hand upon his wife's clothed breast successively to 25 seconds, 30 seconds, 40 seconds, one minute, one-and-a-half minutes, two minutes, and three minutes; and her snuggling up to him. None of these scenes produced any disturbance. On opening his eyes, Mr. B. stated that "having got over the hump last time", he no longer cared what his wife had done in the past. Recovery from the obsession has now lasted 9 months.

The contrast between the marked effects of the desensitization and the limited impact of the "eidetic" treatment affords us a valuable object lesson. In the desensitization, the relaxation systematically overcame the anxiety engendered by images of progressively greater liberties taken by Mrs. B.'s lover; desensitizing Mr. B. to the idea of her having permitted such liberties — which was precisely the therapeutic target. In the "eidetic" treatment, the images mobilizing anger against the seducer produced some improvement, presumably by deconditioning anxiety for which the seducer was the stimulus. Practicing images of aggression towards the 'errant' Mrs. B. only led to hostility towards her. Since both eidetic images were off the main therapeutic target, neither could have been the vehicle for full recovery.

CASE 11

Desensitization of a Multimensional Automobile Phobia, With Temporary Therapist Substitution[2]

Mrs. C. was a 39-year-old woman who complained of fear reactions to traffic situations, and whom I first saw on April 6, 1960. Her story was that on February 3, 1958, while her husband was taking her to work by car, they entered an intersection on the green light. She suddenly became aware of a large truck that, disregarding the red signal, was bearing down upon the car from the left. She remembered the moment of impact, being flung out of the car, flying through the air, and then losing consciousness. Her next recollection was of waking in the ambulance on the way to the hospital. She was found to have injuries to her knee and neck, for the treatment of which she spent a week in the hospital.

On the way home, by car, she felt unaccountably frightened. She stayed at home for two weeks, quite happily, and then, resuming normal activities, noticed that, while in a car, though relatively comfortable on the open road, she was always disturbed by seeing any car approach from either side, but not at all by vehicles straight ahead. Along city streets she had continuous anxiety, which, at the sight of a laterally approaching car less than half a block away, would rise to panic. She could, however, avoid a reaction by closing her eyes before reaching an intersection. She was also distressed in other situations that in any sense involved lateral approaches of cars. Reactions were extraordinarily severe in relation to making a left turn in the face of approaching traffic on the highway.

[2]This account is adapted from a previous description (Wolpe, 1962) of a patient's treatment at the University of Virginia.

Execution of the turn, of course, momentarily placed the approaching vehicle to the right of her car, and there was a considerable rise in tension even when the vehicle was a mile or more ahead. Left turns in the city disturbed her less because of slower speeds. The entry of other cars from side streets even as far as two blocks ahead into the road in which she was traveling also constituted a "lateral threat.". Besides her reactions while in a car, she was anxious while walking across streets, even at intersections with the traffic light in her favor, and even if the nearest approaching car were more than a block away.

During the first few months of Mrs. C.'s neurosis, her panic at the sight of a car approaching from the side would cause her to grasp the driver by the arm. Her awareness of the annoyance this occasioned subsequently led her to control this behavior, for the most part successfully, but the fear was not diminished.

Questioned about previous related traumatic experiences, she recalled that ten years previously a tractor had crashed into the side of a car in which she was a passenger. Nobody had been hurt, the car had continued its journey, and she had been aware of no emotional sequel. No one close to her had ever been involved in a serious accident. Though she had worked in the Workmen's Compensation Claims office, dealing with cases of injury had not been disturbing to her. She found it incomprehensible that she should have developed this phobia; in London during World War II, she had accepted the dangers of the blitz calmly, without ever needing to use sedatives.

Her early history revealed nothing of significance. In England, during World War II, she had been engaged to a pilot, who was killed. After his death, she had lost interest for a time in forming other associations. Her next serious association was with her husband, whom she had met in 1955. They had married in May, 1957, about nine months before the accident. Until the accident, the marital relationship had been good. Sexual relations had been satisfactory, most often with both partners achieving orgasm. Since the accident, however, she had been negatively influenced by adverse comments that her husband had made about her disabilities, so that sexual behavior had diminished. Nevertheless, when coitus occurred, she still had orgasm more often than not.

The plan of therapy was to confine subsequent interviews as far as possible to the procedures of systematic desensitization.

In the second interview, training in relaxation and the construction of hierarchies were both initiated. Mrs. C. was schooled in relaxation of the arms and the muscles of the forehead. Two hierarchies were constructed. The first related to traffic situations in open country. There was allegedly a minimal reaction if she was in a car driven by her husband and they were 200 yards from a crossroad and if, 400 yards away, at right angles, another car was approaching. Anxiety increased with increasing proximity. The second hierarchy related to lateral approaches of other cars while that in which she was traveling had stopped at a city traffic light. The first signs of anxiety supposedly appeared when the other car was two blocks away. (This, as will be seen, was a gross understatement of the patient's reactions.) The interview concluded with an introductory desensitization session. Having hypnotized and relaxed Mrs. C., I presented to her imagination some presumably neutral stimuli. First she was asked to imagine herself walking across a baseball field and then that she was riding in a car in the country with no other cars in sight. Following this, she was presented with the allegedly weak phobic situation of being in a car 200 yards from an intersection and seeing another car 400 yards on the left. She afterwards reported no disturbances to any of the scenes.

At the third interview, instruction in relaxation of muscles of the shoulder was succeeded by a desensitization session in which the following scenes were presented: 1. The patient's car, driven by her husband, had stopped at an intersection, and another car was approaching at right angles two blocks away. 2. The highway scene of the previous session was suggested, except that now her car was 150 yards from the intersection and the other car 300 yards away. Because this produced a finger-raising (signaling felt anxiety), after a pause she was asked to imagine that she was 150 yards from the intersection and the other car 400 yards. Though she did not raise her finger at this, it was noticed that she moved her legs. (It was subsequently found that these leg movements were a very sensitive indicator of emotional disturbances.) Consequently, at the fourth interview, I subjected Mrs. C. to further questioning about her reactions to automobiles, from which it emerged that she was continuously tense in cars but had not thought this worth reporting, so trifling was it beside the terror experienced at the lateral approach of a car. She now also stated that all the car scenes imagined during the sessions had aroused anxiety, but too little, she had felt, to deserve mention. While relaxed under hypnosis, Mrs. C. was asked to imagine that she was in a car about to be driven around an empty square. As there was no reaction to this, the next scene presented was being about to ride two blocks on a country road. This evoked considerable anxiety!

At the fifth interview, it was learned that even the thought of a journey raised Mrs. C.'s tension, so that if, for example, at 9 a.m. her husband were to say, "We are going out driving at 2 p.m.", she would be continuously apprehensive, and more so when actually in the car. During the desensitization session (fourth) at this interview, I asked her to imagine that she was at home expecting to go for a short drive in the country in four hours' time. This scene, presented five times, evoked anxiety that did not decrease on repetition. It was now obvious that scenes with the merest suspicion of exposure to traffic were producing more anxiety than could be mastered by Mrs. C.'s relaxation potential.

A new strategy therefore had to be devised. I introduced an artifice that lent itself to controlled manipulation. On a sheet of paper I drew an altogether imaginary completely enclosed square field, which was represented as being two blocks (200 yards) long (see Figure 9). At the southwest corner (lower left) I drew her car, facing north (upwards), in which she sat with her husband and at the lower right corner another car, supposed to be that of Dr. Richard W. Garnett, a senior staff psychiatrist, which faced them at right angles. Dr. Garnett (hereafter "Dr. G.") was 'used' because Mrs. C. regarded him as a trustworthy person.

This imaginary situation became the focus of the scenes presented in the sessions that followed. At the fifth desensitization session, Mrs. C. was asked to imagine Dr. G. announcing to her that he was going to drive his car a half-block towards her and then proceeding to do so while she sat in her parked car. As this elicited no reaction, she was next made to imagine him driving one block towards her, and then, as there was again no reaction, one-and-a-quarter blocks. On perceiving a reaction to this scene, I repeated it three times, but without effecting any decrement in the reaction. I then 'retreated,' asking her to imagine Dr. G. stopping after traveling one block and two paces towards her. This produced a slighter reaction, which decreased on repeating the scene, disappearing at the fourth presentation. This was the first evidence of change, and afforded grounds for a confident prediction of successful therapy.

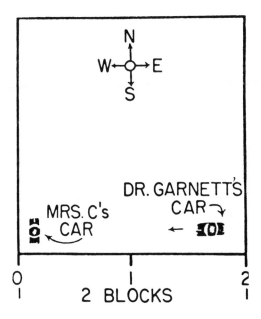

FIG. 9. Imaginary enclosed square where Doctor Garnett makes progressively closer advances to Mrs. C.'s car (See text).

At the sixth session, the imagined distance between Dr. G.'s stopping point and Mrs. C.'s car was decreased by two or three paces at a time, and at the end of the session he was able to stop seven-eighths of a block short of her (a total gain of about 10 paces). The following are the details of the progression. In parenthesis is the number of presentations of each scene required to reduce the anxiety response to zero:

1. Dr. G. approaches four paces beyond one block (3).

2. Six paces beyond one block (3)

3. Nine paces beyond one block (2)

4. Twelve paces beyond one block, i.e., one and one-eighth block (4)

At the seventh session, Mrs. C. was enabled to tolerate Dr. G.'s car reaching a point half-a-block short of her car without disturbance; at the eighth session, three-eighths of a block (about 37 yards); at the tenth, she was able to imagine him approaching within two yards of her without any reaction whatsoever.

The day after this, Mrs. C. reported that for the first time since her accident she had been able to walk across a street while an approaching car was in sight. The car was two blocks away but she was able to complete the crossing without quickening her pace. At this, the eleventh session, I began a new series of scenes in which Dr. G. drove in front of the car containing Mrs. C. instead of towards it, passing at first 30 yards ahead, and then gradually closer, cutting the distance eventually to about three yards. Desensitization to all this was rather rapidly achieved during this session. Thereupon, I drew two intersecting roads in the diagram of the field (Figure 10.) A traffic light was indicated in the middle, and the patient's car, as shown in the diagram, had 'stopped' at the red signal. At first, Mrs.

C. was asked to imagine Dr. G.'s car passing on the green light. As anticipated, she could at once accept this without anxiety; it was followed by Dr. G.'s car passing one way and a resident physician's car in the opposite direction. The slight anxiety this aroused was soon eliminated. In subsequent scenes, the resident's car was followed by an increasing number of students' cars, each scene being repeated until its emotional effect declined to zero.

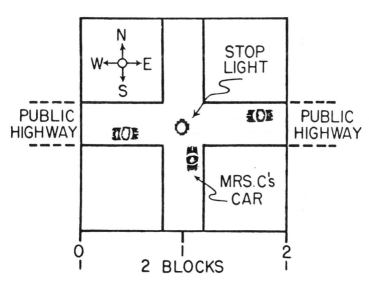

FIG. 10. Imaginary enclosed square with crossroads and traffic light added. Other cars pass while Mrs. C's car has stopped at the red light (See text).

At the twelfth session, the roadway at right angles to Mrs. C.'s car was made continuous with the public highway system (as indicated by the dotted lines) and now, starting off again with Dr. G., we added the cars of the resident and the students, and subsequently those of strangers. Imagining two unknown cars passing the intersection produced a fair degree of anxiety and she required five presentations at this session and five more at the next before she could accept it entirely calmly. However, once this was accomplished, it was relatively easy gradually to introduce several cars passing from both sides.

We now began a new series of scenes in which, with the traffic light in her favor, she was stepping off the curb to cross a city street while a car was slowly approaching. At first, the car was imagined a block away, but during succeeding sessions the distance gradually decreased to ten yards.

At this point, to check upon transfer from the imaginary to real life, I took Mrs. C. to the Charlottesville business center and observed her crossing streets at an intersection controlled by a traffic light. She went across repeatedly with apparent ease and reported no anxiety. But in the car, on the way there and back, she showed marked anxiety whenever a car from a side street threatened to enter the street in which we drove.

Soon afterwards, the opportunity arose for an experiment relevant to the question of 'transference.' A medical student had been present as an observer during four or five sessions. Early in May I had to leave town for a week to attend a conference. I decided to let the student continue therapy in my absence. I asked him to conduct the fifteenth desensitization session under my supervision. I corrected his errors by silently passing him written notes. Since he eventually performed quite well, he agreed to carry on treatment during my absence, and conducted the eighteenth to the twenty-third sessions entirely without supervision. His efforts were directed to a new series of scenes in which, while Mrs. C. was being driven by her husband along a city street, Dr. G.'s car made a right turn into that street from a cross street on their left. At first, Dr. G. was imagined making this entry two blocks ahead, but after several intervening stages it became possible for her to accept it calmly only half a block ahead. The student therapist then introduced a modification in which a student instead of Dr. G. drove the other car. The car was first visualized as entering two blocks ahead and the distance then gradually reduced to a half-block in the course of three sessions, requiring 63 scene presentations, most of which were needed in a very laborious advance from three-quarters of a block.

At this stage, the substitute therapist experimentally inserted a scene in which Mrs. C.'s car was making a left turn in the city while Dr. G.'s car approached from the opposite direction four blocks ahead. This produced such a violent reaction that the substitute therapist became apprehensive about continuing treatment. However, I returned the next day. Meanwhile, the point had been established that a substitute therapist could make satisfactory progress. (Under continuing guidance, but not in my presence, the student therapist went on to conduct two entirely successful sessions the following week.)

I now made a detailed analysis of Mrs. C.'s reaction to left turns on the highway in the face of oncoming traffic. She reported anxiety at doing a left turn if an oncoming car was in sight. Even if it was two miles away she could not allow her husband to turn left in front of it.

To treat this most sensitive reaction, I again re-introduced Dr. G. into the picture. I started by making Mrs. C. imagine (while hypnotized and relaxed) that Dr. G.'s car was a mile ahead when her car began the turn. But this was too disturbing and several repetitions of the scene brought no diminution in the magnitude of anxiety evoked. It seemed possible that there would be less anxiety if the patient's husband were not the driver of the car since his presence at the time of the accident might have made him a conditioned stimulus to anxiety. Thus I presented the scene with Mrs. C.'s brother as the driver of the car. With this altered feature, Dr. G.'s making a left turn a mile ahead evoked much less anxiety, and after four repetitions it declined to zero. We were gradually able to decrease the distance so that she could eventually imagine making the turn with Dr. G.'s car only about 150 yards away (see Table 5). Meanwhile, when she was able to 'do' the turn with Dr. G. three-eighths of a mile away, I introduced two new left-turn series: a strange car approaching with her brother driving and Dr. G. approaching with her husband driving — both a mile away initially. Work on all three series went on concurrently. When Mrs. C. could comfortably imagine her brother doing a left turn with the strange car five-eighths of a mile ahead, I resumed the original series in which her husband was the driver, starting with a left turn while the strange car was a mile ahead. This now evoked relatively little anxiety; progress could be predicted, and ensued. The interrelated decrements of reaction to this group of hierarchies are summarized in Fig. 11.

Other series of related scenes were also subjected to desensitization. They are listed in Table 5, in order of commencement, but there was much overlapping of incidence. One comprised left turns in the city in front of oncoming cars. Since cars in the city move relatively slowly, she felt less 'danger' at a given distance. At first, we dealt with left turns while an approaching car was about two blocks away, and in the course of several sessions gradually decreased the distance until Mrs. C. could comfortably 'do' a left turn with the other car slowly moving 15 yards ahead. The series where Mrs. C. was crossing streets as a pedestrian was extended, and she was enabled in imagination to cross under all normal conditions. She reported complete transfer to

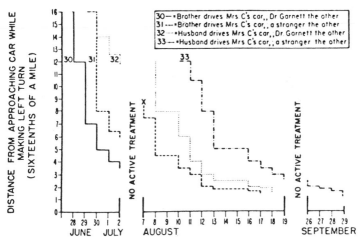

FIG. 11. Temporal relations of "distances accomplished" in imagination in desensitization series 30, 31, 32 and 33. X: indicates some relapse in Hierarchy 31 following a taxi ride in which the driver insisted on exceeding the speed limit. The status of Hierarchy 32 was not tested before the relapse in 31 was overcome.

the reality. A series that was started somewhat later involved driving down a through street with a car in a side street slowing to a stop. At first, the side street was 'placed' two blocks ahead. The distance was gradually decreased as desensitization progressed, and eventually she could without anxiety drive past a car slowing to a stop. A series intercurrently employed to desensitize her in a general way to the feeling that a car was 'bearing down upon her,' was not part of any real situation. In our imaginary square field (Figure 9), I 'placed' two parallel white lines, scaled to be about 20 feet long and 10 feet apart. During the session I said, "You are walking up and down along one white line and Dr. G. drives his car up to the other at one mile per hour . . ." This was not disturbing; but at subsequent visualizings the speed was gradually increased, so that quite soon the distance between the lines decreased to five feet. At four miles per hour there was some anxiety. This was soon eliminated, and several presentations of scenes from this series during each of 10 sessions made it possible for Mrs. C. calmly to imagine Dr. G. driving up to his white line at eighteen miles per hour while she strolled along hers.

The total effect of desensitization to these interrelated series of stimulus situations was that Mrs. C. became completely at ease in all normal traffic situations — both in crossing streets as a pedestrian and riding in a car. Improvement in real situations took place in close relation with the improvement during sessions. A direct demonstration of the transfer of improvement with respect to crossing streets at traffic lights has been described above.

TABLE 5.

SUMMARY OF DATA CONCERNING HIERARCHIES

No. of Hierarchy	Content of Hierarchy	No. of Presentations of Scenes from Each Hierarchy	Progress
0	Baseball field (control scene)	1	No disturbance
1	Approaching highway crossroads which another car approaches laterally (two distance variables—own distance and that of other car)	15	Nil
2	Stationary at city intersection while other cars approach (two blocks maximum)	2	Nil
3	About to be driven from country lodge—starting from distance of two blocks (temporal variable)	9	Nil
4	Approached by Dr. G.'s car on imaginary field (Fig. 9) starting two blocks away	41	+
5	As No. 4, but Dr. G. starts each advance from one block away	50	+
6	Dr. G. drives his car to pass in front of hers (decreasing passing distance (30 yards to 3 yards)	10	+

(Table 5. Continued)

7-8	Mrs. C. stopped by red in imaginary field (Fig. 10) and increasing variety and number of medical school cars pass on green	10	+
9-10	As No. 7 but the crossroad now continuous with public highway and increasing variety and number of strange cars pass (Fig. 10)	27	+
11	Walking across road at intersection while a car moves towards her (decreasing distances from 1½ blocks to 10 yards)	30	+
12	Goes through on green with increasing number of strange cars stationary at right and left	4	No disturbance from outset
13	As her car passes on green, Dr. G.'s car advances at side (decreasing distance from ½ block to 10 yards)	25	+
14	While Mrs. C.'s car moves slowly in town, Dr. G.'s car turns into her lane from side street (2 blocks to ¼ block) (Sessions by student, see text)	39	+
15	As No. 14, but strange car (2 blocks to ½ block) (Sessions by student, see text)	62	+

(Table 5. Continued)

16	Dr. G.'s car makes left turn across path of her slowly moving car (2 blocks to ¾ block) (Sessions by student, see text)	22	+
17	As No. 16, but student's car (2 blocks to ¾ block) (Sessions by student, see text)	26	+
18	Mrs. C.'s car in city turns left while Dr. G. advances (Handled alternately by student and author) (6 blocks to 3¾ blocks)	22	+ with difficulty
19	On highway (Fig. 10) turns left in front of tractor moving 5 mph. (1 mile to ¼ block)	36	+
20	Turns left in car while at fixed distance of ½ block a car whose driver is instructed by Dr. G. is advancing. Its speed was gradually increased from 5 to 30 mph.	93	+
21	Turns left while two strange cars advance a block ahead. Speed of the cars increased gradually from 15 mph to 26 mph.	25	+
22	While driving in taxi in through street, sees a car moving very slowly to stop at intersection ahead. Distance decreased from 1 block to 5/16 block	35	+

(Table 5.   Continued)

23	As No. 22, but the other car decelerates from normal speed. Distance gradually decreased from ½ block to zero from line of intersection	102	+
24	Walking across intersection at green light, while car a block away approaches. Increasing speeds 10-20 mph.	5	+
25	Stepping off curb to cross at unguarded intersection while car on left approaches at 10 mph. Decreasing distance 1 block to 3/8 block	137	+ very difficult progress from ½ block on
26	Does left turn in city while a car approaches at 10 mhp. Decreasing distance from 7/8 to 5/8 block	67	+ very difficult progress from ¾ block on
27	She walks back and forth in the imaginary enclosed field parallel to a white line up to which Dr. G. drives his car at 1 mph. Her distance from the line decreases from 10 yds. to 4½ yds.	23	+
28	While she keeps constant parallel distance of 5 yds. from white line, Dr. G.'s speed increases from 1 to 18 mph.	68	+

(Table 5. Continued)

29	Steps off curb at unguarded intersection while car on *right* approaches at 10 mph. Distances 1 block to 5/8 block	14	+
30	On highway in car driven by brother, does left turn in face of approaching car driven by Dr. G. Distance between them decreases from 1 mile to 350 yards	70	+
31	As 30, but stranger drives other car. Distances from 1 mile to 150 yds.	126	+
32	As 30, but Mrs. C.'s husband drives her car. Distances from 1 mile to 175 yds.	117	+
33	As 30, but Mrs. C.'s husband drives her car and stranger drives the other. Distances from 1 mile to 150 yds.	100	+
34	In taxi that does U-turn while a car approaches in city. Distances 2 blocks to 1 block	6	+
35	Driven by husband does left turn in city in face of slowly oncoming car. Distances of ½ block to 15 yds.	29	+
36	In sight of oncoming car, enters highway from side road after stopping. Distances ¼ to 1/8 mile	43	+
	Total Scenes	1491	

The patient's progress was slow but consistent. Because she lived about 100 miles away, treatment was episodic. At intervals of from four to six weeks she would come to Charlottesville for about two weeks and be seen almost every day. Noteworthy reduction in the range of real situations that could disturb her occurred in the course of each period of active treatment, and practically none during the intervals. She was instructed not to avoid exposing herself during these intervals to situations that might be expected to be only slightly disturbing; but if she anticipated being very disturbed to close her eyes, if feasible, for she could thus 'ward off' the situation. Every now and then, particular incidents stood out as landmarks in her progress. One day in late August, driving with her brother in a through street in her home town, she saw a car slowing down before a stop sign as they passed it. Though the car did not quite stop, she had no reaction at all, though gazing at it continuously. This incident demonstrated the transfer to life of the desensitization of the relevant hierarchy (No. 23) which had been concluded shortly before. Since then, similar experiences had been consistently free from disturbance.

At the conclusion of Mrs. C.'s treatment, she was perfectly comfortable making a pedestrian crossing even though the traffic was creeping up to her. Left turns in a car on a highway were quite comfortable with fast traffic up to about 150 yards ahead. When the closest approaching car was somewhat nearer, her reaction was slight anxiety, and not panic, as in the past. In all other traffic situations her feeling was entirely normal. Another effect of the treatment was that she no longer had headaches due to emotional tension.

In all, 57 desensitization sessions were conducted. The number of scene presentations at a session generally ranged from 25 to 40. Table 5 records a total of 1491 scene presentations, which does not include a small number of test scenes that were not continued because they were too disturbing when presented. The last session took place on September 29, 1960.

When Mrs. C. was seen late in December, 1960, she was as well as she had been at the end of treatment. Her sexual relations with her husband were progressively improving. At a follow-up telephone call on June, 1961, she stated that she had fully maintained her recovery and had developed no new symptoms. Her relationship with her husband was excellent and sexually at least as satisfying as before the accident. A further call, on February 19, 1962, elicited the same general report, with the additional information that two near-misses of accidents had had no lasting consequences.

CASE 12

"Spontaneous" Reversal of Homosexuality After Overcoming General Interpersonal Anxiety[3]

Mr. R., a 32-year-old hairdresser, was first seen in April, 1954. Seven years previously he had become aware of a slowly progressive diminution in his general enjoyment of life. He had emigrated to South Africa early in 1952 and soon after began to suffer from a persistent feeling of tension, combined with a varying amount of depression. Over the next two years he was treated unsuccessfully by several psychiatrists who gave him electroshock therapy, injections of vitamins and some psychoanalytic psychotherapy.

Mr. R. was born in a small town in Sweden and had an only sister, seven years younger. His father

[3] A shorter account of this case appears in Stevenson and Wolpe (1960).

was a very good-natured religious man, who never smoked, drank or lost his temper. He was extremely submissive in all his personal relations and much dominated by his wife, a very ambitious woman who could never be satisfied. She had been very anxious for R. to do credit to her by becoming someone important, and was very resentful when he did not turn out to be a particularly good scholar. She would repeatedly say how disappointed she was to have borne a son, and treated him like a girl — forbidding him to play football, for example. She used to force him to stay at home and amuse his sister when he would rather be playing with his friends. If anything went wrong, she would invariably blame him, screaming at him and not infrequently beating him. His predominant feeling towards her was fear. He also felt an impulse to please her and, particularly in later years, condoned her harshness towards him by the thought that she knew no better.

Mr. R. disliked school, was a poor scholar and had few friends in childhood. On leaving school at 16 he was sent to work on a farm, but soon left this to take up ladies' hairdressing. This greatly angered his mother but he continued in this career notwithstanding her objections.

At the time of puberty, Mr. R. found himself attracted to men, although at first socially rather than sexually. As he became older, he experienced no sexual attraction for women and when they occasionally made advances towards him he became extremely anxious and experienced no sexual arousal. In contrast, he found pleasure in the company of men and had formed a succession of attachments to men with whom he had sexual relations. But he thought homosexuality sinful and shameful, and became increasingly anxious about his sexual behavior. He had struggled against his homosexual inclinations and behavior and tried unsuccessfully to fortify himself with religious advice and practices. Failure to master his homosexual impulses along with family stresses, had led to mounting anxiety from which he had sought relief by emigrating to South Africa when he was 30. He thought that such a drastic geographical change might effect a psychological change. However, this did not occur, and in South Africa he found himself continuing homosexual behavior in unstable relationships and experiencing the rising anxiety which finally brought him to treatment.

The above history required nearly five interviews. These did not discover any causal sexual trauma, did not elicit any emotions of marked intensity and were not accompanied by any change in the patient's condition. Toward the end of the fifth interview, because it seemed clear that his excessive devotion to religious matters was responsible for many of his stresses, an effort was made to provide a different perspective and he was given a copy of Winwood Reade's *Martyrdom of Man* to read. At his sixth interview a week later he reported having read the book; and though upset by the criticisms of religion at first, he felt afterwards that his ideas about it had been clarified. He could see that he had taken sin, particularly in relation to sexuality, too seriously. His reactions in many common social situations were discussed and it became evident that in most of them he was extremely fearful and submissive. He found arguments of any kind so unpleasant that he would avoid them at almost any cost. If a customer at the beauty shop made an unjust criticism of him he would let her get away with it and feel helpless and tearful. He had lent considerable sums of money to certain of his friends and was quite unable to ask for repayment, even after a year or two had elapsed since the loan.

The mode of development of unadaptive fears was explained to him, and its therapeutic implications. The five interviews of the next two months were devoted to guiding him in the use of assertive behavior for overcoming his social fears. He proved an apt pupil and soon became much more firm and positive in all his behavior. In two months, his symptoms had almost completely disappeared and he was almost always completely at ease with his customers. In the meantime, he had formed a couple of new homosexual attachments, each of which, although satisfying while it lasted, had petered out in less than a month. He asked whether I could help him overcome his homosexuality; I gave a negative answer, because Kallman's (1952) twin studies had then convinced me that it had a genetic basis.

Mr. R. did not come again until August 23, (i.e., after an interval of two months). He had continued to advance in the handling of his personal relationships and had been free from symptoms. The quality of his work had greatly improved and as a consequence, his clientele had practically doubled. He had been offered an administrative post which would begin a year later at a mission hospital in one of the African tribal reserves, and had been enthusiastically studying to equip himself for it.

When next seen on October 18, he said that he had again felt considerably depressed in the past two weeks because of uncertainties associated with the mission hospital job. The mission people were not particularly cooperative and if the project fell through all his study would be in vain. At the same time, though better than ever at hairdressing, he was becoming dissatisfied with his present billet because of the generally uninteresting clientele as well as a feeling that it was rather pointless and no real service to humanity. He was told that any work that ministered to human needs constituted a service, and was advised to give up the idea of going to the mission. A week later he reported feeling much relieved after having told the mission people that he had decided to withdraw. On November 29, he said that he was feeling fine and getting on very well, especially at his work, which was giving him great satisfaction so that he had abandoned the idea of changing. All the same, he was interested to experience what it would be like to work in some other country like England or the United States.

He was seen again eight months later when he told the following story. Since his treatment he had given up worrying about the sexual problem and had been doing just what he pleased. He had formed a very pleasant homosexual association, but after two months had noticed that he was no longer responding to his friend sexually. A week or two later when he tried to have sex with another man to whom he felt attracted, there was similarly a failure to sexual response. "It felt funny." Two or three later attempts with other men also failed and Mr. R. now felt that, "If a man were to touch me I would hit him."

A few months earlier, Mr. R. had met a girl called Jean whom he had found very likeable. She had an attractive personality and many tastes and interests in common with his own, and he had grown fond of her. He had sometimes thought, "I would marry her if I was normal." When his associations with males became unsatisfactory, he began to take Jean out. It was very pleasant, and before long he wanted to see her every day. For about three months the relationship was purely platonic, but one night after a party when they were both slightly drunk and Jean became sentimental he kissed her and found to his surprise that it was pleasant. From this time onward he began to respond to her in a sexual way and one evening became so excited during petting that he was sure he could have had coitus. This kind of reaction had recurred consistently ever since. She easily roused him to erections, and even holding her hand was exciting. Intercourse had not been attempted because she was "not that kind of girl". He asked whether he should go ahead and marry her and was told that no objection could be seen. The next week he reported that Jean would probably accept his proposal of marriage although she had not yet given a definite answer. He felt wonderful and expected at any moment to wake from a dream. He had decided to migrate to England and said that if they married Jean was willing to accompany him. It was confirmed at this interview that he had previously not felt the slightest physical attraction towards women, although he had always liked their company. In his male associations he had taken the active role on about ninety percent of occasions.

Because of his inexperience with courtship, Mr. R. sadly mishandled his affair with Jean, arousing her resistance by unbridled eagerness. When next seen late in July 1955, (at his 21st interview) he reported that she had rejected him, to his great distress, and he was consequently soon leaving for England on his own. Parting advice to him was to make love only to women to whom he felt some positive attraction.

In January 1956, he wrote a letter from London. He said that after a party he had taken a woman home who had suggested that he spend the night with her, but he had refused on the grounds of tiredness. However, a few nights later he had had dinner at her apartment and, at the end of a pleasant evening, she had suggested that he spend the night with her. Although strongly attracted, he had felt very much afraid, excused himself, and got up to go home. But when he opened the front door it was raining heavily. He decided to go to bed with her and risk the chagrin of failure. To his delight, however, his sexual performance was completely successful. At the time of writing he had made love to this woman almost every night for a month, always with complete success, and with greater enjoyment than he had ever experienced with men. He was jubilant. He regarded this as his final vindication, feeling that he need now never again feel inferior to other men.

I had follow-up interviews with Mr. R. in 1956 and again in 1957. He had continued to be free from neurotic reactions, remained completely heterosexual and had begun part-time studies in business administration.

In January 1959, I received a letter from him stating that he had married a South American girl. His sex life was still in every way satisfactory, and his wife was expecting a baby.

The favorable sequence of events is explained as follows. Mr. R's anxieties evidently originated in his childhood association with his harsh, perpetually screaming mother. Although he was fearful and apologetic towards everybody, men were further than women along the gradient of generalization from his mother. During adolescence he had a pleasant feeling of warmth and affection towards men, which naturally inclined him to seek a greater closeness with which was bound up the expression of his sexual impulses. Sexual satisfaction with men reinforced his tendencies to consort with them. Direct instigation of assertive behavior with a wide range of individuals led to an extinction of his fear of people. When this had been accomplished, and he was able to survey the world of men and women without anxiety, preference for females spontaneously emerged — a preference presumably established by social factors of early life.

Case 13

A Washing Compulsion Overcome by Systematic Desensitization to Urinary "Contamination" Using Both Imaginary and Real Stimuli[4]

Mr. T. was an eighteen-year-old youth with a very severe washing compulsion. The basis of this was a fear of contamination by urine, and most especially his own urine, mainly because he dreaded to contaminate others with it. When the treatment to be described began, the patient was almost completely impotentiated by his neurosis. After urinating, he would spend up to 45 minutes in an elaborate ritual of cleaning up his genitalia, followed by about two hours of hand washing. When he woke in the morning, his first need was to shower, which took him about four hours to do. To these 'basic requirements' of his neurosis were added many others occasioned by the incidental contaminations inevitable on any day. It is scarcely surprising that Mr. T. had come to conclude that getting up was not worth the effort, and for two months had spent most of his time in bed.

[4]This case first published in slightly different form in a paper on complex neurotic states (Wolpe, 1964).

The neurosis evidently originated in an unusual domestic situation. Until he was 15, Mr. T.'s parents had compelled him to share a bed with his sister, two years older, because she had a fear of being alone. The very natural erotic responses aroused by this kind of proximity to the girl had made him feel very guilty and ashamed. Anger towards his parents for imposing this on him led to hostile and at times destructive phantasies about them. Horrified at these, he had come to regard himself as despicable. His urine had subsequently become the prime focus of his 'repulsiveness'.

Treatment in the first place consisted of conventional desensitization. Since he was even disturbed at the idea of anybody else's independent contamination with urine, the first scene he was asked to imagine was the sight of an unknown man dipping his hand into a forty cubic foot trough of water into which one drop of urine had been deposited. Even this scene produced some disturbance in Mr. T. at first, but it waned and disappeared in the course of a few presentations. The concentration of urine was then 'increased' until the man was imagined to be inserting his hand into pure urine. At each stage a particular scene was repeated until it no longer evoked any anxiety.

During the course of these procedures, which occupied about five months of sessions taking place about five times a week and lasting, as a rule, about twenty minutes, there was considerable improvement in Mr. T.'s clinical condition. For example, his handwashing time went down to about 30 minutes and his shower time to just over an hour; and he no longer found it necessary to interpose the *New York Times* between himself and his chair during interviews.

A new series of imaginary situations was now started in which Mr. T. himself was inserting his hand into increasingly concentrated solutions of urine. During this time it became evident that there was diminishing transfer between what Mr. T. could imagine himself doing and what he actually could do. Whereas he could unperturbedly imagine himself immersing his hand in pure urine, to do so in actuality was out of the question.

It was therefore decided to resort to desensitization *in vivo* (p. 161). Relaxation was to be opposed to increasingly strong *real* stimuli evoking anxiety. Accordingly, Mr. T. was, to begin with, exposed to the word "urine" printed in big block letters. This evoked a little anxiety which he was asked to relax away. The next step was to put him at one end of a long room and a closed bottle of urine at the other end. Again, he had to relax away the anxiety; and then step by step the bottle of urine was moved closer until eventually he was handling it with only minimal anxiety which again he was able to relax away. When the bottle of urine was no longer capable of evoking anxiety, the next series of manoeuvres was started. First of all, a very dilute solution of urine (1 drop to a gallon) was applied to the back of his hand and he was made to relax until all anxiety disappeared; and then, from session to session the concentration was gradually increased. When he was able to endure pure urine, his own urine began to be used; and finally, he was made to 'contaminate' all kinds of objects with his uriniferous hands — magazines, doorknobs, and people's hands.

The numerous acts of desensitization outlined were completed at the end of June 1961. By then Mr. T. had achieved greatly increased freedom of movement; he was dressing daily, his hand washing time had gone down to 7 minutes and his shower time to 40 minutes, and his cleaning-up ritual was almost eliminated. In September 1961, he went back to school and was seen only occasionally until March 1962. During this time, without active treatment, he made virtually no further progress. In March 1962, he began weekly sessions and improvement was resumed. When last seen in June 1962, his handwashing time was 3 minutes and his shower time 20 minutes. He said that he was coming to think of urine as "sticky and smelly and nothing else". In February 1965, he reported that handwashing took him about 10 seconds, and he "wasn't even using soap." He was leading a normal life. In September 1967, a telephone call conveyed that his recovery had been maintained.

CHAPTER XIV

Evaluation of
Behavior Therapy

Psychotherapists very easily acquire a belief in the efficacy of their own methods because, as has repeatedly been shown (e.g. Landis, 1937; Wilder, 1945; Eysenck, 1952), forty percent or more of neurotic patients improve markedly with conventional therapies (not behavior therapy) despite widely differing theories and practices. Success with this degree of frequency provides more than enough intermittent reinforcement to maintain therapeutic habits very strongly. But the fact that the beneficial effects are rather uniform indicates that they are not attributable to specific features of the individual therapies, but to some process that is common to all of them — presumably the emotional impact on the patient of the therapist, a trusted and supposedly wise and competent person to whom he entrusts himself. Nobody who is aware of these non-specific therapeutic effects should claim special potency for his particular practices unless they yield either a percentage of recoveries substantially above the common average or greater rapidity of recovery.

Thus the only basis on which behavior therapy could justifiably displace the present widely-accepted and well-organized psychoanalytically-oriented practices would be evidence that it is substantially more effective in overcoming neurotic disturbances, psychotherapy's most rewarding target. It is because there are factual grounds for believing that behavior therapy does exceed the common average in *both* percentage and speed of recoveries that its techniques are confidently offered in this volume. This confidence falls short of the assurance that would be engendered if we could point to impeccably controlled and replicated clinical trials supporting the methods, but it is a considerable confidence, based partly on impressive clinical experience, and partly on a few very well controlled experimental studies.

CLINICAL STUDIES

An increasing number of reports of the successful treatment of individual cases or small groups treated by behavior therapy have been appearing during the past decade. Many of them have been conveniently brought together in two volumes edited by Eysenck (1960, 1964). A feature of these case reports that is unusual in the literature of psychotherapy is that they almost invariably display *clear temporal relationships between specific interventions and therapeutic change.*[1] This, together with a highly predictable replicability of effects is really more impressive than any statistical comparisons at present available.

[1] The cases in Chapter XIII are typical.

There have been several uncontrolled statistical studies. In my survey (1958) of the results of a private practice of behavior therapy, 89 per cent of 210 patients had either apparently recovered or were at least 80 per cent improved in a mean of about 30 therapeutic sessions. The criteria were those suggested by Knight (1941) (see page 275). No case diagnosed as neurotic was refused treatment if time was available. Psychotics and psychopaths were not knowingly accepted, and, if treated through error of diagnosis, were transferred to other therapists when the mistake was discovered. Lazarus (1963) reported that of 408 patients who consulted him, 321 (78 per cent), derived marked benefit on "very stringent criteria".

TABLE 6.

UNCONTROLLED OUTCOME STUDIES OF DIFFERENT
TYPES OF THERAPY

Series	No. of Cases	Apparently cured or much Improved	Percentage recoveries
Behavior Therapy			
Wolpe (1958)	210	188	89.5
Lazarus (1963)	408	321	78.0
Psychoanalytic Therapy			
(Brody, 1962) Completely analyzed cases only	210	126	60
General Hospital Therapy			
(Hamilton and Wall, 1941)	100	53	53

Note: The *total* patient population in the psychoanalytic group was 595.

Table 6, comparing the results of the foregoing two studies with those of a typical series from a general hospital, and two psychoanalytic series, shows a substantially higher percentage of recoveries for behavior therapy. However, the series are not matched and therefore the validity of the comparison can be disputed. A controlled comparison would nevertheless not necessarily be more favorable to psychoanalysis. More important than the relative percentages is the fact that the number of sessions spent in therapy is overwhelmingly in favor of behavior therapy. The mean number for psychoanalysis is in the region of 600 — 3 or 4 times a week for 3 or 4 years (Masserman, 1963); while the mean for behavior therapy is about 30. The practical implication of the contrast seems inescapable.

The following uncontrolled statistical reports on the results of behavior therapy are of interest but really do not have much evaluative relevance to the battery of techniques described in this book — for reasons that will be given. Hussain (1964) has claimed a 95 per cent "complete or almost complete removal of symptoms" in 105 patients whose disturbed habits were treated by hypnotic suggestions based on the reciprocal inhibition principle; but the details of his method are not very clear, and the criteria of change are not reported in detail. Burnett and Ryan (1964) treated 100 patients by giving them relaxation training, and desensitization to both imaginary and real situations — in groups, and sometimes individually. Treatment continued for 5 weeks on the average. A one-year follow-up could only be carried out on 25 of the patients, of whom 15 (60 percent) were found to be either apparently cured or much improved. The brief exposure of the patients to behavior therapy, and the predominance of group procedures tends to bias the outcome negatively because they do not permit a full exploitation of the resources available. Nevertheless, the 60 per cent recovery rate after such brief therapy, seems quite noteworthy; and the authors were encouraged by their findings.

McConaghy (1964) having obtained a much lower improvement rate with behavior therapy than any of the foregoing, states that his results contrast "very unfavorably with Wolpe's". Of 18 patients he treated, four were markedly improved and five moderately so. These rather poor figures are not surprising in the light of the following facts. Fifteen of McConaghy's 18 cases had failed to respond to, or were considered unsuitable for, conventional psychiatric treatment; at least three were psychotic; avoidance therapy was used in no less than six of the remainder without any prior attempt to decondition underlying emotional reactions; and when treatment was instituted on the desensitization model it was always *in vivo* — which makes it difficult to ensure control of inhibition of anxiety.

Controlled Comparative Studies of Outcome

There have been several controlled outcome studies comparing systematic desensitization with various forms of nonbehavioristic psychotherapy. Lazarus (1961) compared the results of treating phobias, such as claustrophobia (fear of enclosed spaces) and acrophobia (fear of heights), by two different forms of group therapy. The patients were separated into matched pairs, and then by the toss of a coin one member of a pair was placed in a desensitization group and the other in a conventional 'dynamic' group. After 21 sessions, 72 per cent of the patients in the desensitization groups had recovered, compared with 12 per cent in the 'dynamic' groups.

Paul (1965) in an ingeniously designed experiment, compared desensitization with two other methods in the treatment of students with severe fears of speaking in public. He enlisted the services of five experienced psychotherapists whose 'school' affiliation ranged from Freud to Sullivan. Nine cases were allotted to each therapist who was required to use three different methods — each in three subjects. The methods were (1) the therapist's own customary type of insight therapy; (2) a stylized procedure involving suggestion and support called "attention-placebo" therapy; and (3) systematic desensitization, which the therapist had to be trained to administer. Each patient received five therapeutic sessions. The results showed significantly superior effectiveness for systematic desensitization on a variety of measures. In terms of conventional clinical change (Table 7), 86 per cent of the patients treated by desensitization were much improved and 14 per cent improved. This compares with 20 per cent much improved and 27 per cent improved for the insight group. In the attention placebo group none were much improved and 47 per cent improved.

Another noteworthy series of controlled investigations is due to Lang and Lazovik (1963) and Lang, Lazovik and Reynolds (1965). Their subjects were students who had severe phobic reactions to harmless snakes. They treated some of them by systematic desensitization, and compared the results with those of two control groups — one that received no treatment and another that received "pseudotherapy" (i.e. relaxation training followed by interviews focusing on problems of 'living', with the patient in a state of relaxation.) The desensitized students improved very much more than either of the

TABLE 7.

PERCENTAGE BREAKDOWN OF CASES IN TRADITIONAL
"IMPROVEMENT" CATEGORIES FROM STRESS CONDITION DATA

Treatment Group N	Unimproved		"Improvement" Classification		
			Slightly Improved	Improved	Much Improved
Desensitization	15	—	—	14%	86%
Insight	15	7%	4%	27%	20%
Attention-Placebo	15	20%	33%	47%	—
Treatment-Control	29	55%	28%	17%	—

Gordon L. Paul (1966)

TABLE 8.

T-TESTS OF MEAN FEAR CHANGE SCORES FROM
PRE- TO POST-TREATMENT IN SNAKE PHOBIAS

Groups	Avoidance test	Fear thermometer	FSS No. 38	Fear survey
Combined control vs. Desensitization	2.57*	2.12*	2.19*	1.25
Combined control vs. 15 or more	3.26†	3.44†	3.99‡	2.52*
Combined control vs. Less than 15	0.14	0.41	1.85	0.41
Less than 15 vs. 15 or more	2.33*	3.28*	5.00‡	2.26*
Pseudotherapy vs. No treatment	1.67	0.48	0.58	0.12

*d < 0.05. † p < 0.01. ‡ p < 0.001.
Lang, Lazovik and Reynolds, *J. Abnorm. Psychol.* (1965).

control groups as shown by a snake avoidance test, and by the patient's self-rating of fear reaction to snakes (Table 8.) The difference is significant at the 0.001 level when 15 or more hierarchy items have been desensitized.

Moore (1965) is the author of the first well-planned and well-executed controlled investigation dealing with patients applying for treatment at a clinic. She used a balanced incomplete block design (in which the patients are their own controls) to compare the effects on cases of asthma of 3 forms of treatment — 1. reciprocal inhibition therapy; 2. relaxation therapy; 3. relaxation combined with suggestion. During the first 4 weeks of treatment, both subjectively, and objectively as measured by maximum peak flow of respired air, all three groups improved, but the reciprocal inhibition group more than the others. After this time, progress continued in the reciprocal inhibition group, while the other two began to regress. Eight weeks from the beginning of treatment, in terms of maximum peak flow, the difference in degree of improvement of the reciprocal inhibition group was significant at the .001 level (Fig. 12).

In contrast to the above are the 'controlled studies' of Cooper (1963), Gelder, Marks, Sakinovsky and Wolff (1964) and Gelder and Marks (1965) which purport to compare the results in clinical practice, of behavior therapy with those of conventional 'dynamic' psychotherapy. Though their work is conscientious, it has serious flaws, some of which, biassing it negatively against behavior therapy, will be mentioned.[2] A behavior analysis, such as described in this book, is not generally performed, the 'deconditioning' being on the whole applied to the patient's complaints as presented. Desen-

[2]The comments that follow are partly based on personal correspondence with Dr. M. G. Gelder.

sitization *in vivo* is almost the exclusive technique in contrast to the considerable range that a well-schooled behavior therapist can offer. The therapists who carried out the behavior therapy were often unskilled, and sometimes novices. It is significant that in later studies (Gelder *et al*, 1967; Gelder & Marks, 1968), using conventional desensitization, the inexperienced therapists obtained better results than before.

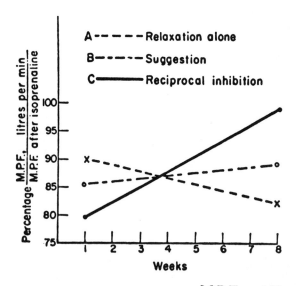

Change in percentage efficiency. $\dfrac{\text{M.P.F.} \times 100.}{\text{M.P.F. after isoprenaline.}}$

Fig. 12. Comparative effects of three treatment schedules on maximum peak flow of inspired air in asthmatic patients (Moore, 1965).

THE CRITERIA OF THERAPEUTIC CHANGE

The central goal of psychotherapy is the same as that of any other branch of therapeutics — the lasting removal of the sources of suffering and disability. Since the behavior therapist views the therapeutic task as a matter of eliminating persistent unadaptive *habits*, an appropriate way of measuring his success would be to classify and enumerate the unadaptive habits before therapy, and then, after therapy, to assess to what extent each habit has been eliminated. In making such assessments the therapist can employ several kinds of information — the report of the patient, clinical observation, the observations of the patient's associates, and psychophysiological studies. The last-named are basic, and necessarily figure prominently in research.

The clinical criteria for therapeutic change that have been generally adopted by behavior therapists are those delineated by Knight (1941.) They are potentially useful for comparative outcome research, and were in fact proposed for the purpose of improving psychoanalytic research. Knight's criteria are as follows:

1. Symptomatic improvement
2. Increased productiveness at work
3. Improved adjustment and pleasure in sex
4. Improved interpersonal relationships
5. Enhanced ability to handle ordinary psychological conflicts and reasonable reality stresses.

One or more of these criteria are relevant to all cases of neurosis. "Symptomatic improvement" is almost always relevant, but a neurosis need not interfere with all or any of the specified functions. A man with neurotic anxieties in work situations may have a completely satisfying sex life and be at ease in social situations.

"Symptomatic improvement" in this context does not mean palliation by means such as drugs, but *fundamental* change in the sense that the stimuli that used to call forth inappropriate anxiety or other unadaptive responses no longer can do so *under the same conditions*. What the patient perceives as a symptom, the therapist perceives as a habit. By deconditioning the anxiety-response habit that is the basis of the anxiety symptom, he brings about a commensurate diminution of the symptom. If there have been other reactions that have depended on the presence of the anxiety, they, too, diminish or cease — whether they have appeared in the form of migraine, asthma, neurodermatitis, fibrositis, stammering, frigidity, impotence or homosexuality. The decline of the secondary manifestations of neurosis can thus also be used as a measure of improvement. Moore's investigation of the treatment of asthma (p. 273) provides a good example of this. See also Table 1, pp. 24-25.

There is one major reform that should be incorporated into future outcome studies. Marks and Gelder (1965) have drawn attention to the confusing consequences of the traditional practice of lumping together all kinds of neuroses. Although categorization is not always easy, particularly in cases with complex neuroses, it would facilitate comparisons, and make it possible to determine to what extent different syndromes may require different measures. The customary practice of comparing different therapies on the basis of their effects on widely differing assortments of phobias, tics, sexual deviations, and so forth must present a strange spectacle to the scientific outside observer. Actually, it is a practice that is due to the general acceptance of psychoanalytic theory, which plays down the outward features of neuroses in the belief that the 'real' pathology is 'inside'.

IS BEHAVIOR THERAPY SUPERFICIAL?

The opinion is frequently expressed that the effects of behavior therapy are "superficial" and do not remove the basic neurosis, and that relapse and symptom substitution are to be expected. This opinion presupposes the truth of the psychoanalytic view of neurosis — a view which there are many reasons to doubt (Wohlgemuth 1923, Salter 1952, Eysenck 1953, Wolpe and Rachman 1960, Wolpe 1961a). After behavior therapy has been successful, recurrence of symptoms is very unusual. Every instance of it that has been investigated has been clearly found to be due to re-conditioning. The only 'relapse' among the 45 patients followed up from two to seven years that I reported in 1958 was in a man who was known to be seeing another psychiatrist. Symptom substitution is only found when therapy is carried out without attention to the autonomic core of neurotic reactions. (See pp. 24-26 and also some of McConaghy's (1964) cases referred to above).

A related question is whether behavior therapy is able to effect 'personality change'. If personality is defined as a person's totality of habits, it is obvious that the elimination of a neurotic habit is a kind of personality change. When a patient is rid of his neurotic habits, he is usually thereby made more free to behave effectively in various directions. Motor habits, for example, are often changed — movements become easier and more graceful, or stuttering stops, when the patient is freed from neurotic tension. A great variety of possible changes is implied in Table 1 (Chapter III). Those who usually raise this issue of personality change do not, as a rule, trouble to define it. When they do, the way will be open for comparing behavior therapy with psychoanalysis as instruments of 'personality change'.

Another current variation on the "superficiality" theme is that behavior therapy is useful for simple cases but not for complex ones. In 1964 I made a re-examination of some previously published results, dividing 86 cases into simple and complex. A neurosis was regarded as complex if it had one or more of the following features: (a) more than one family of stimuli conditioned to neurotic responses; (b) reactions to which the conditioned stimuli are obscure and determined with difficulty; (c) reactions that include unadaptiveness in important areas of general behavior (character neuroses); (d) obsessional neuroses; and (e) reactions that include pervasive anxiety. Of the 86 cases reviewed, 65 were *complex* in one or more of the senses defined. Fifty-eight of these (89 per cent) were judged either apparently cured or much improved. This percentage was exactly the same as that obtained for the whole group. However, the median number of sessions for the complex group was 29 and the mean 54.8 in contrast to a median for the non-complex remainder of 11.5 and a mean 14.9. Thus while complex cases respond to behavior therapy as often as simple ones do, therapy takes longer.

Willoughby
Personality Schedule

Instructions: The questions in this schedule are intended to indicate various emotional personality traits. It is not a test in any sense because there are no right and wrong answers to any of the questions.

After each question you will find a row of numbers whose meaning is given below. All you have to do is to draw a ring around the number that describes you best.

0 means "No", "never", "not at all", etc.
1 means "Somewhat", "sometimes", "a little", etc.
2 means "About as often as not", "an average amount", etc.
3 means "Usually", "a good deal", "rather often", etc.
4 means "Practically always", "entirely", etc.

1. Do you get stage fright? — 0 1 2 3 4
2. Do you worry over humiliating experiences? — 0 1 2 3 4
3. Are you afraid of falling when you are on a high place? — 0 1 2 3 4
4. Are your feelings easily hurt? — 0 1 2 3 4
5. Do you keep in the background on social occasions? — 0 1 2 3 4
6. Are you happy and sad by turns without knowing why? — 0 1 2 3 4
7. Are you shy? — 0 1 2 3 4

8. Do you day-dream frequently? — 0 1 2 3 4

9. Do you get discouraged easily? — 0 1 2 3 4

10. Do you say things on the spur of the moment and then regret them? — 0 1 2 3 4

11. Do you like to be alone? — 0 1 2 3 4

12. Do you cry easily? — 0 1 2 3 4

13. Does it bother you to have people watch you work even when you do it well? — 0 1 2 3 4

14. Does criticism hurt you badly? — 0 1 2 3 4

15. Do you cross the street to avoid meeting someone? — 0 1 2 3 4

16. At a reception or tea do you avoid meeting the important person present? — 0 1 2 3 4

17. Do you often feel just miserable? — 0 1 2 3 4

18. Do you hesitate to volunteer in a class discussion or debate? — 0 1 2 3 4

19. Are you often lonely? — 0 1 2 3 4

20. Are you self-conscious before superiors? — 0 1 2 3 4

21. Do you lack self-confidence? — 0 1 2 3 4

22. Are you self-conscious about your appearance? — 0 1 2 3 4

23. If you see an accident does something keep you from giving help? — 0 1 2 3 4

24. Do you feel inferior? — 0 1 2 3 4

25. Is it hard to make up your mind until the time for action is past? — 0 1 2 3 4

Revised Willoughby
Questionnaire For
Self-Administration

Instructions: The questions in this schedule are intended to indicate various emotional personality traits. It is not a test in any sense because there are no right and wrong answers to any of the questions.

After each question you will find a row of numbers whose meaning is given below. All you have to do is to draw a ring around the number that describes you best.

0 means "No", "never", "not at all", etc.
1 means "Somewhat", "sometimes", "a little", etc.
2 means "About as often as not", "an average amount", etc.
3 means "Usually", "a good deal", "rather often", etc.
4 means "Practically always", "entirely", etc.

1. Do you get anxious if you have to speak or perform in any way in front of a group of strangers? — 0 1 2 3 4

2. Do you worry if you make a fool of yourself, or feel you have been made to look foolish? — 0 1 2 3 4

3. Are you afraid of falling when you are on a high place from which there is no real danger of falling — for example, looking down from a balcony on the tenth floor? — 0 1 2 3 4

4. Are you easily hurt by what other people do or say to you? — 0 1 2 3 4

5. Do you keep in the background on social occasions? — 0 1 2 3 4

6. Do you have changes of mood that you cannot explain? — 0 1 2 3 4

7. Do you feel uncomfortable when you meet new people? — 0 1 2 3 4

8. Do you daydream frequently, i.e. indulge in fantasies not involving concrete situations? — 0 1 2 3 4

9. Do you get discouraged easily, e.g. by failure or criticism? — 0 1 2 3 4

10. Do you say things in haste and then regret them? — 0 1 2 3 4

11. Are you ever disturbed by the mere presence of other people? — 0 1 2 3 4

12. Do you cry easily? — 0 1 2 3 4

13. Does it bother you to have people watch you work even when you do it well? — 0 1 2 3 4

14. Does criticism hurt you badly? — 0 1 2 3 4

15. Do you cross the street to avoid meeting someone? — 0 1 2 3 4

16. At a reception or tea do you go out of your way to avoid meeting the important person present? — 0 1 2 3 4

17. Do you often feel just miserable? — 0 1 2 3 4

18. Do you hesitate to volunteer in a discussion or debate with a group of people whom you know more or less? — 0 1 2 3 4

19. Do you have a sense of isolation, either when alone or among people? — 0 1 2 3 4

20. Are you self-conscious before 'superiors' (teachers, employers, authorities)? — 0 1 2 3 4

21. Do you lack confidence in your general ability to do things and to cope with situations? — 0 1 2 3 4

22. Are you self-conscious about your appearance even when you are well-dressed and groomed? — 0 1 2 3 4

23. Are you scared at the sight of blood, injuries, and destruction even though there is no danger to you? — 0 1 2 3 4

24. Do you feel that other people are better than you? — 0 1 2 3 4

25. Is it hard for you to make up your mind? — 0 1 2 3 4

Fear Inventory

The items in this questionnaire refer to things and experiences that may cause fear or other unpleasant feelings. Write the number of each item in the column that describes how much you are disturbed by it nowadays.

	Not At All	A Little	A Fair Amount	Much	Very Much
1. Noise of vacuum cleaners					
2. Open wounds					
3. Being alone					
4. Being in a strange place					
5. Loud voices					
6. Dead people					
7. Speaking in public					
8. Crossing streets					
9. People who seem insane					
10. Falling					
11. Automobiles					
12. Being teased					
13. Dentists					
14. Thunder					
15. Sirens					
16. Failure					

	Not At All	A Little	A Fair Amount	Much	Very Much
17. Entering a room where other people are already seated					
18. High places on land					
19. Looking down from high buildings					
20. Worms					
21. Imaginary creatures					
22. Strangers					
23. Receiving Injection					
24. Bats					
25. Journeys by train					
26. Journeys by bus					
27. Journeys by car					
28. Feeling angry					
29. People in authority					
30. Flying insects					
31. Seeing other people injected					
32. Sudden noises					
33. Dull weather					
34. Crowds					
35. Large open spaces					
36. Cats					
37. One person bullying another					
38. Tough looking people					
39. Birds					
40. Sight of deep water					
41. Being watched working					
42. Dead animals					
43. Weapons					
44. Dirt					
45. Crawling insects					
46. Sight of fighting					
47. Ugly people					

	Not At All	A Little	A Fair Amount	Much	Very Much
48. Fire					
49. Sick people					
50. Dogs					
51. Being criticized					
52. Strange shapes					
53. Being in an elevator					
54. Witnessing surgical operations					
55. Angry people					
56. Mice					
57. Blood a — Human b — Animal					
58. Parting from friends					
59. Enclosed places					
60. Prospect of a surgical operation					
61. Feeling rejected by others					
62. Airplanes					
63. Medical odors					
64. Feeling disapproved of					
65. Harmless snakes					
66. Cemeteries					
67. Being ignored					
68. Darkness					
69. Premature heart beats (Missing a beat)					
70. Nude Men (a) Nude Women (b)					
71. Lightning					
72. Doctors					
73. People with deformities					

	Not At All	A Little	A Fair Amount	Much	Very Much
74. Making mistakes					
75. Looking foolish					
76. Losing control					
77. Fainting					
78. Becoming nauseous					
79. Spiders					
80. Being in charge or responsible for decisions					
81. Sight of knives or sharp objects					
82. Becoming mentally ill					
83. Being with a member of the opposite sex					
84. Taking written tests					
85. Being touched by others					
86. Feeling different from others					
87. A lull in conversation					

Bernreuter S-S Scale
& Scoring Key

1. Yes No ? Would you rather work for yourself than carry out the program of a superior whom you respect?
2. Yes No ? Do you usually enjoy spending an evening alone?
3. Yes No ? Have books been more entertaining to you than companions?
4. Yes No ? Do you feel the need of wider social contacts than you have?
5. Yes No ? Are you easily discouraged when the opinions of others differ from your own?
6. Yes No ? Does admiration gratify you more than achievement?
7. Yes No ? Do you usually prefer to keep your opinions to yourself?
8. Yes No ? Do you dislike attending the movies alone?
9. Yes No ? Would you like to have a very congenial friend with whom you could plan daily activities?
10. Yes No ? Can you calm your own fears?
11. Yes No ? Do jeers humiliate you even when you know you are right?
12. Yes No ? Do you think you could become so absorbed in creative work that you would not notice the lack of intimate friends?

13. Yes No ? Are you willing to take a chance alone in a situation of doubtful outcome?

14. Yes No ? Do you find conversation more helpful in formulating your ideas than reading?

15. Yes No ? Do you like to shop alone?

16. Yes No ? Does your ambition need occasional stimulation through contacts with successful people?

17. Yes No ? Do you have difficulty in making up your mind for yourself?

18. Yes No ? Would you prefer making your own arrangements on a trip to a foreign country to going on a prearranged trip?

19. Yes No ? Are you much affected by praise, or blame, of many people?

20. Yes No ? Do you usually avoid taking advice?

21. Yes No ? Do you consider the observance of social customs and manners an essential aspect of life?

22. Yes No ? Do you want someone with you when you receive bad news?

23. Yes No ? Does it make you uncomfortable to be 'different' or unconventional?

24. Yes No ? Do you prefer to make hurried decisions alone?

25. Yes No ? If you were to start out in research work would you prefer to be an assistant in another's project rather than an independent worker on your own?

26. Yes No ? When you are low in spirits do you try to find someone to cheer you up?

27. Yes No ? Have you preferred being alone most of the time?

28. Yes No ? Do you prefer traveling with someone who will make all the necessary arrangements to the adventure of traveling alone?

29. Yes No ? Do you usually work things out rather than get someone to show you?

30. Yes No ? Do you like especially to have attention from acquaintances when you are ill?

31. Yes No ? Do you prefer to face dangerous situations alone?

32. Yes No ? Can you usually see wherein your mistakes lie without having them pointed out to you?

33. Yes No ? Do you like to make friends when you go to new places?

34. Yes No ? Can you stick to a tiresome task for long without someone prodding or encouraging you?

35. Yes No ? Do you experience periods of loneliness?

36. Yes No ? Do you like to get many views from others before making an important decision?

37. Yes No ? Would you dislike any work which might take you into isolation for a few years, such as forest ranging, etc.?

38. Yes No ? Do you prefer a play to a dance?

39. Yes No ? Do you usually try to take added responsibility upon yourself?

40. Yes No ? Do you make friends easily?

41. Yes No ? Can you be optimistic when others about you are greatly depressed?

42. Yes No ? Do you try to get your own way even if you have to fight for it?

43. Yes No ? Do you like to be with other people a great deal?

44. Yes No ? Do you get as many ideas at the time of reading as you do from a discussion of it afterwards?

45. Yes No ? In sports do you prefer to participate in individual competitions rather than in team games?

46. Yes No ? Do you usually face your troubles alone without seeking help?

47. Yes No ? Do you see more fun or humor in things when you are in a group than when you are alone?

48. Yes No ? Do you dislike finding your way about in strange places?

49. Yes No ? Can you work happily without praise or recognition?

50. Yes No ? Do you feel that marriage is essential to your happiness?

51. Yes No ? If all but a few of your friends threatened to break relations because of some habit they considered a vice in you, and in which you saw no harm, would you stop the habit to keep friends?

52. Yes No ? Do you like to have suggestions offered to you when you are working a puzzle?

53. Yes No ? Do you usually prefer to do your own planning alone rather than with others?
54. Yes No ? Do you usually find that people are more stimulating to you than anything else?
55. Yes No ? Do you prefer to be alone at times of emotional stress?
56. Yes No ? Do you like to bear responsibilities alone?
57. Yes No ? Can you usually understand a problem better by studying it out alone than by discussing it with others?
58. Yes No ? Do you find that telling others of your own personal good news is the greatest part of the enjoyment of it?
59. Yes No ? Do you generally rely on your judgment?
60. Yes No ? Do you like playing games in which you have no spectators?

Bernreuter Key *

1. Yes No ?
2. Yes No ?
3. Yes No ?
4. Yes No ?
5. Yes No ?
6. Yes No ?
7. Yes No ?
8. Yes No ?
9. Yes No ?
10. Yes No ?
11. Yes No ?
12. Yes No ?
13. Yes No ?
14. Yes No ?
15. Yes No ?
16. Yes No ?
17. Yes No ?
18. Yes No ?
19. Yes No ?
20. Yes No ?
21. Yes No ?
22. Yes No ?
23. Yes No ?
24. Yes No ?
25. Yes No ?
26. Yes No ?
27. Yes No ?
28. Yes No ?
29. Yes No ?
30. Yes No ?
31. Yes No ?
32. Yes No ?
33. Yes No ?
34. Yes No ?
35. Yes No ?
36. Yes No ?
37. Yes No ?
38. Yes No ?
39. Yes No ?
40. Yes No ?
41. Yes No ?
42. Yes No ?
43. Yes No ?
44. Yes No ?
45. Yes No ?
46. Yes No ?
47. Yes No ?
48. Yes No ?
49. Yes No ?
50. Yes No ?
51. Yes No ?
52. Yes No ?
53. Yes No ?
54. Yes No ?
55. Yes No ?
56. Yes No ?
57. Yes No ?
58. Yes No ?
59. Yes No ?
60. Yes No ?

* Underlined answer scores one point.

Bibliography

ABRAHAM, D. (1963) Treatment of encopresis with imipramine, *Amer. J. Psychiat. 119*:891.

AHSEN, A. (1965) *Eidetic Psychotherapy*, Lahore, India, Nai Matboat Press.

ANANT, S. (1967) A note on the treatment of alcoholics by a verbal aversion technique, *Canad. Psychol. 80*:19.

ARNOLD, M. B. (1945) The physiological differentiation of emotional states, *Psychol. Rev. 52*:35.

ASHEM, B. and DONNER, L. (1968) Covert sensitization with alcoholics: a controlled replication, *Behav. Res. Ther. 6*:7.

AX, A. F. (1953) The physiological differentiation of anger and fear in humans, *Psychosom. Med. 15*:433.

AYLLON, T. (1963) Intensive treatment of psychotic behavior by stimulus satiation and food reinforcement, *Behav. Res. Ther. 1*:53.

AYLLON, T. and AZRIN, N. H. (1968) *The Token Economy: A Motivational System for Therapy and Rehabilitation*, New York, Appleton, Century, Croft.

AYLLON, T. and MICHAEL, J. (1959) The psychiatric nurse as a behavioral engineer, *J. Exp. Anal. Behav. 2*:323.

AZRIN, N. H. and HOLZ, W. C. (1966) Punishment in W. K. Honig (ed.) *Operant Behavior*, New York, Appleton, Century, Croft.

BACHRACH, A J., ERWIN, W. J., and MOHR, J. P. (1965) The control of eating behavior in an anorexic by operant conditioning techniques, in L. Ullman and L. Krasner (eds.) *Case Studies in Behavior Modification*, New York, Holt, Rhinehart, and Winston.

BAIN, J A. (1928) *Thought Control in Everyday Life*, Funk and Wagnals.

291

BANDURA, A. (1968) Modelling approaches to the modification of phobic disorders in *Ciba Foundation Symposium: The Role of Learning in Psychotherapy,* London: Churchill.

BANDURA, A., BLANCHARD, E. D. and RITTER, B. (1968) The relative efficacy of desensitization and modelling therapeutic approaches for inducing behavioral, affective, and attitudinal changes, Stanford Univ. Unpublished manuscript.

BANDURA, A., GRUSEC, J. and MENLOVE, F. (1967) Vicarious extinction of avoidance behavior, *J. Pers. Soc. Psychol.* 5:16.

BARKER, J. C. and MILLER, M. B. (1968) Recent developments and some future trends in the application of aversion therapy, unpublished manuscript.

BERGER, B. (1968) Personal communication.

BERKUN, M. M. (1957) Factors in the recovery from approach-avoidance conflict, *J. Exp. Psychol.* 54:65.

BLAKEMORE, C. B. (1965) The application of behavior therapy to a sexual disorder in H. J. Eysenck (ed.) *Experiments in Behavior Therapy,* Oxford, Pergamon Press.

BLEWETT, D. B. and CHWELOS, N. (1959) Handbook for the therapeutic use of LSD-25: individual and group procedures, mimeo.

BRADY, J. P. (1966) Brevital-relaxation treatment of frigidity, *Behav. Res. Ther. 4:* 71.

BREGER, L. and McGAUGH, J. L. (1965) Critique and reformulation of "Learning Theory" approaches to psychotherapy and neuroses, *Psychol. Bull. 63:*338

BRODY, M. W. (1962) Prognosis and results of psychoanalysis in J. H. Nodine and J. H. Moyer (eds.) *Psychosomatic Medicine,* Philadelphia, Lea and Febiger.

BURCHARD, J. and TYLER, V. (1965) The modification of delinquent behavior through operant conditioning, *Behav. Res. Ther. 2:*245.

BURNETT, A. and RYAN, E. (1964) Conditioning techniques in psychotherapy, *Canad. Psychiat. Ass. J. 9:*140.

CAMPBELL, D., SANDERSON, R. E. and LAVERTY, S. G. (1964) Characteristics of a conditioned response in human subjects during extinction trials following a single traumatic conditioning trial, *J. Abn. Soc. Psychol. 68:*627.

CAUTELA, J. (1966) Treatment of compulsive behavior by covert sensitization, *Phycol. Rec. 16:33.*

CAUTELA, J. (1967) Covert sensitization, *Psychol. Rep. 20:459.*

CHURCH, R. (1963) The varied effects of punishment, *Psychol. Rev. 70:369.*

CLARK, D. E. (1963) The treatment of monosymptomatic phobia by systematic desensitization, *Behav. Res. Ther. 1:63.*

COOKE, G. (1966) The efficacy of two desensitization procedures: an analogue study, *Behav. Res. Ther. 4:17.*

COOPER, J. E. (1963) A study of behavior therapy, *Lancet 1:411.*

COSTELLO, C. G. (1964) Lysergic acid diethylamide (LSD-25) and behavior therapy, *Behav. Res. Ther. 2:117.*

DALTON, K. (1964) *Pre-menstrual Syndrome,* Springfield, Illinois, Thomas Co.

DAVISON, G. C. (1964) A social learning therapy programme with an autistic child, *Behav. Res. Ther. 2: 149.*

DAVISON, G. C. (1965) The Influence of Systematic Desensitization, Relaxation and Graded Exposure to Imaginal Aversive Stimuli on the Modification of Phobic Behavior, Ph.D. Dissertation, Stanford Univ. Published (1968) under the title, Systematic desensitization as a counterconditioning process, *J. Abn. Psychol. 73:91.*

DAVISON, G. C. (1967) The elimination of a sadistic fantasy by a client-controlled counterconditioning technique, *J. Abn. Psychol. 73:84.*

DENGROVE, E. (1968) Personal communication.

DESTOUNIS, N. (1963) Enuresis and imipramine, *Amer. J. Psychiat. 119:893.*

DROOBY, A. S. (1964) A reliable truce with enuresis, *Dis. Nerv. Syst. 25:97.*

DROOBY, A. S. (1964ª) Personal communication.

DRVOTA,, S. (1962) Personal communication.

DUNLAP, K. (1932) *Habits: Their Making and Unmaking,* New York, Liveright.

DWORKIN, S., RAGINSKY, B. B. and BOURNE, W. (1937) Action of anasthetics and sedatives upon the inhibited nervous system, *Current Res. Anaesth. 16:283.*

ERWIN, W. J. (1963) Confinement in the production of

human neuroses: the barber's chair syndrome, *Behav. Res. Ther.* 1:175.

EYSENCK, H. J. (1952) The effects of psychotherapy: an evaluation, *J. Consult. Psychol.* 16:319.

EYSENCK, H. J. (1957) *The Dynamics of Anxiety and Hysteria,* London, Routledge & Kegan Paul.

EYSENCK, H. J. (1953) *Uses and Abuses of Psychology,* London, Penguin Books.

EYSENCK, H. J. (1959) Learning theory and behavior therapy, *J. Ment. Sci.* 105:61.

EYSENCK, H. J. (1960) *Behavior Therapy and the Neuroses,* Oxford, Pergamon Press.

EYSENCK, H. J. (1963) *Experiments with Drugs,* New York, Pergamon Press.

EYSENCK, H. J. (1964) *Experiments in Behavior Therapy,* Oxford, Pergamon Press.

FARRAR, C. H., POWELL, B. J. and MARTIN, L. K. (1968) Punishment of alcoholic consumption by apneic paralysis, *Behav. Res. Ther.* 6:13.

FEINGOLD, L. (1966) Personal communication.

FELDMAN, M. P. and MAC-CULLOCH, M. J. (1965) The application of anticipatory avoidance learning to the treatment of homosexuality. I. theory, technique and preliminary results, *Behav. Res. Ther.* 2:165.

FELDMAN, M. P. and MAC-CULLOCH, M. J. (1967) Aversion therapy in the management of homosexuals, *Brit. Med. J.* 1:594.

FRANK, J. D. (1961) *Persuasion and Healing,* New York, Shocken Books.

FRANKL, V. (1960) Paradoxical intention: a logotherapeutic technique, *Amer. J. Psychother.* 14:520.

FRANKS, C. M. (1965) *Conditioning Techniques in Clinical Practice and Research,* New York, Springer.

FREEMAN, H. L. and KENDRICK, D. C. (1960) A case of cat phobia: treatment by a method derived from experimental psychology, *Brit. Med. J.* 1:497.

FREUND, K. (1960) Some problems in the treatment of homosexuality in H. J. Eysenck (ed.) *Behavior Therapy and the Neuroses,* Oxford, Pergamon Press.

FRIEDMAN, D. E. (1966) A new technique for the systematic desensitization of phobic symptoms, *Behav. Res. Ther.* 4:139.

FRIEDMAN, D. E. and SIL-
VERSTONE, J. T. (1967)
Treatment of phobic patients
by systematic desensitization, *Lancet 1*:470.

FRY, W. H. (1962) The marital content of an anxiety syndrome, *Family Process 1*:
245.

GARFIELD, Z. H., DARWIN,
P. L. SINGER, B. A. and
McBREARTY, J. F. (1967)
Effect of *in vivo* training
on experimental desensitiza-
tion of a phobia, *Psychol.
Rep. 20*:515.

GELDER, M. G. and MARKS,
I. M. (1965) A controlled ret-
rospective study of behavior
therapy in phobic patients,
Brit. J. Psychiat. 111:561.

GELDER, M. G. and MARKS,
I. M. (1968) Desensitization
and phobias, a cross-over
study, *Brit. J. Psychiat. 114*:
223.

GELDER, M. G., MARKS, I.
M., SAKINVOSKY, I. and
WOLFF, H. H. (1964) Be-
havior therapy and psychotherapy for phobic disorders:
alternative or complement-
ary procedures? Paper read
at Sixth International Cong.
of Psychother, London.

GELDER, M. G., MARKS, I. M.
and WOLFF, H. H. (1967)
Desensitization and psychotherapy in the treatment of
phobic states: a controlled
enquiry, *Brit. J. Psychiat.
113*:53.

GELLHORN, E. (1967) *Princi-
ples of Autonomic-Somatic
Integrations*, Minneapolis,
Univ. Minnesota Press.

GERZ, H. O. (1966) Experience with the logotherapeutic
technique of paradoxical intention in the treatment of
phobic and obsessive-com-
pulsive patients, *Amer. J.
Psychiat. 123*:548.

GETZE, G. (1968) Adverse ap-
peal to senses cuts smoking,
Los Angeles Times. Reprint-
ed by Z. Wanderer, Center
for Behavior Therapy, Bev-
erly Hills, Calif.

GLYNN, J. D. and HARPER,
P. (1961) Behavior therapy
in transvestism, *Lancet 1*:
619.

GOLD, S. and NEUFELD, I.
(1965) A learning theory approach to the treatment of
homosexuality, *Behav. Res.
Ther. 2*:201.

GOLDBERG, J. and D'ZURIL-
LA, T. J. (1968) A demon-
stration of slide projection
as an alternative to imaginal stimulus presentation in
systematic desensitization
therapy, *Psychol. Reps.*, In
Press.

GRANVILLE-GROSSMAN, K.
L. and TURNER, P. (1966)
The effect of propranolol on
anxiety, *Lancet 1*:788.

GRAY, J. A. (1964) *Pavlov's Typology,* Oxford, Pergamon Press.

GRINKER, R. R. and SPIEGEL, J. P. (1945) *War Neuroses,* Philadelphia, Blakiston.

GUTHRIE, E. R. (1935) *The Psychology of Human Learning,* New York, Harper & Bros.

GUTTMACHER, A. F. (1961) *Complete Book of Birth Control,* New York, Ballantine.

HAMILTON, D. M. and WALL, J. H. (1941) Hospital treatment of patients with psychosomatic disorders, *Amer. J. Psychiat. 98:551.*

HERZBERG, A. (1941) *Active Psychotherapy,* London, Research Books.

HOMME, L. E. (1965) Perspectives in psychology - XXIV control of coverants, the operants of the mind, *The Psychol. Rec. 15:501.*

HORSLEY, J. S. (1936 Narcoanalysis: a new technique in shortcut psychotherapy, *Lancet 1:55.*

HULL, C. L. (1943) *Principles of Behavior,* New York, Appleton-Century.

HUSSAIN, A. (1964) Behavior therapy using hypnosis, in J. Wolpe, A. Salter and L. J. Reyna *The Conditioning Therapies,* New York, Holt, Rinehart & Winston.

JACOBSON, E. (1938) *Progressive Relaxation,* Chicago, Univ. of Chicago Press.

JACOBSON, E. (1939) Variation of blood pressure with skeletal muscle tension and relaxation, *Ann. Int. Med. 12:1194.*

JACOBSON, E. (1940) Variation of pulse rate with skeletal muscle tension and relaxation, *Ann. Int. Med. 13:1619.*

JAMES, B. (1962) Case of homosexuality treated by aversion therapy, *Brit. Med. J. 1:768.*

JONES, H. G. (1960) Continuation of Yates' treatment of a tiquer, in H. J. Eysenck *Behavior Therapy and the Neuroses,* Oxford, Pergamon Press.

JONES, H. G. (1960) The behavioral treatment of enuresis nocturna, in H. J. Eysenck *Behavior Therapy and the Neuroses,* Oxford, Pergamon Press.

JONES, M. C. (1924) Elimination of children's fears, *J. Exp. Psychol. 7:382.*

JONES, M. C. (1924[a]) A laboratory study of fear. The case of Peter, *J. Genet. Psychol. 31:308.*

KALLMAN, F. (1952) Comparative twin studies on the

genetic aspects of male homosexuality, *J. Nerv. Ment. Dis.* 115:283.

KALLMAN, F. (1953) *Heredity in Health and Mental Disorder*, New York, W. W. Norton & Co., Inc.

KANTOROVICH, N. V. (1929) An attempt at associative reflex therapy in alcoholism, *Psychol. Abst.* No. 4282, 1930.

KENNEDY, W. A. and FOREYT, J. (1968) Control of eating behavior in an obese patient by avoidance conditioning, *Psychol. Rep.* 22: 571.

KIMMEL, H. D. (1967) Instrumental conditioning of autonomically mediated behavior, *Psychol. Bull.* 67:337.

KNIGHT, R. P. (1941) Evaluation of the results of psychoanalytic therapy, *Amer. J. Psychiat.* 98:434.

KOLVIN, I. (1967) Aversive imagery treatment in adolescents, *Behav. Res. Ther.* 5: 245.

KONDAS, O (1965) The possibilities of applying experimentally created procedures when eliminating tics, *Studia Psychol.* 7:221.

KRASNOGORSKI, N. I. (1925) The conditioned reflexes and children's neuroses, *Amer. J. Dis. Child.* 30:754.

LANDIS, C. (1937) A statistical evaluation of psychotherapeutic methods, in L. Hinsie *Concepts and Problems of Psychotherapy*, New York, Columbia Univ. Press.

LANG, P. J. (1964) Experimental studies of desensitization psychotherapy, in J. Wolpe, A. Salter and L. J. Reyna, *The Conditioning Therapies*, New York, Holt, Rinehart, Winston.

LANG, P. J. (1966) Personal communication.

LANG, P. J. (1967) Personal communication.

LANG, P. J. (1968) Appraisal of systematic desensitization techniques with children and adults. II. Process and mechanisms of change, theoretical analysis and implications for treatment and clinical research, in C. M. Franks (ed.) *Assessment and Status of the Behavior Therapies and Associated Developments*, New York, McGraw-Hill (in press).

LANG, P. J. and LAZOVIK, A. D. (1963) The experimental desensitization of a phobia, *J. Abn. Soc. Psychol.* 66:519.

LANG, P. J. LAZOVIK, A. D. and REYNOLDS, D. (1965) Desensitization, suggestibility and pseudotherapy, *J. Abn. Psychol.* 70:395.

LANGLEY, J. N. and ANDERSON, H. K. (1895) The innervation of the pelvic and adjoining viscera, *J. Physiol.* 19:71.

LATHROP, R. G. (1964) Measurement of analog sequential dependency, *Human Factors* 6:233.

LaVERNE, A. A. (1953) Rapid coma technique of carbon dioxide inhilation therapy, *Dis. Nerv. Syst.* 14:141.

LAZARUS. A A. (1961) Group therapy of phobic disorders by systematic desensitization, *J. Abn. Soc. Psychol.* 63:504.

LAZARUS, A. A. (1963) The results of behavior therapy in 126 cases of severe neurosis, *Behav. Res. Ther.* 1:69.

LAZARUS, A. A. (1967) In support of technical eclecticism, *Psychol. Reps.* 21:415.

LAZARUS, A. A. and ABRAMOVITZ, A. (1962) The use of "emotive imagery" in the treatment of children's phobias, *J. Ment. Sci.* 108:191.

LEAHY, M. R. and MARTIN, I. C. A. (1967) Successful hypnotic abreaction after twenty years, *Brit. J. Psychiat.* 113:383.

LEMERE, F. and VOEGTLIN, W. L. (1950) An evaluation of the aversion treatment of alcoholism, *Qrt. J. Stud. Alcoh.* 11:199.

LEUKEL, F. and QUINTON, E. (1964) Carbon dioxide effects on acquisition and extinction of avoidance behavior *J. Comp. Physiol. Psychol.* 57:267.

LEURET, F. (1846) *De Traitement Moral de la Folie,* Paris. Quoted by Stewart (1961).

LEVIS, D. J. and CARRERA, R. N. (1967) Effects of ten hours of implosive therapy in the treatment of outpatients: a preliminary report, *J. Abn. Psychol.* 72:504.

LINDSLEY, O. R. (1956) Operant conditioning methods applied to research in chronic schizophrenia, *Psychiat. Res. Rep.* 5:118.

LITTLE, J. C. and JAMES, B. (1964) Abreaction of conditioned fear after eighteen years, *Behav. Res. Ther.* 2:59.

LONDON, P. (1964)*The Modes and Morals of Psychotherapy,* New York: Holt, Rinehart & Winston.

LOVIBOND, S. H. (1963) The mechanism of conditioning treatment of enuresis, *Behav. Res. Ther.* 1:17.

LUBLIN, I. (1968) Aversive conditioning of cigarette addiction, Paper read at 76th Meeting of American Psychological Ass'n., San Francisco.

MALLESON, N. (1959) Panic and phobia, *Lancet 1*:225.

MASSERMAN, J. H. (1963) Ethology, comparative biodynamics, and psychoanalytic research, in J. Scher *Theories of the Mind*, New York, The Free Press.

MASSERMAN, J. H. and YUM, K. S. (1946) An analysis of the influence of alcohol on the experimental neuroses in cats, *Psychosom. Med. 8*:36.

MASTERS, W. H. and JOHNSON, V. E. (1966) *Human Sexual Response*, Boston, Little, Brown Co.

MASTERS, W. H. and JOHN, SON, V. E. (1967) Personal communication.

MAX, L. W. (1935) Breaking up a homosexual fixation by the conditioned reaction technique. A case study, *Psychol. Bull. 32*:734.

MAXWELL, R. D. H. and PATERSON, J. W. (1958) Meprobamate in the treatment of stuttering, *Brit. Med. J. 1*: 873.

McCONAGHY, N. (1964) A year's experience with nonverbal psychotherapy, *Med. J. Austral. 1*:831.

McGUIRE, R. J. and VALLANCE, M. (1964) Aversion therapy by electric shock: a simple technique, *Brit. Med. J. 1*:151.

MESMER, A. (1779) Quoted by C. L. Hull (1933), Hypnosis and Suggestibility, New York, Appleton Century.

MEYER, V. (1957) The treatment of two phobic patients on the basis of learning principles, *J. Abn. Soc. Psychol. 58*:259.

MEYER, V. (1963) Paper read at Behavior Therapy Seminar, University of London.

MIGLER, B. and WOLPE, J. (1967) Automated desensitization: a case report, *Behav. Res. Ther. 5*:133.

MILLER, G. E. (1967) Personal communication.

MILLER, N. E. and DiCARA, L. V. (1968) Instrumental learning of vasomotor responses by rats: learning to respond differentially in the two ears, *Science 159*:1485.

MILLER, N. E., HUBERT, E. and HAMILTON, J. (1938) Mental and behavoral changes following male hormone treatment of adult castration hypogonadism and psychic impotence, *Proc. Soc. Exp. Biol. Med. 38*:538.

MILLER, R. E., MURPHY, J. V. and MIRSKY, I. A. (1957) Persistent effects of chlorpromazine on extinction of an avoidance response, *Arch. Neurol, Psychiat. 78*:526.

MOORE, N. (1966) Behavior therapy in bronchial asthma: a controlled study, *J. Psychosom. Res. 9*:257.

MOWRER, O. H. and VIEK, P. (1948) Experimental analogue of fear from a sense of helplessness, *J. Abn. Soc. Psychol. 43*:193.

MURPHY, I. C. (1964) Extinction of an incapacitating fear of earthworms, *J. Clin. Psychol. 20*:396.

NAPALKOV, A. V. and KARAS, A. Y. (1957) Elimination of pathological conditioned reflex connections in experimental hypertensive states, *Zh. Vyssh. Nerv. Deiat. 7*: 402.

OSGOOD, C. E. (1946) Meaningful similarity and interference in learning, *J. Exp. Psychol. 38*:132.

PALMER, H. A. (1944) Military psychiatric casualties, *Lancet, 2*:492.

PAUL, G. L. (1966) *Insight versus Desensitization in Psychotherapy,* Stanford, Stanford Univ. Press.

PAUL, G. L. (1968) Two-year follow-up of systematic desensitization in therapy groups, *J. Abn. Psychol. 73*: 119.

PAUL, G. L. and SHANNON, D. T. (1966) Treatment of anxiety through systematic desensitization in therapy groups, *J. Abn. Psychol. 71*: 124.

PAVLOV, I. P. (1927) *Conditioned Reflexes,* trans by G. V. Anrep, New York, Liveright.

PAVLOV, I. P. (1941) *Conditioned Reflexes and Psychiatry,* trans. by W. H. Gantt, New York, International Publ.

PHILPOTT, W. M. (1967) Personal communication.

PITTS, F. N. and McCLURE, J. (1967) Lactate metabolism in anxiety neurosis, *New Eng. J. Med. 277*:1329.

PREMACK, D. (1965) Reinforcement theory, in D. Levine (ed.) *Nebraska Symposium on Motivation,* Lincoln, Univ. Nebraska Press.

RACHMAN, S. (1965) Studies in desensitization I. The separate effects of relaxation and desensitization, *Behav. Res. Ther. 3*:245.

RACHMAN, S. and TEASDALE, J. D. (1968) Aversion therapy, in C. L. Franks (ed.) *Assessment and Status of the Behavior Therapies and Associated Developments,* New York, McGraw Hill.

RAFI, A. A. (1962) Learning theory and the treatment of tics, *J. Psychosom. Res. 6:* 71.

RAYMOND, M. J. (1956) Case of fetishism treated by aversion therapy, *Brit. Med. J. 2:* 854.

READE, W. (1872) *The Martyrdom of Man,* London, Watts & Co. (1943).

REED, J. L. (1966) Comments on the use of methohexitone sodium as a means of inducing relaxation, *Behav. Res. Ther. 4:323.*

REYNA, L. J. (1964) Conditioning therapy, learning theories and research, in J. Wolpe, A Salter and L. J. Reyna (eds.) *Conditioning Therapies,* New York, Holt, Rinehart, Winston.

RITTER, B. J. (1968) The group treatment of children's snake phobias using vicarious and contact desensitization procedures, *Behav. Res. Ther. 6:1.*

ROTHBALLER, A. B. (1959) The effects of catecholamines on the central nervous system, *Pharm. Rev. 11:494.*

SALTER, A. (1949) *Conditioned Reflex Therapy,* New York, Creative Age.

SALTER, A. (1952) *The Case Against Psychoanalysis,* New York, Holt, Rinehart, Winston.

SALZER, H. M. (1966) Relative hypoglycemia as a cause of neuropsychiatric illness, *J. Natn'l. Med. Ass'n. 58:12.*

SANDERSON, R. E., CAMPBELL, D. and LAVERTY, S. G. (1963) Traumatically conditioned responses acquired during respiratory paralysis, *Nature 196:1235.*

SANDISON, R. A. (1954) Psychological aspects of the LSD treatment of the neuroses, *J. Ment. Sci. 100:508.*

SARGANT, W. and DALLY, P. (1962) The treatment of anxiety states by antidepressant drugs, *Brit. Med. J. 1:* 6.

SCHWITZGEBEL, R. R. and KOLB, D. A. (1964) Inducing behavior change in adolescent delinquents, *Behav. Res. Ther. 1:297.*

SEMANS, J. H. (1956) Premature ejaculation, a new approach, *South Med. J. 49:* 353.

SEMANS, J. H. (1962) Personal communication.

SHORVON, H. J. and SARGANT, W. (1947) Excitatory abreaction with special reference to its mechanism and the use of ether, *J. Ment. Sci. 93:709.*

SIMONOV, P. V. (1962) Stanislavskii method and physiology of emotions, mimeo.

SIMONOV, P. V. (1967) Studies of emotional behavior of humans and animals by Soviet physiologists, paper read at Conference on Experimental Approaches to the Study of Behavior, New York.

SINGH, H. (1963) Therapeutic use of thioridazine in premature ejaculation, *Amer. J. Psychiat. 119*:891.

SKINNER, B. F. (1953) *Science and Human Behavior,* New York, Macmillan & Co.

SKINNER, B. F. and LINDSLEY, O. R. (1954) Studies in behavior therapy, status reports II and III, Office of Naval Research Contract N5 ori-7662.

SLATER, S. L. and LEAVY, A. (1966) The effects of inhaling a 35% carbon dioxide, 65 per cent oxygen mixture upon anxiety level in neurotic patients, *Behav. Res. Ther. 4*:309.

SOLOMON, R. L. (1964) Punishment, *Amer. Psychol. 19*:239.

STAMPFL, T. G. (1964) Quoted by London (1964).

STAMPFL, T. G. and LEVIS, D. J. (1967) Essentials of implosive therapy: a learning-theory-based psychodynamic behavioral therapy, *J. Abn. Psychol. 72*:496.

STAMPFL, T. G. and LEVIS, D. J. (1968) Implosive therapy, a behavoral therapy, *Behav. Res. Ther. 6*:31.

STETTEN,, D. (1968) Basic Sciences in Medicine: the example of gout, *New Eng. J. Med., 278*:1333.

STEVENS, S. S. (1957) On the psychophysical law, *Psychol. Rev. 64*:153.

STEVENS, S. S. (1962) The surprising simplicity of sensory metrics, *Amer. Psychol. 17*:29.

STEVENSON, I. and WOLPE, J. (1960) Recovery from sexual deviation through overcoming non-sexual neurotic responses, *Amer. J. Psychol. 116*:737.

STEWART, M. A. (1961) Psychotherapy by reciprocal inhibition, *Amer. J. Psychiat. 188*:175.

SULZER, E. S. (1965) Behavior modification in psychiatric adult patients, in L. Ullman and L. Krasner (eds.) *Case Studies in Behavior Modification,* New Work, Holt, Rinehart, and Winston.

SUZMAN, M. M. (1968) Propanolol relieves anxiety symptoms, *Mod. Med.* May:36.

TAYLOR, J. G. (1955) Personal communication.

TAYLOR, J. G. (1963) A behavioral interpretation of obsessive compulsive neurosis, *Behav. Res. Ther.* 1:237.

TERHUNE, W. S. (1948) The phobic syndrome, *Arch. Neurol. Psychiat.* 62:162.

THOMAS, E. J. (1968) Selected sociobehavoral techniques and principles: an approach to interpersonal helping, *Social Work* 13:12.

TURSKY, B., WATSON, P. D. and O'CONNELL, D. N. (1965) A concentric shock electrode for pain stimulation, *Psychophysiol,* 1:296.

ULLMAN, L. P. and KRASNER, L. (1965) *Case Studies in Behavior Modification,* New York, Holt, Rinehart & Winston.

ULRICH, R., STACHNIK, T. and MABRY, J. (1966) *Control of Human Behavior,* Glenview, Ill., Scott-Foresman & Co.

VOEGTLIN, W. and LEMERE, F. (1942) The treatment of alcohol addiction, *Qrt. J. Stud. Alcoh.* 2:717.

WALTON, D. (1964) Experimental psychology and the treatment of a tiquer, *J. Child Psychol. Psychiat.* 2: 148.

WATSON, J. B. and RAYNER, P. (1920) Conditioned emotional reactions, *J. Exp. Psychol.* 3:1.

WEINREB, S. (1966) The effects of inhaling spirit of ammonia upon anxiety level in neurotic patients, mimeo.

WILDER, J. (1945) Facts and figures on psychotherapy, *J. Clin. Psychopath.* 7:311.

WILLIAMS, C. D. (1959) The elimination of tantrum behavior by extinction procedures, case report, *J. Abn. Soc. Psychol.* 59:269.

WILLOUGHBY, R. R. (1934) Norms for the Clark-Thurston Inventory, *J. Soc. Psychol.* 5:91.

WINKELMAN, N. W. (1955) Chlorpromazine in the treatment of neuropsychiatric disorders, *J. A. M. A.* 155:18.

WOHLGEMUTH, A. (1923) *A Critical Examination of Psychoanalysis,* London, Allen and Unwin.

WOLBERG, L. (1948) *Medical Hypnosis,* New York, Grune & Stratton.

WOLPE, J. (1948) An Approach to the problem of neurosis based on the conditioned response, unpublished manuscript, M. D. Thesis, Univ. of the Witwatersrand.

WOLPE, J. (1952) Objective psychotherapy of the neuroses, *S. A. Med. J.* 26: 825.

WOLPE, J. (1952[a]) Experimental neurosis as learned

behavior, *Brit. J. Psychol.* 43:243.

WOLPE, J. (1954) Reciprocal inhibition as the main basis of psychotherapeutic effects, *Arch. Neurol. Psychiat.* 72: 205.

WOLPE, J. (1956) Learning versus lesions as the basis of neurotic behavior, *Amer. J. Psychiat.* 112:923.

WOLPE, J. (1958) *Psychotherapy by Reciprocal Inhibition,* Stanford, Stanford Univ. Press.

WOLPE, J. (1961) The systematic desensitization treatment of neuroses, *J. Nerv. Ment. Dis.* 112:189.

WOLPE, J. (1961ᵃ) The prognosis in unpsychoanalyzed recovery from neurosis, *Amer. J. Psychiat.* 118:35.

WOLPE, J. (1962) Isolation of a conditioning procedure as the crucial psychotherapeutic factor, *J. Nerv. Ment. Dis.* 134:316.

WOLPE, J. (1963) Quantitative relationships in the systematic desensitization of phobias, *Amer. J. Psychiat.* 119:1062.

WOLPE, J. (1964) Behavior therapy in complex neurotic states, *Brit. J. Psychiat.* 110: 28.

WOLPE, J. (1965) Conditioned inhibition of craving in drug addiction: a pilot experiment, *Behav. Res. Ther.* 2: 285.

WOLPE, J. and FRIED, R. (1968) Psychophysiological correlates of imaginal presentations of hierarchical stimuli. I. The effect of relaxation, Unpublished manuscript.

WOLPE, J. and LANG, P. J. (1964) A fear survey schedule for use in behavior therapy, *Behav. Res. Ther.* 2: 27.

WOLPE, J. and RACHMAN, S. (1960) Psychoanalytic evidence: a critique based on Freud's case of little Hans, *J. Nerv. Ment. Dis.* 131:135.

WOLPIN, M. and PEARSALL, L. (1965) Rapid deconditioning of a fear of snakes, *Behav. Res. Ther.* 3:107.

WOLPIN, M. and RAINES, J. (1966) Visual imagery, expected roles and extinction as possible factors in reducing fear and avoidance behavior, *Behav. Res. Ther.* 4:25.

YATES, A. J. (1958) The application of learning theory to the treatment of tics, *J. Abn. Soc. Psychol.* 56:175.

Author Index

Subject Index